To Donna & Mike,
  Hope you find so
recipes! Enjoy our ——— you!
  Frances Calhoun Schaffer

Enjoyed sharing the eclipse
         with you.
Best wishes!
  Dave Schaffer,
         Illustrator
  8/21/17

Frances Schaffer's

Shortcuts to Gourmet Cooking
Encore

Illustrations by David Schaffer
Edited by Sandra Bauer

INFUSIONMEDIA
Lincoln, Nebraska

Infusionmedia

140 North 8th Street #214

Lincoln, NE 68508-1353

www.infusion.media

Printed in the United States

First Edition

10 9 8 7 6 5 4 3 2 1

Library of Congress Control Number: 2015944049

ISBN: 978-0-9916455-2-7

Cover photo by Charl Ann Mitchell

Illustration by Carrie Arnold reprinted with permission of Bill Lagos

Modern family photographs by Hal Maggiore Photography

"Two-Dice Icon" on page 58 by Steaphan Greene/Wikimedia Commons

To my main critics—my husband and five children.

Back row: Tony, Dave, and Chris. Middle row: Greg and Jude.

Front row: Fran and Leslie.

Contents

Foreword

Times change. With retirement, Fran and Dave Schaffer are off on a busy new chapter in their lives. So far it has included travel, a mission trip, benefit dinners, TV appearances, and renewing old acquaintances and family ties. One thing hasn't changed. Fran's abiding interest in well-prepared, healthful food, nicely presented. Every year she enters a number of her tasty, all-natural creations in the Nebraska State Fair, winning many first-place blue ribbons and Best of Division awards while creating interest in her cooking style. (You'll find several of her blue ribbon recipes in this book.)

Lately Fran has become even more interested in, even concerned, about the nutritional aspects of how we shop for and prepare our foods. Without the responsibility of the restaurant, she has had more time to research the latest trends and experiment on ways to make food healthier. She has also become more aware than ever of how busy our lives have become, and this has led her to find more shortcuts in preparing meals ... adapting recipes to the Crock-Pot, using the microwave, planning ahead. It all sparked her interest in doing a second cookbook. And to those readers, former customers, and friends who were disappointed that their favorite dishes did not appear in *Family Favorites*, a chance to make that up with an *Encore* was especially appealing.

And so it began ... where else but in her kitchen? The last vestiges of a restaurant kitchen are gone, the steam table and oversized appliances have disappeared, and it is once again the Schaffer family kitchen. Its warm woods and glass-beveled cupboard fronts give it a cozy atmosphere. On one side of the room is a sturdy and inviting wooden dining table. It is here that Fran is at her laptop, surrounded by papers, clippings, old cookbooks, and the like, working on the new book. She stops occasionally to add another ingredient to a Crock-Pot meal, to slide pans of raised bread dough into the oven, or to deftly remove cookies from a baking sheet.

I join her here to "cuss" and discuss, to agree and disagree, to change and rearrange in hopes that Fran's message will reach and touch her readers.

The end product is a timely book. More and more articles in all types of media, from newspapers and magazines to television and the Internet, are touting all-natural cooking, and more and more healthful food supermarkets—Whole Foods and Trader Joe's are just two examples—are becoming accessible to consumers. And some regular supermarkets now have specialty sections dedicated to all-natural and organic foods, as well as special dietary needs like gluten free.

But above all, this is a very personal cookbook. Fran will be the first to tell you she is not a professional chef or trained dietitian. She is a cook with a lifetime of experiences, and the invaluable lessons of her mother and Nonna to guide and inspire. And in case you think this is just a serious, no-fun cookbook, check out the delicious desserts, cakes, cookies, and candy. Fran definitely has a sweet tooth, but even her candy is healthful.

Finally, I must mention the delightful sketches by Dave Schaffer, even more charming in this book.

I hope you enjoy reading Fran's recipes and stories as much as I did while helping her put them all together. I have cooked for many years, but I have learned so many things from Fran, and I hope you do, too.

Sandie and Don Bauer.

Preface

Wow! How my life has changed. When I was in school and college, the thought of writing an essay scared me to death. Now, I am the author of a four-hundred-page cookbook.

When talking with Jane Palmer, a longtime food writer for the Omaha *World-Herald*, she asked me if I was planning to write another cookbook. I told her, "Absolutely not" ... I didn't know what I would write about—but here I am. What's happened?

One day while shopping in Skagway, one of our local supermarkets, I noticed a specialty flour on sale. It was white whole-wheat flour.* Was it bleached? Was the color of the flour white? Did it have the sometimes bitter taste of regular (red) whole-wheat flour? It was at a bargain price, so I bought two bags so I could answer all my questions. To my surprise, the answers to all my questions were "No!"

This started me on a new mission. I began making everything I could think of with white whole-wheat flour or a blend of unbleached and white whole-wheat flours ... noodles, spaghetti, cakes, cookies, pie crust, etc. The idea of a second cookbook began to emerge ... one that would incorporate new and helpful information about nutrition.

With retirement, I found other ways to use my skills and learn new ones. Karen Mayer asked me if I would help with a benefit for her church. It was advertised as a "Night at Nonna's." Many of my loyal customers thought I had opened my restaurant again. This led to other benefit dinners. When I had Nonna's, I was too busy to volunteer; so now I was glad to give back to the community that had given so much to me and my family. The beauty of volunteering is you can say "no" according to your schedule. Another plus was that these experiences made me think more and more about another book.

In 2010 the Nebraska State Fair relocated from Lincoln to Grand Island, and I started entering my recipes into open class, winning many blue ribbons and some Best of Division.

*White whole-wheat flour is flour milled from hard white spring wheat, rather than traditional red wheat. White whole wheat has all of the nutrients (bran, germ, and endosperm) of red whole wheat but is lighter in color and milder in flavor, requiring less added sweetener. The reason for its milder taste is because it's an albino wheat without the red hull that contains the strongly flavored phenolic acid and tannins that are in red wheat.

It was educational and offered me an opportunity to experiment and polish my recipes, which I am now eager to share.

When I wrote my first cookbook, *Family Favorites*, I told about my experiences with our family when we were on the Feingold Diet, but that was forty years ago. Now everyone's idea of a healthy diet is different; there are many diets—all natural, organic, gluten free, paleo—and the list goes on and on. Everyone feels their diet is the best and will assure you that it will cure all your ills, heart disease, gastrointestinal problems, ADHD; it's never ending. The way to solve these problems is to have recipes with options. By changing the types of flour and sugars, by using organic products to avoid hormones and additives, you can take any recipe, use the foods you can tolerate, and usually you will have good results. This is called being creative.

Many of the recipes in this book, *Encore*, can be used for any type of diet; if an option isn't listed, choose a similar ingredient that you can tolerate. This is how new recipes are made. I can tell you from experience, I have had many failures in cooking and other things too, but the successes always overshadow your failures.

There is nothing I like to do better than to find interesting recipes and change them into all natural ingredients: Bloody Mary Mix, page 118, and Carbonara Pasta Salad, page 331. Most of the time, the end product is not only healthier but also saves you time and money. Always remember, the producers of processed foods not only have to pay for ingredients but also the cost of a factory to make them, plus advertising, delivery, and a discount to the store to sell the product. Usually, they use the cheapest ingredients in order to make a profit. Not only do they use artificial sweeteners and flavors for taste, plus artificial colors for presentation, but they use additives and preservatives for shelf life.

In October 2009 I started to be a regular guest cook on our area TV station, NTV's *The Good Life*. The second Tuesday of each month, I demonstrate a recipe from my cookbook, give cooking tips, and explain how it is more healthy and economical to cook from scratch. Soon I was asked to speak at book clubs, church groups, and other organizations ... never knew I was a speaker.

While on TV, I try to emphasize how cooking from scratch is easy, saves you time and money, is healthier for your family (lower doctor and dentist bills), and you can do it with your family. When you replace all your staples with natural ingredients, it takes less time to cook from scratch than going to the store, shopping, bringing all those processed foods into your house, and then putting them away. Home cooking is not just about food, it is about family members sitting down and eating together. It promotes unity and harmony as family members recount their daily activities and have good discussions and many laughs.

When I wrote the first book, our economy was better than we are experiencing now. Food prices have skyrocketed since I closed Nonna's, and there is more emphasis on good nutrition for us as adults and especially for our children. Our first lady, Michelle Obama, is concerned about child obesity, but our children are facing other problems such as ADHD, Asperger's, and autism. Could this be food related? I sometimes believe "we can't see the forest for the trees."

A couple of years ago an article was in the Omaha *World-Herald*, "Five Chemicals to Avoid in Food." The article stated that food manufacturers aren't going to advertise the fact that controversial chemicals are actually in their food. If you want to be informed and eat healthier, here are five chemicals to avoid so you can eat without worry.

1. Sodium nitrates and sodium nitrites
2. Artificial sweeteners, especially aspartame
3. Artificial food colorings and dyes; the European Union, India, and Japan have banned food with these colorings
4. BHA and BHT, common food preservatives
5. Perfluorooctanoic acid used in food packaging and cookware.

This article was written in 2012, and in the early 1970s Dr. Ben Feingold warned about all of the above: artificial colors and flavors, nitrates and nitrites, BHA and BHT, and plastics that we used to store our foods. (Read more Feingold information in the appendix at the back of this book.)

When did these conditions become problematic? In my opinion it started after World War II when we began to package our foods and put chemicals in the food to increase shelf life and colorings for presentation.

When families had gardens, canned their foods, and cooked at home, we weren't concerned about these conditions. How do we remedy these situations, the cost of foods, obesity, ADHD, and possibly autism? We might start by cooking from scratch, just like our mothers and grandmothers did. This way we would be aware of what we are eating, the taste, nutritional value, calories, and, let's not forget, presentation.

While scanning the Internet, I came upon an article, "22 Ways to Fight Rising Food Prices." Number one was, "Eat at Home." This one suggestion would solve many of these problems we adults and our children are facing. Home cooking can be a family affair. It doesn't have to be mom's duty; many men enjoy it as well, and it is something in which you can (and should) have your children participate. This is an activity that can bring your family together. With all of the appliances at our disposal, this adventure is not labor-intensive. Having the staples in your kitchen rather than packages and cans, you will spend less time because it is faster to whip up a recipe than shop for premade food. Plus, it will probably reduce the time and money you spend in the doctor's office, pharmacy, and school conferences.

I intend for this to be a good reference for any kind of a diet you may be on. So please read the stories and the recipes, check the options, helpful hints, healthful hints, and glossaries. If you don't have a certain ingredient, substitute a similar one; you might discover you like it better, as with Oatmeal Coconut Cookies, page 193 in *Family Favorites*. I have created three to four different recipes from the original recipe.

I'm also going to emphasize healthful foods without artificial additives; recipes using white whole-wheat, unbleached, and gluten-free flours; and how to be more economical.

You have to think of cooking as a creative art, and an "art" that saves you money (no packaged foods and fewer prescription medications) and time (less shopping, school conferences, and doctor visits). It is time that we question why so many of our children are obese or having an increase in behavioral and learning problems and do something that may be more helpful than giving them another pill. Home cooking (cooking from scratch) has no side effects. The only reaction you will get is happy, smiling faces.

Acknowledgments

During the 22 years of being the owner of Nonna's, I adhered to a simple policy of business … hire employees who are dependable, have good work ethics, and are always willing to be there for you when needed. Why make changes? There will be differences of opinions in any business that can be intense and lead to heated discussions, but in the end, we usually are on the same page.

Without Sandra Bauer, I would have never ventured to start another cookbook. She continues to be the crutch I need to edit my writings and find all my grammatical errors I fail to catch.

To my artist in residence, husband David, whose artistic talent never ceases to amaze me. He is the main reason this book is in color.

To my lifelong friend and artist, Charl Ann Mitchell, for the beautiful color photo; Aaron Vacin for the cover art work; Hal Maggiore for the family portraits; plus Bev Harvey for editing.

To Bill Lagos for the gift of Carrie Arnold's original painting of Frank's Bar, which is the divider page for the Italian section …another reason this book is in color.

To all the people who shared their recipes, NTV's (Channel 13) *The Good Life*, for the opportunity to demonstrate these recipes, and the Nebraska State Fair for the opportunity to have my recipes judged.

And finally to Cris Trautner, my publisher, who once again rescued me with this cookbook venture. Cris and Sandie are the two most important ingredients in this recipe (cookbook).

To all of you, I give my heartfelt thanks. Without you this book would still be a dream.

How This Cookbook Works

Like its predecessor, *Shortcuts to Gourmet Cooking & Family Favorites*, this book, *Encore*, still subscribes to the idea that cooking from scratch, using all-natural ingredients, and nicely presenting your food can make any meal gourmet, and it will not use all your time and energy. That it tastes good, is nutritious, and looks nice is all that matters. But this book goes even deeper into making your food healthier, delving into the hazards of using certain processed foods and the danger of additives, preservatives, and chemical processing—and how you can avoid them by using alternative ingredients and methods. It also shows ways to save money and time by substituting less expensive ingredients for higher-priced ones, and it demonstrates that cooking from scratch is always less expensive than eating out or buying prepared food. In this book there will be many recipes using the Crock-Pot that can help busy families eat tastier, healthier meals in less time.

Options: Many of the basic recipes are followed by alternative ones, allowing you to make several dishes from the same recipe or just give the basic recipe a different twist. For instance, the potato roll recipe can be used to make a variety of dinner rolls with just a few changes. My fresh egg white whole-wheat pasta can be made into everything from spaghetti to tortellini. Some options involve only simple changes or additions in seasonings and flavorings.

Step Method: Instead of all ingredients being listed first, followed by the method, I have put down the ingredients and method together in individual steps. The ingredients are listed in bold so that you can scan the recipe and see that you have all of them. In some cases when an ingredient is divided, the total amounts needed are given at the beginning of the recipe.

Helpful Hints: Scattered throughout the book are ideas I have either read about or discovered through years of cooking. They may make your cooking and baking easier and answer questions about problems you may have encountered.

Healthful Hints: Tips on how to buy certain foods to make a dish more healthy.

Glossary: At the beginning of each section there is a brief glossary of words found in that section.

Icons to Guide You: Symbols placed by a recipe give nutritional information about it.

🍎 means all natural

♥ means low cholesterol

GF means gluten free

🐝 means honey is used in the recipe

Equipment

While I have become a staunch believer in homemade-from-scratch cooking with minimal use of processed food, I have never been one to say you have to stand over a hot stove all day. I use and recommend the many labor-saving devices available to us today. There are some silly, faddish small appliances that periodically make their appearances, such as doughnut makers and pizza bakers, but I am talking about sturdy, hard-working, multiple-use appliances that will last for years. Some are quite expensive, but consider them as investments the same as you do your stove, refrigerator/freezer, or dishwasher. The important small electrical appliances are

- **Microwave oven** (you probably already own one)
- **KitchenAid Stand Mixer** or other heavy-duty mixer with meat grinder and shredder attachments
- **Food processor and/or blender** (both are best)
- **Rival Crock-Pot or other slow cookers** in small, medium, and large sizes

- **Pasta machine with a motor**, if you plan to make your own pasta (I have had an Imperia for twenty years)
- **White Mountain Ice Cream Freezer** or other six-quart electric freezer

In addition to these appliances and the usual pots, pans, and utensils, I especially recommend the following for use with the recipes in this book:

- **Pyrex cups** in one-, two-, four-, and eight-cup sizes
- **Glass bowls** and bakeware with lids (microwave safe) in different sizes—DO NOT USE plastic or Styrofoam in the microwave
- **Wire whisks** ... small, medium, and large
- **Wooden spoons** ... one with a hole in the center to stabilize a candy thermometer
- **Scoops** ... large for ice cream (¼ cup), medium for large cookies (2 ½ Tablespoons), and small for regular cookies (1 ½ Tablespoons)
- **Baker's pin** ... a rolling pin without handles, usually an eighteen-inch long, two-inch diameter wooden dowel that is perfect for rolling out pie dough and cookie dough directly on a cookie sheet without sides; great for holiday cut-out cookies
- **Double dough roller** to smooth and even dough, pastries, and candies, such as pizzas, pie and crumb crusts, toffee and peanut brittle, and bar cookies.
- **Garlic press**
- **Cheese grater for Parmesan cheese**; I recommend the KitchenAid attachment using the fine grater
- **Pasta crimper and pastry wheel**
- **Spring-form pan**, preferably more than one, for cheesecakes
- **Large stainless steel pot with insert/strainer** for cooking pasta
- **Thermometers**, three kinds—meat, food or instant-read, and candy

One important thing about equipment: KNOW YOUR OVEN! I cook with electric, convection, and gas ovens, and I get different results from each. So take the time to figure out how your oven—and your microwave oven—bakes or cooks. All times and temperatures in this book are approximate.

Staples

Jordan

Glossary

bread crumbs. Small particles of dried bread for breading, topping, stabilizing, thickening, and coating.

broth. A flavorful liquid made from cooking water with meat, poultry, vegetables, or fish. Forms the base for many soups and as a cooking liquid for many dishes.

clove. An individual section of the garlic bulb.

cream soup. A soup base made by blending and cooking fat and flour, then adding milk, water, or other flavorful liquids and cooking until thick and creamy. A variety of cream soups may be made by adding meat, vegetables, cheese, etc. May be used as is or as an ingredient in other dishes, sauces, etc.

croutons. Toasted bread cubes used to garnish and lend crunch to soups, salads, etc.

drippings. Juices that exude from meat and poultry during roasting, frying, pan browning (ground beef); wonderful for making soups, gravies, and as flavorings.

gelatin. A translucent substance derived from collagen obtained by boiling or otherwise cooking skin, tendons, ligaments, and bones of meat animals. It may be used to make broth. Commercial gelatin is usually granulated and is used to thicken and set juices in making molded desserts or salads. Sometimes found in candy, marshmallows, yogurt, and commercial ice cream.

IQF. Individually Quick Frozen. A method of freezing pieces of food singly on a flat surface, such as a baking sheet, before packaging; prevents foods from sticking together so you can use as much or as little as you wish.

roux. Fat and flour blended together and cooked over low heat to serve as a thickener for soups, sauces, and gravies. It forms the basis for cream soups.

staples. Basic ingredients, usually kept on hand, to be used in cooking and preparing food.

stocks. Broth; also, any juices saved from cooking meat, fish, or vegetables.

whipping cream. Same as heavy cream; full fat cream, at least 36% milkfat. Used to make *whipped* cream and butter.

Staples

So many readers were appreciative of my Staples section in *Family Favorites* that I decided to expand it. There are so many types of simple, basic items, like flour, sugar, salts, etc., that used to be more or less one-ingredient items but are now more complicated. We need to know more about them so we can make informed choices. I have added more information about them to the staples list. Of course, I have kept my personal list of what I consider essential, inexpensive ingredients to have in making nutritious meals. They include old bread (crumbs and croutons); parts of chicken that were not favorites (chicken broth); juices of meats, chicken, and vegetables that once found their way into the garbage but were given new life as flavorful ingredients in other dishes. In addition, I found simple ways to prepare and preserve certain foods so that I don't have to run to the store for them at the last minute. With a little advance planning and preparation you can get along with fewer cans, packages, and processed foods. This is especially true for those on restricted diets; they want to know what is in their finished product. I hope this rather unique list is helpful in your cooking.

Bread Crumbs and Croutons

Crumbs are bread crumbled into small fragments for use in cooking. Save all *homemade* **bread, buns, bagels, rolls**, etc. Put into a pan and place in oven for 20 minutes at 350 degrees. Turn off oven but leave bread in oven overnight. With a KitchenAid mixer's fine shredder attachment, or a food processor, grind the bread into crumbs. Store in a resealable plastic bag. Use for breading chicken, fish, meats, or any recipe that calls for bread crumbs, such as meatballs, ravioli, cabbage rolls, or lasagna.

Croutons are small pieces of dried bread, sometimes seasoned, used as a garnish for soups, salads, and other dishes. Use leftover **homemade garlic bread** or any **flavored bread**. Place bread on a cookie sheet in a single layer. With a pizza cutter, cut the bread into ½-inch squares. Toast in oven for 10 minutes at 350 degrees. Store in a resealable plastic bag for later use.

Fat

Oils come from vegetables and seeds, such as extra virgin olive oil (olives) and canola oil (rapeseeds). Both oils are monounsaturated and are considered to be very healthy. They have been my only choices, but now I'm adding coconut oil to my list.

Coconut oil is refined from the meat of mature coconuts, so there is no coconut flavor or aroma. It has "0" grams of trans fat (page 197). In temperatures below 76 degrees, coconut oil is solid, and above 76 degrees, it becomes liquid. Coconut oil is great for baking, cooking, and popping corn, and it can replace butter, shortening, and liquid oils in your recipes.

Butter comes salted or unsalted, which is a personal preference. I use either depending on the price. If I had to restrict my salt intake and had salted butter available, I would reduce the amount of salt used in my recipe. I never use margarine because of the artificial colors and additives, plus recent studies show that the trans-fatty acids that occur in the processing of margarine are not healthy or desirable in your diet. There are a few additive-free margarines available in health-food stores, but they are usually soft margarines that are not recommended for baking. Butter is naturally yellow. If butter is colored, it is listed as an additive in the ingredients.

Shortenings change like the weather, so it is important to check your labels every time you purchase them. I use only unflavored—*never butter flavored*—and avoid any shortenings with the additives BHA, BHT, or TBHQ. I have found that many store brands have less additives than name brands.

Lard is rendered from pig fat and has recently come back into favor because most home-rendered lard is additive free (which needs to be refrigerated or frozen, see page 283–284). This is not the case for lard that is on the store shelves and is not refrigerated; check your labels.

Flavorings

Natural flavorings are oils extracted from fruit peelings (lemon, orange, lime), leaves (mint), and nuts (almond), or steeped in alcohol (vanilla bean). I have noticed that several of my bottles of flavoring extracts have the word "pure" on the label. They don't have any artificial additives, but my raspberry extract *does not* have "pure" on its label, and it has Red 40 food coloring. Why? It is a flavoring not a *coloring*! Once again, read your labels.

Fruit-flavored schnapps are other flavorings I use in cooking. I use schnapps in sorbet and frozen yogurt because it not only adds flavor, it also makes the sorbet and yogurt easier to scoop. Many kinds of schnapps are naturally flavored and uncolored—strawberry, raspberry, peach, apricot, and blueberry. If I can't find the flavor (raspberry for raspberry sorbet) without color, I often substitute strawberry or any other fruit schnapps that is uncolored; it doesn't affect the taste. Artificial colors and flavors have been linked to behavioral changes in children, also possibly allergies, migraines, and cancer. Artificial dyes are banned in the European Union as well as Japan and India. (Look up "eight foods we eat that other countries ban" on Google for more information.)

Flours

Flour is a powder that is made by grinding cereal, grains, beans, seeds, or roots. It is the main ingredient for breads. In this book we are going to focus on three specific flours: unbleached, white whole wheat, and gluten free.

Unbleached flour whitens by letting the flour oxidize (mix with oxygen in the air, a natural aging process) for approximately ten days; however, this process is more expensive due to the time required. Bleached flour is white flour treated with chlorine or peroxide to whiten it (freshly milled flour is yellowish). Many European countries have prohibited bleaching flour.

White whole-wheat flour is flour milled from hard white spring wheat rather than traditional red wheat. In England whole-wheat flour is more commonly made from white whole wheat instead of red as in the United States. White whole-wheat flour has all of the nutrients (bran, germ, and endosperm) of red whole wheat but is lighter in color and milder in flavor, requiring less added sweetener. The reason for its milder taste is it does not contain the strongly flavored phenolic acid and tannins that are in red whole wheat. I have found that you can use it to make noodles, bread, cake, pie crust, and cookies, and I have discovered little difference when I used unbleached flour for these products. The big plus is you have all the nutrition of whole-wheat flour and the taste and texture of white flour. *It is a win-win situation.* Try it. I'm sure you will be pleased with the results.

Gluten-free flour is not made from a specific grain like gluten flours (wheat, rye, and barley) but is a combination of ingredients. It is one or a mixture of flours (rice, corn, soy, potato, tapioca, beans, sorghum, quinoa, millet, pure buckwheat, amaranth, teff, and Montina) and thickeners such as corn starch, arrowroot, tapioca, xanthan, guar gum, and potato starch. Baking with these flours can be very difficult at times, and you need to experiment with them. Expect some failures. Your breads will be dense and not as light as with regular wheat flours.* The taste and texture is different; I like it toasted. Making muffins, bars, and regular cookies are the easiest, and they taste more like the gluten recipes. On most packages of gluten-free flours the labels say "all purpose flour," but with the recipes it usually asks for other thickeners besides the ones in the flour. These flours are always changing, but I have found one that I feel is the closest to an "all purpose flour." It is "Premium Gold Gluten Free." I have been able to use this cup for cup as I would with regular flour. I was even able to make noodles with this flour. This is a challenge in cooking, but if you have celiac disease or intestinal problems, it is worth all the trouble. All the recipes in this book have been tested more than one time, and I continue to try new ones. Good luck!

*Flour made from wheat, barley, rye, and related
components, including durum, graham, kamut,
semolina, or spelt, are prohibited on a
gluten-free diet.

Vegetables

Garlic. Being an Italian cook, one of the most important staples in my kitchen is garlic. I use it in everything except dessert. The garlic press is good for small amounts, but when I'm making large quantities for benefit dinners, I want to have plenty on hand. Since *Family Favorites* was published, I have found **fresh peeled garlic cloves** in the refrigerated section of the produce department in some supermarkets. With my KitchenAid grinder attachment with the finest holes, I'm able to grind 2 pints of garlic from this one sack. Seal the lids tightly; you can even put the jars in a resealable plastic bag. Then I have garlic anytime I need it. If it has been in the refrigerator any length of time, it may discolor, but it's still good. When a recipe calls for *freshly squeezed garlic*, I use this already *prepared garlic*: **1 teaspoon prepared garlic equals 1 medium garlic clove**.

Onions, Celery, and Sweet Bell Peppers. Whenever I chop any of the above, I use the **whole pepper**, **onion**, and sometimes the **whole bunch of celery**. I then store the remaining in a resealable plastic bag for future use. If you are not going to use them soon, *freeze*. However, after they have been frozen, you can only use them in cooking. Do *not* use them with fresh foods.

Use garlic in sauces, stews, butters, oils, and many other dishes. For a change, use green-stemmed garlic (called green garlic); it is not fully matured and has a milder taste.

Vinegars

Vinegar is a sour-tasting liquid used as a condiment or preservative and comes in many flavors. My choice is **apple-cider vinegar** ... not *apple-cider-flavored* vinegar.

Balsamic vinegar has been made in Modena, Italy, for nearly one thousand years using white Tebbiano grapes that are simmered for hours until they become carmelized. The syrup is aged in a succession of barrels made from different woods for no less than twelve years ... no wonder it is so expensive! Cheaper balsamic vinegars are aged a shorter time in larger barrels and mixed with wine vinegar; they also have color added.

White balsamic vinegar uses a blend of white grapes and white wine vinegar and is cooked at a low temperature to avoid any darkening. The flavors of the two balsamic vinegars are very similar, although dark balsamic vinegar is slightly sweeter and syrupy. White has more of a clean aftertaste. The main reason one would use white balsamic vinegar is mostly aesthetic; this variety is often used when the color of white sauces or foods would be affected by the dark color of the traditional balsamic vinegar. After reading all this, seeing the difference in cost, and reading the additives in white balsamic vinegar (high-fructose corn syrup and sulfites), I will stay with my old standby, **apple-cider vinegar.***

*White distilled vinegar is approved for the Feingold Diet, not vinegars made from grapes or apples; these fruits have natural salicylates and are not used in the first phase of the diet.

Salts

A frequent question asked by many cooks is "Which salt is the best?" There are our basic varieties, and ounce for ounce, they contain a similar amount of sodium. Salt is a natural ingredient and is essential to our body. It is the abuse of salt, as of anything, that causes problems. To remove salt completely from most food makes food bland and tasteless. Example: Hot cereal such as oatmeal without salt makes it taste like paste.

Table salt is much less expensive but is refined and treated to prevent clumping. It comes either "plain" or "iodized." Iodized salt has the element iodine added. Iodine is necessary for proper thyroid function; it was added to salt beginning in 1924 because people weren't getting enough iodine in their diets to eliminate the possibility of goiters. Now, if you eat a healthy, balanced diet, you probably are getting enough iodine and don't need iodized salt.

Sea salt is very trendy, and most people who use sea salt use a certain type because of its flavors (minerals), which depend on the body of water from which the salt is drawn. My experience with sea salt is it's not usually as salty as regular salt. So, for salting water for pasta, you have to use more. Also, sea salt costs per pound about ten times more than table salt ($5.00 versus $0.50); for that reason, I never use sea salt in boiling water and reserve it for seasoning food. Sea salt contains trace amounts of iodine.

Kosher salt is sold in larger crystals and is less processed than table salt. It sells for $.55 per pound and is called a budget-friendly substitute for sea salt. The term "kosher salt" comes from its use in making meat kosher by removing surface blood, not from its being made in accordance with the guidelines for kosher food as written in the Torah. One salt manufacturer distinguishes between "kosher certified" and "koshering salt." Koshering salt has a small flake-like form useful in treating meat, whereas kosher certified salt is salt that has been certified as such by an appropriate religious body.

Halite, commonly known as rock salt, is the mineral form of sodium chloride. It is typically colorless and white but may be colored. Rock salt is often used for managing ice because it causes ice to melt. In cooking it is used as a flavor enhancer and to cure food such as bacon and fish. I use rock salt and ice to freeze my homemade ice cream.

Salty. Our brains are programmed so that a little salt tastes good, and a lot tastes bad. This ensures we consume just enough to maintain the salt balance our bodies need to function. But your palate can adapt to crave too much salt, as in the case of those who eat the typical American diet. If you cut back on salt, your taste buds will adjust to be satisfied with less.

When Nonno Frank was put on a low-sodium diet, Nonna used herbs, spices, and vegetables to enhance his food. The ones I remember were freshly squeezed garlic, onions, celery (especially celery leaves and seeds), basil, oregano, tomatoes, bell peppers. By using these herbs, spices, and vegetables, you can dramatically reduce the amount of salt used. But it is important NOT to use garlic, celery, or onion salts or powders for seasonings. They add additional sodium and often give the food a bitter taste. USE FRESH!

Varieties of salt.

Sweeteners

What can you do to get your sugar fix? There are many, many kinds of sugars and sweeteners without additives. Turn to natural sweeteners for your drinks and food alike. Honey, corn, maple, and agave syrups; molasses; white, brown, raw sugars; and stevia are just a few natural sweeteners to which you can turn. Not only will they wreak less havoc on your body but your support of these sweeteners instead will, eventually, help to slow the production of artificial sweeteners.*

White granulated sugar. This is the white sugar we probably use the most ... in baking, to sweeten foods and beverages. It is the all-purpose sweetener without additional flavors beyond sweetness. It is made up of two simple sugars, sucrose and glucose; they come from either sugar cane or sugar beets. It is 99% pure.

Confectioner's or powdered sugar. This is a combination of fine crystals of granulated sugar mixed with a small amount of corn starch to make a light, fluffy powder. It is essential in making frostings such as butter cream, cream cheese, simple confectioner's icing. It is also called for in some cookie recipes and is sometimes sprinkled on cakes, fruits, pancakes, and French toast.

Brown sugar. True brown sugar is sugar crystals derived from molasses with natural flavor and color. It is similar to white sugar in sweetness but has a mild, distinctive flavor. It is used in baking, especially cookies and on cereals. Some refiners make brown sugar by adding syrup to refined sugar.

*I never use artificial sweeteners, such as aspartame, Splenda, Sweet 'N Low, or Equal. Search for "artificial sweeteners side effects" on Google.

Turbinado sugar or raw sugar. Turbinado is refined to remove the impurities in raw sugar. Crunchy texture and golden brown color enhance fruits and complements a cup of coffee. Can be used in baking and is especially good sprinkled on the tops of muffins and quick breads.

Honey. This is one of the oldest sweeteners, sweeter than sugar. Honey can have a range of flavors, from dark and strong to light and mildly flavored. It can be used in many recipes calling for sugar and is often used as a topping in the place of jellies, jams, syrups, and as a sweetener in beverages.

Maple syrup. This syrup is made from the boiled-down sap of the maple tree. It adds a pleasant flavor to foods and is great for baking. Be sure to buy 100% maple syrup, not maple-flavored syrup. It is expensive due to the fact that it takes forty gallons of sap to produce one gallon of syrup. Maple sugar is made by further processing the syrup and is often found in candies.

Karo Light Corn Syrup. This is a light-colored syrup, often used in candy making, produced by actions of enzymes and/or acids on corn starch. It does more than sweeten; it improves the product (see page 170). I specify Karo Light Corn Syrup because it doesn't have high-fructose corn syrup and undesirable additives and flavorings. You may find some store brands that are additive free, but be careful and always read the labels. High-fructose corn syrup is produced by additional processing, making it more sweet. It is used in many processed foods. I do not use it.

Agave syrup. This nectar is a natural liquid sweetener made from the juice of the agave cactus. It is sweeter than regular sugar but does not create a sugar rush and is much less disturbing to the body's blood sugar level.

Stevia. Derived from the leaves from a shrub of South American origin, stevia doesn't metabolize as sugar, so it has no effect on insulin levels. Dissolves easily in liquids, making it ideal for beverages, smoothies, sauces, and ice cream. It is 150 to 300 times sweeter than sugar, so heavily concentrated, it is somewhat trickier to use in baked goods.

Broths for Soups and Flavorings

As food prices continue to rise, we always try to find ways to cut costs. Many times we throw away good food that we don't care for or that we don't know how to use. That was me when I used hindquarters for our Italian chicken. I always cut off the chicken backs on the thighs and threw the backs into the garbage. Carolyn McCullough, an employee at Nonna's, suggested that we use the backs and other chicken parts for making broth. First, we cooked them in a Crock-Pot, and then we tried cooking them in smaller amounts in the microwave. Now when I buy hindquarters in ten-pound packages, I remove the backs, then package and freeze them in twos for making broth. When I need chicken broth for soups or gravy, these "throwaways" come in handy.

Quick Microwave Chicken Broth 🍎❤GF

In an 8-cup Pyrex glass bowl, assemble:
1 to 2 chicken backs or a neck and ribs, any fat, or the equivalent of these items you have saved
1 or 2 stalks celery, chopped
1 to 2 Tablespoons onion, chopped
1 teaspoon salt

Fill container with:
Water to make 8 cups

Sprinkle over top of mixture:
1 teaspoon parsley
¼ teaspoon tarragon

Cook in the microwave on high for 20 minutes. Stir well, then allow the mixture to steep for 1 to 2 hours. This is a wonderful chicken broth, and it costs pennies. Thrifty and delicious! Strain, and the broth is ready to be used in soups, sauces, gravies, or as a flavoring. Store in containers that fit the way you will be using the broth; refrigerate or freeze. If you refrigerate overnight, then skim off the fat; you will have a lovely, fat-free broth.

If you need a large amount of broth, you can repeat this quick method several times or use the Crock-Pot or soup kettle. Just increase all the ingredients proportionately and, of course, the cooking time.

Other Sources of Chicken Flavoring

- Another way to have chicken flavoring for soups, gravies, etc., is to save the drippings off roast chicken or Italian chicken. If drippings are stuck to the pan, a little water will liquefy them. Place in the refrigerator and let the fat come to the top. Separate the fat from the meat gelatin. Store the fat and gelatin in *separate* plastic bags and freeze. Use a larger bag so you can keep adding to your store of goodies.
- Chicken fat is a good substitute for butter when making a gravy.
- The gelatin is excellent for making soup. Depending on how much you have saved, you can often make soup with just the gelatin, water, noodles, and a cut-up chicken breast. A wonderful, nonfat soup!

Option 🍎 ♥ GF

- **Vegetable broth.** You can make this the same as chicken broth using assorted vegetables such as cabbage, carrots, beans, peas, etc., in place of the meat (see roasted root vegetables, page 367).

Helpful Hints

- Get an extra clear broth by placing a paper coffee filter in your strainer.

Beef and Other Meat Stocks 🍎❤GF

Drain the drippings off browned ground beef you are using in other dishes and allow it to stand in the refrigerator until the fat is solid. Remove and discard the fat and save the **meat gelatin**. This is wonderful for soups and gravies. Again, use a larger bag and accumulate a supply of gelatin.

For larger amounts of beef broth, the Crock-Pot method is still your best bet, since making beef broth requires a longer cooking time than chicken. **Oxtails** make a lovely, clear beef broth.

Now that you know your broths, you can find recipes for soups that use them in the Soup section of this book on page 345.

Top: Removing fat from meat gelatin.
Middle: Meat gelatin in the mixing bowl.
Bottom: Storing and freezing the meat gelatin.

Cream Soups Used as an Ingredient ❦ ♥ GF

Cream soups, such as cream of mushroom, celery, and chicken, are usually used in a recipe as an ingredient rather than a soup entrée. Other cream soups, such as cream of tomato, broccoli, and asparagus, are served as a soup alone or with a sandwich or salad. In this section we will feature the "ingredient" cream soups and feature the "entrée" cream soups in the Soup section of the book beginning on page 345. After making any one of these soups, you will understand the technique for all the soups is very similar. These soups are in *Family Favorites* but are adapted here to cook in the microwave. See Options for gluten-free substitutions.

Cream of Mushroom Soup ❦ ♥

In an 8-cup Pyrex glass bowl, melt and mix well:
2 Tablespoons butter
2 Tablespoons fresh or canned mushrooms, thinly sliced
Cook in microwave on high for 1 to 2 minutes.

Using a wire whisk, add and mix well:
¼ cup white whole-wheat or unbleached flour
Return to microwave on high and cook for 1 minute.

Add to **mixture**:
1 cup water
Cook in microwave on high until it thickens, 2 to 3 minutes.

Add to **mixture** to make **soup**:
additional cup water or 1 cup milk (whole, 2%, 1%, or skim)

salt and pepper to taste

Cook on high until **soup** is thick and hot.

Cream of Celery Soup 🍎❤

In an 8-cup Pyrex glass bowl, add and mix well:

2 Tablespoons butter

2 Tablespoons celery, finely chopped

1 Tablespoon white or yellow onion, finely chopped

Microwave on high for 2 minutes.

Using a wire whisk, add and mix well:

¼ cup white whole-wheat or unbleached flour

Return to microwave on high and cook for 1 minute.

Add and mix well:

1 cup water

Microwave on high until **mixture** thickens, 1 to 2 minutes.

Add and mix well to make **soup**:

additional cup water or 1 cup milk (whole, 2%, 1%, or skim)

salt and white pepper to taste

Cook in microwave on high until **mixture** thickens and is hot.

Cream of Chicken Soup 🍎❤

In an 8-cup Pyrex glass bowl, melt and mix well:
2 Tablespoons butter
1 Tablespoon white or yellow onion, finely chopped
1 Tablespoon celery, finely chopped
Microwave on high for 2 minutes.

Using a wire whisk add and mix well:
¼ cup white whole-wheat or unbleached flour
Return to microwave on high and cook for 1 minute.

Add and mix well:
1 cup chicken broth, page 13
Microwave on high until mixture thickens, 1 to 2 minutes.

Add and mix well to make **soup**:
additional cup water or 1 cup milk (whole, 2%, 1%, or skim)
¼ teaspoon tarragon
salt and white pepper to taste
Cook in microwave on high until **mixture** thickens and is hot.

Option 🍎❤GF

- ■ **GF** Substitute **¼ cup gluten-free flour or 1 ½ Tablespoon corn starch** for **white whole-wheat flour or unbleached flour**.

Individually Quick Frozen Foods (IQF) 🍎♥GF

There is a new way of freezing foods separately before packaging them. You can freeze large quantities, and you can remove as few or as many as you need when they are not all frozen together in a block. Basically, all you do is place individual foods on baking sheets and freeze before you package them. This is especially good for freezing seasonal fruit for use throughout the year. You will find several recipes that call for IQF foods in this book.

Fruit

Strawberries, raspberries, blueberries, and other berries 🍎♥GF

Wash berries, hull those that need it, and place on baking sheets. Slide into freezer and allow to freeze solidly. Then place in plastic containers or resealable plastic bags.

Peaches 🍎♥GF

Blanch to remove skins, cut in half, and remove pit. Place on baking sheets and freeze solidly. Store in resealable plastic bags or plastic containers. I use five-quart ice cream buckets.

Other Foods

You will also find this method useful in freezing other foods, such as rolls. Instead of loading up your freezer with TV dinners, pizzas, and other prepared foods, stock up on nutritious fruits and foods you yourself have prepared.

God's Pharmacy

It's been said that God first separated the salt water from the fresh, made dry land, planted a garden, made animals and fish ... all before making a human. He made and provided what we'd need before we were born. These are best and more powerful when eaten raw. We're such slow learners … God left us a great clue as to what foods help what part of our body!

Italian Cooking

Glossary

al dente. Degree of doneness of pasta. Soft but still firm, never slack. To test doneness, bite the pasta; you should be able to see a tiny bit of raw pasta in the center.

Alfredo. Sauce made with cream and butter, sometimes cheese.

antipasto. Literally means "before the meal"; the first course of a traditional formal Italian meal. It has become more of an informal appetizer and a stand-alone party snack food. Usually a platter of small bits of food such as olives, cheeses, cured meats, artichokes, tomatoes, and other vegetables. Note: There is no such thing as *antipasta*, meaning "before the pasta."

béchamel. A cream sauce made of butter, flour, and cream. It was named after Louis Béchamel, a steward to King Louis XIV.

bolognese. Meat-based tomato sauce for pasta; originated in Bologna, Italy. Various recipes call for ground beef or different types of minced or finely chopped meats; flavored with small amounts of carrots, celery, and onion.

carbonara. Italian pasta dish based on eggs, cheese, and cream with bacon or pancetta. Most familiar version is fettuccine or spaghetti carbonara, which has crispy bacon or pancetta bits on top of Alfredo sauce.

fettuccine. Pasta that is long like spaghetti and flat like a noodle.

garlic. A bulbous plant of the lily family, made up of small sections called cloves, used for seasoning meats and salads.

garnish. To decorate (food) with something of color or flavor.

gastronomy. The art or science of good eating.

marinara. Sauce made with tomatoes and seasoned with garlic and spices.

pancetta. Italian-style bacon. Made from pork belly, it is cured but not smoked as regular bacon is; pancetta and bacon can be used interchangeably in many dishes.

pasta. The dough used to make spaghetti, linguine, fettuccine, angel hair, or any other macaroni product.

pesto. A ground sauce made of fresh basil, garlic, cheeses, and olive oils. Frequently has ground nuts, such as pine nuts.

polenta. Italian for corn meal mush.

ragu. A meat marinara. The word ragu means "to excite the appetite."

semolina flour. Granular, high-protein flour with coarse particles of wheat remaining after processing. Used particularly in pasta.

Going Back

After *Family Favorites* was published, I received many wonderful letters and comments, especially from people in Wyoming. After leaving Hartville, Nonna and Uncle Frank continued to have Italian dinners in their homes in Torrington and Cheyenne. Many people from Wyoming and surrounding states remembered eating their Italian dinners and were glad to have a cookbook not only for the recipes but for the stories of Wyoming. When I went to Hartville, Torrington, Casper, and Guernsey for book signings, many friends of my grandparents would have a story about them: "Mrs. Brazzale cooked the dinner for my wedding," "I mowed Mr. Brazzale's grass.," "My parents bought their tavern." I felt so at home hearing all these wonderful stories about my family and how much they were loved.

When going to Hartville, the first persons I usually contact are Deana (Testolin) Orr and Marion Jean Testolin Offee. Their grandparents were my grandparents' closest friends, and they had the Mercantile Store right across the street from Nonno's bar. Both Marion Jean and Deana have homes in Hartville and let us stay there when we come. After turning off the highway at Guernsey to drive the last six miles to Hartville, I roll down the windows of the car, drive slowly, and smell the wonderful scent of Wyoming ... maybe sage. And then there are the sights and sounds of birds and animals grazing in the hills . It is so serene. Soon we see the schoolhouse that has been converted

From left: Mary, Laurel Goddard, and Deana (Testolin) and Butch Orr.

Jon and Fran in front of Nonno's Bar.

Joker, the Shetland pony I rode in the cattle round-up in Wheatland, Wyoming.

into a museum and make the final curve into the village of Hartville. Memories begin to flood my mind of the adventures my brother Jon, sister Mary, and I had in this wonderful Italian, Greek, and Mexican community.

One Sunday I received a phone call from Laramie, Wyoming. "Are you the little redheaded granddaughter of Mrs. Brazzale that spent a couple of weeks at our ranch?" I immediately said, "Yes!" This was one of my most memorable times in Wyoming. The person calling was Joanne Sommers Bromley; I spent two weeks on the Sommers' ranch near Wheatland. At the ranch, I went on a cattle roundup and got to ride on a Shetland pony named Joker. We had a cookout at Wood's cabin near Laramie Peak. On a Saturday night there was a barn dance, and since I didn't bring any dress-up clothes, they altered a skirt and blouse for me to wear. They had a cousin, Wayne Sommers, who was probably coerced into asking me to dance. What a thrill—I was ten years old at the time. It was there I saw my first Jackalope. They assured me that it was a cross between a large jack rabbit and an antelope. What ten- year-old wouldn't believe this? But the problem was I believed it for many years and still get teased whenever one is mounted on a wall. I was just a kid from Nebraska; what was I to believe? After Nonno and Nonna retired, the bar went through a succession of owners including Dante and his son Tony Testolin and Joanne's parents, Hal and Wilma (Tic) Sommers. The tavern was named the Venice Bar and continued to house the Italian dinners in the basement. People from as far away as western Nebraska and northern Colorado would come to this bar for one of these Italian meals. Many people who have purchased my cookbook *Family Favorites* have often commented that

Tony Testolin, the son of Dante, and his cousin Lena Marie Balzan Dawson at the Family Favorites *book signing in Wheatland, Wyoming.*

they have had an Italian meal at this bar.

At a book signing at a Wheatland truck stop, two people from my past came walking through the door; it was Tony Testolin and his cousin Lena Marie Balzan Dawson. Tony was the son of Dante, and his sister, Kathleen, and I would help him deliver groceries to customers in Sunrise. We would sit in the back of a pickup ... how did we ever survive without a seat belt? Lena Marie, her twin sisters, Marilyn and Carolyn, and I began our culinary skills by making mud pies and decorating them with rocks and gravel. At another book signing in Torrington, John Russ brought pictures of his mother and a picture of Nonna's boarding house in Sunrise. It was the first time I had seen a picture of the boarding house where my mother had been raised. John said he didn't know which boarding house was Nonna's because there were three boarding houses in a row. They were called the "Three Bs," ... Brazzale, Balzan, and Besso. Celestina Balzan Testolin was my mother's best friend and stood up for my parents when they were married.

Another person I wanted to meet was Bill Logas. He was a friend of my mother and the person who allowed me to use the sketches by Carrie Arnold in *Family Favorites*. Each year, Carrie would sketch a Christmas card of Hartville or Sunrise for Bill, and he would send them to his friends. Every Christmas you can imagine how happy friends of Bill were to receive a card. Everyone I know who received these cards kept them, including my mother. When I saw this picture of Frank's Bar with Nonna and me, I knew I wanted this picture in my cookbook, plus the other familiar sketches of Hartville and Sunrise After the book was published, we planned a trip to Wyoming and Colorado; I called Bill and asked him if we could take him out to lunch ... his choice. After lunch, he took us to his apartment so we could continue our visit. On the walls

The three boarding houses called the Three Bs, Balzan's, Besso's, and Brazzale's.

of his apartment were all the original paintings of Hartville and Sunrise by Carrie Arnold. A few years later, we called him again to go out for lunch. When he got into the car, he handed me a package; he said, "This is something I want you to have." When I unwrapped it, it was the original painting of Frank's Bar. I was so happy to have it and offered to pay him for it. He refused and said, "I feel this painting belongs to you." This painting begins the Italian section of this book and is one of the reasons I decided to print this book in color.

Back, from left: My mom, Nida Cappozzo, and Nella Morris. Front, from left: Julia Grand Pre and Uncle Frank Brazzale.

Bill Lagos giving me the original painting of Frank's Tavern.

This year I received an email from the Hartville Town Hall requesting some cookbooks. Also written in the email was a message, "If you happened to be in the area, we would like you to come to our meeting about the Hartville museum." I called my sister Mary; she called Deana, and away we went. As soon as we got to Hartville, we stopped at the schoolhouse; several people were there preparing for a visit from the Wyoming Historical Society from Cheyenne. Their visit was to help them organize the museum. The following day we attended the meeting and heard many new stories about Hartville.

One was when the Ku Klux Klan burned a cross on the hill just above Hartville. Why? There were no black people in the village, but there were a lot of immigrants from Italy, Greece, and Mexico. The burning cross caused a large fire on the hillside, and that was the last time there was any trouble with the KKK. After the meeting, we had a tour of the village: Town Hall, Fire Station, the oldest bar in Wyoming, and some new construction on the hillside. Next we went to Sunrise. The mine has been closed for many years and so has the village of Sunrise. One man, who owns the area, gave us a special tour of the existing buildings; then we went to the mining pit. This was

Nonna with a friend.

Sunrise Mine.

something most people, especially women, had never seen. All around were buildings with equipment from days gone by. There is always talk of the possibility of some day the mine reopening or being a tourist attraction. The man who owns Sunrise loves living there. While driving back to Hartville, I asked the lady who was driving, "'Who lives in Hartville now?" The lady told me mostly retired people. But when Mary and I stopped at a house she once owned, we realized this wasn't the case. While Mary was taking pictures of the house, a young lady came out to talk to us. Mary said, "Is this your house?" She said, "Yes." Mary told her that she once owned the house, and the lady invited us in to show us how she had remodeled it. She explained they had bought the house because they loved the area and used it only in the summer months; but they liked living there so much that they decided to bring their business there. They have three homes, one they live in, one for their candle business, and another one. We were overjoyed to hear this, and hopefully there will be many more couples like this who will want to live in this beautiful village of Hartville.

Four Essentials of Italian Cooking

Butter

Since *Family Favorites* was published, butter has come back into favor. I guess Nonna, in all her wisdom, knew best when she never allowed margarine in her house. She used butter for everything that called for shortening or margarine ... pie crust, cookies, cakes, etc. Now, since there is an increased interest in natural foods, not only is butter back in favor but also lard (home rendered) and coconut (palm) oils. When our family was on the Feingold diet, I used only unsalted butter, but now I use regular butter, and, contrary to what some other cooks say, I don't see any difference. If you are worried about too much salt in your diet, decrease the amount of salt called for in the recipe.

Garlic

Garlic is used in all kinds of cooking, not just Italian, and I feel it is the most important Italian flavoring. I never use garlic powder or garlic salt. Garlic powder is ground, dehydrated garlic, and garlic salt is *simply* salt with garlic powder. Expensive salt! Over the years, garlic has not only been used for food but also for its antiseptic capability, inhibiting the action of bacteria. Mashed garlic was applied to wounds before the discovery of antibiotics, and medieval doctors wore masks stuffed with garlic in times of plague. Garlic is traditionally hung, often braided in strands called plaits. Nonna would hang her garlic in the garage for future use. Garlic bulbs should be clean and white with a dried neck and outer skin and feel firm under pressure. If spongy or showing any signs of mold, garlic should be discarded. Garlic may have a greenish hue due to an abundant sulfur compound, but it is safe to eat. One important thing: If you burn garlic, start over because it will take on a strong, unpleasant taste and odor. You want only a golden brown color.

Olive Oil

The olive was native to Asia Minor and spread to the Mediterranean Basin six thousand years ago. Throughout history, kings and nobility have been ceremonially anointed with olive oil. During baptism in the Christian church, holy oil is often olive oil. It is blessed by the bishops of the Catholic Church at the Chrism Mass and used for their sacraments.

The Romans and Greeks had many uses for olive oil. The Greeks anointed winning athletes with olive oil and used olive oil to make their muscles appear supple, while noble ladies maintained the freshness of their skins with it. I remember Nonna telling my mother to use olive oil on her face rather than the facial cream she bought at the department store. It worked for me when I had rosacea. Olive oil was also used to light lamps.

Olives are harvested in November and December. Green olives are picked before they are fully ripened. Black olives are picked when they are ripe or even overripe.

The oil must be extracted from the olives within a week, using a cold process for pressing. The best oil is produced in one or two days. Extra virgin and virgin oil comes from the first pressings and have the most intense flavor. Other olive oils come from subsequent pressings. Since the whole process takes place without any heat, the end result is the pure juice of the olive with all the nutrition of the fruit left in. It is the heat used in processing vegetable oils that makes them less healthful.

There are several classifications of olive oil, *extra virgin* being the top quality in olives and processing—and the most expensive. As a pamphlet from one of the olive oil companies says, it is like a beautiful Italian lady who has never so much as been kissed. It can contain no more than 1% of free oleic acid. *Virgin olive oil*, like extra virgin, is also top quality but for one reason or another does not quite qualify as extra virgin. It is the lovely Italian lady who is pure but slightly more worldly. Then there is olive oil or *pure olive oil*, a blend of refined olive oil and virgin or extra virgin oils. Finally, there is *light olive oil*, which has an even smaller amount of virgin or extra virgin olive oil.

Olive oil from different regions can have different colors and flavors. Italian olive oil is typically dark green with an herbal aroma and grassy flavor. Spanish olive oil is often golden yellow and has a nutty, fruity flavor. Californian olive oil tends to be light in color and flavor.

There are many choices available, and Mom and Nonna always strongly recommended "Italian olive oil." I use Italian extra virgin olive oil in my salads, sauces, and pastas. I use what is called olive oil or pure olive oil for frying.

Parmesan Cheese

After I closed Nonna's I needed to grate some Parmesan cheese. The large Hobart mixer that had the cheese grater attachment had been sold, so I thought I would try my fine shredder attachment to my KitchenAid mixer. I cut the cheese into the size that fit the shredder, froze the cheese, and the next day, grated the cheese. It worked! This was another "Ah-ha Moment" in my life because this was one of the most frequently asked questions, "Where can I find a good cheese grater?" Most people have those small hand-held graters, used in restaurants, that don't grate a large quantity of cheese. Because I still buy a twenty-pound Parmesan wheel that has been aged for ten months, I usually grate five pounds of cheese at a time and place it in the freezer until I'm ready to use it. I still feel any wedge of Parmesan cheese that is hand grated is far superior to any processed grated cheese in a container on the store shelf. *Remember, if the cheese doesn't require any refrigeration, it has additives to prevent molding and ensure shelf life.* After grating cheeses for thirty years, we have learned some helpful hints to ensure finely grated cheese.

Helpful Hints

- If you have a KitchenAid mixer, buy the shredder attachment and use the shredder with the finest grate.
- Cut the cheese into suitable pieces to fit your grater and then freeze these pieces overnight. Frozen cheese will grate finer.
- When grating the cheese, don't apply a lot of pressure to the cheese as its grating. If you do, the cheese will have a coarser grate. Use just enough pressure that the cheese is hitting the grater.
- Store the cheese in tightly covered containers and refrigerate.

- After you grate the cheese, if you don't plan to use all the cheese within a week, freeze the remainder in tightly covered containers. It can be frozen indefinitely.
- You will have small pieces of cheese that will break off that you can't grate. Save those pieces and add them to your pasta before you add the sauce. It is delicious to bite into a "hunk" of Parmesan cheese.

Parmesan cheese, olive oil, butter, and garlic.

Basic Equipment for the Italian Kitchen

Garlic Press

This inexpensive item can be found in most kitchen gadget stores. If you use large quantities of garlic as I do, consult the Staples section, page 7, and equipment notes, page xvi, of this book for grinding larger amounts of freshly squeezed or pressed garlic using the KitchenAid food grinder attachment. Nevertheless, a hand garlic press is always useful if you only have to press one or two cloves in a hurry.

A Pasta Machine with a Motor

If you want to make your own pasta, I highly recommend this. The pasta machine is a must in itself, but the motor makes it even more wonderful, and it will enable you to use your machine without clamping it to a table. I found there was no comparison when I finally got a motor attachment. I like to compare it to using an electric mixer instead of a hand rotary beater. Like Nonna, I have several motors on hand! KitchenAid has pasta attachments, but I prefer the standard motorized pasta machine because it is waist high on the counter.

Ravioli Crimper

This is a necessity if you are making any of the filled pasta dishes to ensure a good, tight seal on your filled pastas. It also can be found where kitchen gadgets are sold.

Fresh Egg Pasta

Pasta is synonymous with Italian cooking. It is the basic ingredient for so very many Italian dishes. It is either commercially produced, which is usually dried, or it is made fresh at home or in restaurants. Fresh egg pasta is truly superior to pasta that is commercially made. Besides better taste and texture, it has a rough surface to which sauces cling. Commercial pasta has a smooth surface to which sauces do not cling, and it takes longer to reach the proper degree of doneness (*al dente*).

Fresh egg pasta is made from flour mixed with eggs and small amounts of water. Additional flavors and colors may be added by using other substances such as spinach for green, carrot for orange, tomato for red. And the Italians also learned to make many shapes of pasta from the same basic recipe … spaghetti, fettuccine, linguine, lasagna, tortellini, etc. *My original recipe called for unbleached white flour, but then I discovered and started using white whole-wheat flour and have also developed a recipe for gluten-free egg pasta. I include all three recipes in this book.*

I learned the basics from my nonna and my mother, but I do not hand mix, knead, roll, and cut my pasta as they did. I learned early on that my KitchenAid mixer could do the job for me. When I decided to open my restaurant, I invested in a heavy-duty commercial mixer.

Another shortcut I highly recommend if you are going to make your own pasta is a **pasta machine *with a motor***.

White Whole-Wheat Egg Pasta

While shopping at a locally owned supermarket, Skagway, I noticed white whole-wheat flour on sale. I couldn't imagine what this was; could it be bleached whole-wheat flour and was the flour's color white? No. It was unbleached, and the color was a light tan. White whole wheat has no major gene for bran color (unlike red that has three bran color genes). You can think of it as an "albino wheat." Did the pasta have a bitter taste, like that noticeable with regular whole-wheat pasta? The answer was "no," again. I couldn't notice any change in taste from regular egg pasta made with unbleached and semolina flours. If you boil some of each together you might notice a slight difference in color, and the taste is not bitter. This recipe is for a domestic KitchenAid mixer using a dough hook. I have seen recipes six pages long describing and illustrating pasta dough making, but with the KitchenAid mixer I have shortened the recipe and time it takes to make the dough. Finding this flour has changed the way I cook and bake; I've tried this flour on breads, cakes, and even pie crust.

Mixing Pasta Dough*

In mixer bowl using dough hook, combine:
2 cups white whole-wheat flour**
1 cup semolina flour
Blend well.

*Check for illustrations on pages 36–37.
**For basic egg pasta dough, substitute an equal amount of unbleached flour for white whole-wheat flour.

Preparing the pasta.

Prepared pasta.

The kneaded pasta ready to cut.

Cutting the pasta in diagonal slices.

Form a well in center of **flour** and add:
3 whole eggs or 6 to 7 egg whites (approximately 1 cup liquid)
With dough hook, mix until the **pasta mixture** has a crumbly appearance.

While continuing to mix, gradually add around the edges of the bowl:
¼ to ½ cup water

Scrape **dough** toward middle with a rubber spatula. Turn out on a board floured with a **blend of semolina and white whole-wheat flours**. Knead in **additional flour** until you reach the desired firmness. The **dough** should be firm, not too hard or soft, moist but not sticky. It is easier to add

Rolling out pasta sheet.

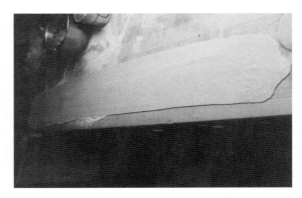

Prepared pasta sheet.

Cutting fettuccine noodles.

Lasagne, fettuccine, linguine, spaghetti, and angel-hair pastas.

more **flour** to make the **dough** firm than it is to add moisture to a dry dough. Store **dough** in a plastic bag at room temperature for 2 hours so **dough** can absorb the liquids. Roll and cut into shapes, preferably with your motorized pasta machine.

Refrigerate or freeze any **dough** that you are not using immediately. **Dough** will keep a week in the refrigerator. Bring back to room temperature before using. If **dough** is too firm, microwave approximately 30 seconds on high, depending on the size of the piece of dough. ***Dough that has been microwaved must be rolled out immediately, because the dough will become hard and stiff, making it impossible to roll into sheets or cut into noodles.***

Rolling and Cutting Pasta Dough

Before cutting, place **dough** on **floured surface**, kneading slightly with a **semolina-and-white-whole-wheat-flour mixture**. Cut the pasta **dough** at an angle into slices approximately 1-inch thick. Flatten with a rolling pin before using the machine. **Flour each piece generously**; be sure it is not sticky.

Pass the pasta through the rollers at the thickest setting. Continue to roll the pasta, reducing the space between the rollers until you get the desired thickness. **Flour generously each pasta sheet** before layering each sheet on top of the other. (See photo illustrations on page 37.)

When all the dough is rolled into sheets of the desired thickness, change the cutting head to make the desired shapes of the noodles. Now it's time to cut the pasta.

The **pasta sheet** should be **lightly floured** to prevent it from sticking to the cutter, then start passing the **pasta** through the cutters.

I didn't have the room or the time it takes to dry pasta, so I *layered my fresh pasta in flat plastic boxes lined with waxed paper. I placed waxed paper between each layer of cut pasta* then placed the boxes in the freezer. The pasta is available as needed. This process prevents your noodles from becoming brittle and breaking into small pieces, as often happens with dried pasta.

Cooking Pasta
(for Noodles, Spaghetti, Fettuccini, Linguini, etc.)

To cook **pasta** correctly, you must start with a large pot that will be able to hold an ample amount of salted, boiling water. For **1 pound of pasta**, you need a pot that will hold **4 to 5 quarts water**. Add **1 Tablespoon salt**. I also prefer one that has an insert that allows you to drain the pasta immediately, instead of using a colander. This way, if you need to boil more pasta, you have your boiling water ready.

After the **pasta** is placed in the **water**, immediately stir the **pasta** to keep it from sticking together. You can test the doneness by biting a noodle. If it tastes and feels chewy, and you see a tiny bit of raw noodle in the center, it is *al dente* and ready to be removed from the water. Drain thoroughly, but do not rinse under cold water because the **pasta** gets slippery and can lose some of its flavor. Check the doneness of **pasta** often; most Americans tend to overcook it.

Approximate Cooking Times

Dried commercial pasta (you can also check the package recommendations):

7 to 12 minutes for most pastas
3 to 5 minutes for angel-hair pasta

Frozen fresh pasta:

5 to 10 minutes

Freshly cut pasta:

3 to 5 minutes for most pastas
2 to 3 minutes for angel-hair pasta

Serving Pasta

Place **pasta** on a *warm* platter or in a large serving bowl. Add **Parmesan cheese** to the noodles before adding the **sauce**. This creates another surface for the **sauce** to adhere to. We always add the **sauce** to the **pasta**, mix well, and then add **additional sauce** in the middle of the **pasta** and **sprinkle with cheese**. Garnish with **fresh herbs**.

Gluten-Free Egg Pasta 🍎 GF

"I DID IT." How often do you hear that phrase when a little child conquers a difficult feat, such as pedaling a tricycle for the first time. That's how I felt the day when I was able to make gluten-free egg noodles. Being an Italian cook, I thought this would be easy, but each time I tried it, it was a disaster. I checked with the gluten-free experts on the Internet, and they seemed to be having the same problems. The ones who had finally made some noodles had so many instructions that it wasn't a good recipe for a book called *Shortcuts to Gourmet Cooking*. There were no shortcuts to be found. I had made up my mind to say in this book, "Don't try this. Just buy gluten-free pasta in the stores." But after I found Premium Gold Gluten-Free All Purpose flour with the top 13 allergen-free ingredients, I decided to give it another try, and it worked. Hooray and Hallelujah!*

In a mixer bowl with a dough hook attachment, add:

1 cup gluten-free all-purpose flour

With the dough hook, make a well in the middle of the **flour**.

In a medium bowl, using a wire whisk, beat:

3 (large) egg yolks

¼ cup water

Pour into the well of the **flour** and mix on medium setting with the dough hook.
The **flour mixture** will appear crumbly.

*After cooking the gluten-free pasta, both Dave and I felt it didn't have the chewiness of wheat pasta, but it was a good substitute for people with celiac and gluten problems. I made it with Chicken Cacciatore, page 48, and it tasted very good.

Continue adding **water** a *little* at a time until it forms a **dough** when you squeeze it together. When it has the appearance of regular pasta dough, store the **dough** in a plastic bag at room temperature for at least 2 hours or more. This helps the **flour** absorb the **egg mixture.** Divide the **dough** in half; with your rolling pin, roll out each piece into ⅛-inch thickness before using your pasta machine. Roll the **dough** through the machine, fold it over, run it through 2 or 3 times until you get a smooth sheet of **pasta**. Then cut it into your choice of **pasta**: spaghetti, linguine, or fettuccine.

For cooking times, see page 38–39.

Back row: Sammy. Middle row, left to right: Zoey, Tony, Cari, Jack. Front row: Gracie.

Crock-Pot Italiano

In this part of the Italian section, you will find recipes that are the same as in *Family Favorites*; however, the method of preparation is different. After we closed Nonna's, we remodeled our kitchen; during that period of time, I didn't have the use of a stove, so I had to use my Crock-Pot. First I tried making meatballs, then chicken cacciatore; why not Italian sausage and so on. I began to tell people about my new discoveries, but it seems they prefer written recipes and instructions, so the addition of this new section, "Crock-Pot Italiano."

Although it takes a longer time to cook your food, I feel the preparation time is the same or faster, no matter if you are a working or stay-at-home mom. The beauty of the Crock-Pot is it cooks evenly on all surfaces of the pot, preventing the scorching of the food. Slow cooking also enhances the flavors.

When using a Crock-Pot, there will be minutes or an hour between the different steps of the recipe, and this is when you might have time to do something else in the house or go shopping. The timer is an invaluable tool when cooking with a Crock-Pot as it is a reminder to check on the cooking progress, add a few more minutes, or start the next step of the recipe. When the food has finished cooking, you can turn your setting to "low" or "warm" and serve when everyone is ready to eat.

Reminder: Alway put the lid back on the Crock-Pot between cooking steps.

Basic Tomato Sauce 🍎♥GF

In a large Crock-Pot on *high* setting, combine:
1 Tablespoon butter
¼ cup olive oil

Sauté in **oil** and **butter** until golden brown:
2 to 5 garlic cloves, freshly squeezed (depending on your taste for garlic)

To the sautéed **garlic**, add and mix well with a wire whisk:
2 (46-ounce) cans tomato juice
1 (12-ounce) can tomato paste
2 teaspoons sweet basil
1 teaspoon oregano
Cook on low heat for approximately 2 to 4 hours until the **sauce** thickens. If too thick, add
another can of tomato juice. This recipe will make approximately **3 quarts of tomato sauce**.

Options

■ Add any of the ingredients below that appeal to your tastes. Experiment and make your
   own trademark spaghetti sauce. Try different combinations for different dishes.

onions	rosemary
leeks	**¼ to ½ teaspoon sugar**
scallions	**dash of cinnamon**
bell peppers	**additional garlic**
carrots	**marjoram**
celery	**parsley**
sautéed mushrooms	**red wine**
whole tomatoes for tomato juice (fresh or canned)	**salt pork in place of butter**

■ Use **green-stemmed garlic** (known as **green garlic**) instead of your regular garlic. It is not
   fully mature and so has a milder taste.

Italian Meatballs 🍎GF

When I first opened Nonna's, I didn't want to use any fillers (bread crumbs) in my meatballs. If you want any honest criticism about your food, just listen to your immediate family. My brother Jim said, "Your meatballs are so tough, they could bounce like a ball! What you need is to add some bread crumbs to your meat balls." I started to add bread crumbs to my meatballs and realized he was right.

Makes: 14 to 16 meatballs

In a Crock-Pot on high setting, melt approximately 5 minutes:
1 Tablespoon butter
2 Tablespoons extra virgin olive oil

Add to **butter/olive oil mixture**:
2 garlic cloves, freshly squeezed
Sauté approximately 15 minutes until **garlic** is *lightly* browned.

While **garlic** is cooking, in a large bowl add and mix thoroughly:
2 pounds (80/20) ground beef
½ cup bread crumbs, page 3
½ teaspoon salt
¼ teaspoon pepper
2 cloves garlic, freshly squeezed
Shape your **meat mixture** into quarter- to 50-cent-sized meatballs and place *evenly* in Crock-Pot with the **garlic mixture**.

Sprinkle with:
2 teaspoons sweet basil
1 teaspoon oregano
Cover and sauté on high setting until completely browned, approximately 45 to 60 minutes.

If you want, you can leave in the **meat drippings** or drain any excess **drippings** from the **meatballs** at this time. *The drippings give the sauce a wonderful flavor.*

Add to the meatballs:

2 (46-ounce) cans tomato juice

1 (12-ounce) can tomato paste

Continue to cook the meatballs on high setting until the **sauce** begins to simmer, then turn the Crock-Pot on low setting. Allow it to cook for at least 2 hours or until you notice the **sauce** becoming thick, then reduce your Crock-Pot setting to warm until you are ready to serve.

Serve on a large, *warm* platter with your choice of **pasta**, arranging **meatballs** around the side, and pour **tomato sauce** over the top. Sprinkle with **Parmesan cheese**.

Option

■ **GF** Substitute **gluten-free bread or crackers** for **bread crumbs**.

My brother Jim Calhoun and his wife, Deb.

Italian Steak Rolls 🍎GF

My nonna served Italian steak rolls in place of meatballs. At my restaurant, the Italian steak roll was a Special of the Week and was served with Italian-style Potatoes (page 336 in *Family Favorites*). The special had quite a following, and when it was advertised in the newspaper, I knew who would be dining at Nonna's that week.

Serves: 10 to 12

Before making this recipe, go to the supermarket and have the butcher thinly slice sirloin or round steak into **10 to 12 (⅛-inch thick) slices.** I use **thin sandwich steaks.**

Have prepared:
1 recipe Basic Tomato Sauce, page 43

In a large bowl, mix together:
2 pounds (80/20) ground beef
1 cup grated Parmesan cheese
1 cup bread crumbs, page 3
½ cup white or yellow onions, finely chopped
1 teaspoon salt
½ teaspoon pepper
4 large eggs
In the mixer, using a dough hook or with your hands, mix the **meat** *thoroughly* with the other ingredients and place it in the refrigerator until ready to use.

To form the **steak rolls,** place a *thin slice* of **steak** on the palm of your left hand; place ⅓ to ½ **cup filling** on the palm side of your hand. Fold the sides of the **steak** toward the center and roll the **filling** into the remainder of the **steak.** Place the **rolls** on a baking sheet.

On the stove top with a Dutch oven or large Crock-Pot on *medium to low* heat, add:

2 Tablespoons butter

¼ cup extra virgin olive oil

2 garlic cloves, freshly squeezed

Allow the **garlic** to *lightly* brown.

Add to lightly browned **garlic**:

Prepared steak rolls

Place seam-side down, closely, side by side in a single layer.

Sprinkle over the top of the **steak rolls**:

1 teaspoon oregano

1 teaspoon sweet basil

Cook on medium to low heat until the **steak rolls** are completely cooked. Drain off most of the **meat juices** and set aside in refrigerator. When cooled, remove the **fat.**

Add to **steak rolls**:

enough tomato sauce to cover the rolls

defatted meat juices

Reduce the heat to low and allow the **steak rolls** to simmer in the **tomato sauce** for 2 or more hours.

To serve: Place a **meat roll** on a warmed plate and cover with **extra tomato sauce.**

Option

■ **GF**   Use **gluten-free bread or gluten-free cracker crumbs** for **bread crumbs**.

Chicken Cacciatore ⬤ ♥ GF

In a Crock-Pot on high setting, melt approximately 10 minutes:
4 Tablespoons (½ stick) butter

Add to **melted butter** and sautée, approximately 30 minutes:
½ medium white or yellow onion, finely sliced
Cook until **onions** are tender and transparent.

Add to the **onion/butter mixture**:
1 (3- to 4-pound) cut-up chicken with the skin side down*

Sprinkle lightly with:
salt and pepper
½ teaspoon basil
½ teaspoon tarragon
Continue to cook on high setting. Turn occasionally until **chicken** is slightly browned on all sides, approximately 1 hour.

When **chicken** is cooked and browned, add:
2 (46-ounce) cans tomato juice
1 (12-ounce) can tomato paste
Mix well and continue to cook the **chicken** on high setting until the **sauce** begins to simmer, then turn to low setting until **sauce** thickens. Turn to warm setting until ready to serve.

To serve, place carefully on a *warm* platter; often the meat of the chicken is so tender that it falls off the bone. It is wonderful with any **pasta** you choose.

Use fresh tarragon in salads, omelets, chicken dishes, or in cream sauces. It can also be used to flavor white wine vinegar.

*Most of the time I only use the breast, thighs, legs, and wings of the chicken for cacciatore. I use the ribs, back, neck, and wing tips for making chicken broth, page 13.

Italian Sausage

Many people when trying a new food will like it or hate it, and you will have a hard time getting them to try a different recipe. I was one of those people. I had eaten Italian sausages at an Italian food festival in Omaha; I did not like the taste of the sauce or the sausage. I don't know about other nationalities, but it seems with Italians everyone's recipe is the best, and I guess I'm just as guilty as anyone else. I have never liked hot-tasting food, and this was why I crossed off this food. It was too hot. But after a persistent customer kept after me to try his recipe and even brought the ingredients, I gave it another try. Not only was the sauce delicious, but the sausages were mild and sweet. This became a favorite of many of my customers. This is one recipe that the longer it cooks, the better it tastes, and if it is a leftover, you can be sure it will be eaten.

Have prepared:
1 recipe Basic Tomato Sauce, page 43

Serves: 4 to 6

In a Crock-Pot on high setting, heat approximately 5 minutes:
¼ cup or less olive oil

Add and sauté in the **oil** until browned on all sides, approximately 45 minutes:
6 to 8 mild sweet Italian sausages
Allow them to simmer in their own juices.

Add to the **sausages** and cook until tender, approximately 15 to 20 minutes:
½ cup white or yellow onions, minced

Add:
3 to 4 cups Basic Tomato Sauce, enough to cover the sausages
Allow the **sauce** to come to a simmer, then place in the Crock-Pot on low setting.

Add, 30 to 60 minutes before serving:
1 cup sweet bell peppers, assorted colors, coarsely cut

To serve, place the **sausages** on warm plates with a generous amount of **sauce**. We served the **Italian sausages** with **angel-hair pasta** at Nonna's.

Crock-Pot Fettuccine Alfredo 🍎

When cooking for a small or large group, timing is everything. You want to have your meal ready when your company arrives and are ready to sit down to eat. Keeping the food ready and warm can be a challenge at times. When I had Nonna's, I had a small steam table, which was a godsend, but I sold it when we closed. First, I tried to keep my food warm by placing the food in a large stainless steel bowl over a large pot of boiling water, and it worked. But then I got a new idea … use my Crock-Pot!

I made Chicken Florentine, page 64, with Fettuccine Alfredo, page 61. I placed the Crock-Pot on the lowest settings (low or warm) before I fried the chicken and boiled the water for the fettuccine noodles. I placed ½ **to 1 cup of chicken broth** (page 13) into one pot and 1½ **cups Alfredo sauce** into the other pot. You can do this about ½ to 1 hour before serving. After frying my **chicken breasts**, I placed them into the Crock-Pot with the **chicken broth** and covered with the lid. At the same time, I cooked the **noodles** until *al dente* and mixed them in the warm **Alfredo sauce**. Then I sprinkled a generous amount of **Parmesan cheese** over the top, mixed well again, and covered with the lid. Every 10 minutes, I would check the fettuccine to see if **additional cheese or sauce** was needed. To my surprise, cooking low in the Crock-Pot made a warm, creamy **fettuccine** and a moist **chicken breast** … better than the steam table. Sometimes I wonder why it takes me so long to figure out some of these "Helpful Hints," but you are never too old to learn something new.

Stuffed, Filled, or Layered Pasta

'So Let the Dice Roll'

Many people associate Italian food with spaghetti and meatballs and other cut pasta, such as linguine, fettuccine, and angel hair, but there are many forms of pasta. The filled, layered, and stuffed pastas are foods we seldom make but often order at a restaurant. They are more time-consuming because they have fillings, but you can make them easier when you use fresh pasta rather than purchased pasta. Before I started Nonna's, I bought all my pasta in a package or box; I had trouble making mannicotti and lasagna because the pasta would break or tear after it was boiled, making a mess. At first I boiled my fresh pasta before I used it, but soon I learned to use fresh-cut pasta with a little more sauce for the noodles to absorb. This made assembling these dishes so much easier and cut my time in half. It gave the food a better flavor. When Nonna would come to visit, we would often make ravioli as a group effort … sort of like an assembly line. One person would roll out the dough; another would fill, cover, press down around each mound, and mark with a fork; the last person would crimp, cut, and place the raviolis into cardboard flats lined with wax paper. To identify the types of ravioli, we would mark them with different types of forks. Using a three-prong fork, we marked beef with two marks and cheese with a crisscross design; for chicken we marked twice with a four-prong fork. While demonstrating ravioli making with my sister, Mary, on a Kansas television station (Nex-Tech), the producer saw the markings on the ravioli and stated, "They look like dice."

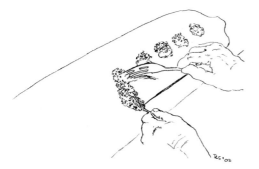

Step 1. Place fillings 2 inches apart.

Step 2. Folding top half of sheet over filling.

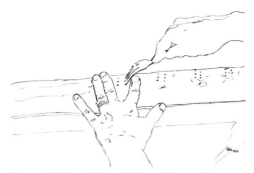

Step 3. With a fork, pricking all mounds through all thicknesses.

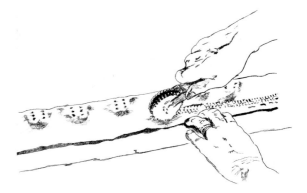

Step 4. Crimping ravioli on bottom edge.

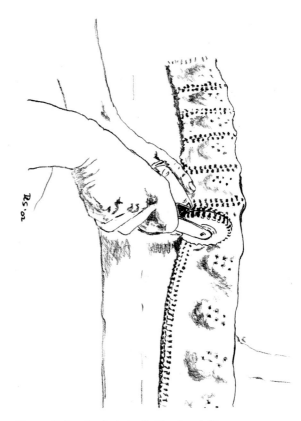

Step 5. Crimping into individual ravioli.

Cheese Ravioli 🍎❤

Ravioli is a pocket-filled pasta that can be made with various types of fillings ... meats, chicken, fish, and cheeses, as well as sauces such as tomato, butter, Alfredo, and pesto. For Italian women such as my nonna, it was a way to use leftover food and make a meal that is now considered gourmet. This is an easy recipe to experiment with using a cheese filling and different sauces. Cheese ravioli has to be a vegetarian's dream.

Have prepared:
1 recipe Pasta Dough, page 34

In a skillet, melt:
½ cup (1 stick) butter

Sauté:
1 white or yellow medium onion finely chopped until tender and transparent
1 (10-ounce) package frozen spinach, thawed and drained well (squeeze out as much liquid as possible).

After **spinach mixture** has cooled, chop finely or run through a meat grinder.

Add to **spinach mixture**:
1 (16-ounce) carton ricotta cheese
½ to 1 cup grated Parmesan cheese
½ teaspoon nutmeg
2 to 3 large eggs
The **mixture** should be firm and hold together, be moist but not ooze liquid. If too moist, add **bread crumbs**, page 3, to get desired consistency.

Roll out **pasta dough** into a long sheet of thin to medium thickness. With a fork, place **½ to 1 teaspoon filling** approximately 2 inches apart on the bottom half of the **pasta sheet**.

Fold the top half of the sheet over the **filling** to the bottom edge. Gently press down and around each mound of **filling**. Then prick each mound through all thicknesses twice with a fork.

With a ravioli crimper, or fluted pastry wheel, cut into squares. Repeat the process until all the **filling** is used.

Cook the **fresh ravioli** in a large pot with a pasta insert/strainer, filled with **6 to 8 quarts of rapidly boiling, salted water**. Boil **ravioli** for about 8 to 15 minutes or until tender. Stir gently to prevent the **ravoili** from sticking to each other. Drain by removing insert.*

To serve: Place on a large, *warm* platter or in a pasta bowl. Sprinkle with **Parmesan cheese**. Top with **Tomato Sauce**, page 43, **Pesto Sauce** (page 77 in *Family Favorites*), or **butter**. Serve immediately.

*If you don't have a pasta insert, use a collander or a sieve to drain the pasta.

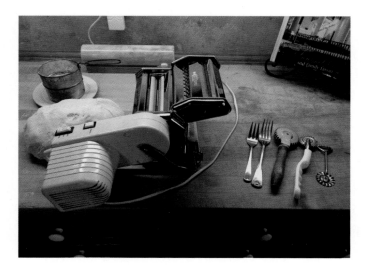

Meadowlark Vegetarian Lasagna 🍎

When I retired, I looked for meaningful things to do. I decided to donate my time to people who were looking for someone to help with fundraisers. I found my calling. One of my callings was from Stuhr Museum. They have a Meadowlark Festival every summer, which is an outdoor event. Pam Price asked me to help Jean Rock of Sutter's Deli with the event in June 2010. I was asked to do a vegetarian lasagna using Alfredo sauce rather than tomato sauce, and this is the recipe we used.

Serves: 12

Have prepared:
1 recipe **Pasta Dough**, page 34
1 recipe **Alfredo Sauce**, page 61
½ to 1 cup bread crumbs, page 3

Also have ready:
1 (16 ounce) package grated Mozzarella cheese
½ cup grated Parmesan cheese
1 (16-ounce) carton ricotta or cottage cheese

In a large skillet, melt:
½ cup (1 stick) butter

Add and sauté until tender and transparent:
1 medium white or yellow onion, finely chopped

Add and cook until most of the moisture is gone:
2 (10-ounce) packages frozen chopped spinach (which has been thawed and squeezed to remove as much moisture as possible)
Remove from heat and allow it to cool in the skillet. This will help the remainder of the moisture to evaporate.

In another skillet, melt:
½ cup (1 stick) butter

Add and sauté for 2 to 3 minutes:
8 ounces mushrooms, freshly sliced
Combine and mix well with **spinach/onion mixture**, then set aside.

Roll out prepared **pasta dough** into long sheets of thin to medium thickness and cut into:
6 (9 × 6-inch) noodles

Assemble the Ingredients

Bake: Preheated 350 degree oven
Time: 45 to 60 minutes

In the bottom of 9 × 13 **greased** pan, pour:
1 ½ cups Alfredo sauce

Over the **sauce**, layer:
2 (9 × 6) noodles
½ the shredded Mozzarella cheese
½ the spinach/mushroom mixture
½ carton ricotta cheese

Sprinkle over the top:
½ cup grated Parmesan cheese
¼ to ½ cup bread crumbs

Pour over top in back and forth motion (drizzle):
½ to ¾ cup Alfredo sauce

Repeat layering.

Cover the **lasagna** with:
Last 2 (9 × 6) noodles
1 ½ to 2 cups Alfredo sauce, enough to cover generously
Bake as instructed above until *browned* at the edges and the center is *firm*. Cover with additional **sauce** and sprinkle with additional **mozzarella cheese**. Cover with foil, turn oven off, and allow the **lasagna** to remain in the oven for ½ hour before serving. This allows the **lasagna** to set up so the **filling** doesn't ooze.

To serve: Cut into 1 ½ by 3-inch pieces. Sprinkle with **Parmesan cheese** and **parsley flakes**.

Helpful Hints

- Freezing: When making **lasagna** ahead of time, put the top layer of **sauce** over the **lasagna** after removing it from the freezer.
- Portion out the leftovers and place in resealable plastic bags. Freeze for later use. These portions can be microwaved as needed.
- Make **lasagna noodles** ahead of time and in the same manner that you do **ravioli** or **cut pasta**. Line each layer with waxed paper.

Presentation of Meadowlark Vegetarian Lasagna.

Manicotti 🍎♥

In my Italian family we had a few favorite dishes, and we never ventured too far from our comfort zone. One day I found manicotti noodles at the supermarket with a recipe on the box; it looked interesting. I tried the recipe but didn't like it because when I tried to stuff the noodles with the manicotti filling, the noodles often split. It was messy. I remedied this problem by using homemade uncooked pasta noodles; it worked like a charm.

Serves: 12 to 14

Have prepared:
1 recipe Fresh Pasta Dough, page 34
1 recipe Basic Tomato Sauce, page 43

In a large mixing bowl, mix:
2 pounds (80/20) ground beef
1 cup bread crumbs, page 3
1 cup grated mozzarella cheese
½ cup grated Parmesan cheese
2 to 3 large eggs
½ teaspoon salt
¼ teaspoon pepper
Mix well and *set aside* for about one hour to allow the **dry ingredients** to absorb the **liquids**.

Assembling the Manicotti

Bake: Preheated 350 degree oven
Time: 45 to 60 minutes

Grease a 9 × 13-inch pan. Pour **1 ½ cups tomato sauce** over bottom of pan. *Set aside.*

Roll out **pasta dough** into a long, medium-thick sheet. I use the third to last notch on the pasta machine. The **pasta sheet** should be the width of the machine, approximately 6 inches.

Using a pastry wheel, cut the **pasta** into 12 to 14 (3-inch strips), so each noodle is 6 × 3-inches. Place a noodle in your left hand and place about ¼ cup of the **filling** on the palm end of the **noodle**. With your right hand, roll the end of the **noodle** with its **filling** to the other end. See illustrations on page 60.

Place **rolls**, *seam side down*, side by side in one layer on top of the **sauce** in pan, leaving a small space between each **manicotti** to distinguish each serving.

Pour over the top of the **manicotti**:
1 ½ cups tomato sauce
Bake until edges becomes slightlybrown. Turn off heat and leave manicotti in the oven for 30 minutes. This allows them to set up so the **filling** doesn't ooze.

Manicotti with Italian green beans and garlic bread.

Manicotti filling.

Cutting the manicotti pasta.

Rolling the filling into pasta.

Manicotti before sauces are added.

Alfredo Sauce 🍎GF

In a glass quart jar, place:
6 Tablespoons (¾ stick) butter
Microwave on high for 1 minute. Set aside.

In a small bowl using a wire whisk, beat:
2 egg yolks*
½ cup half-and-half

In an 8-cup Pyrex glass bowl, place:
1 ½ cups half-and-half
Microwave for 2 minutes or until **cream** is warm-hot.

Add to **hot cream**:
above egg/cream mixture
Mix well with wire whip. Microwave on high for 2 to 3 minutes or until the **sauce** reaches 170 degrees on the food thermometer. Pour this **mixture** into the quart jar with the **melted butter**. Add enough **half-and-half** to fill the quart jar. Refrigerate until needed. This **sauce** can be stored in the refrigerator for up to 2 weeks.

*It has been my experience that fresh farm eggs with bright yellow or orange-colored yolks curdle easier than light-colored yellow yolks.

Bolognese Sauce 🍎 ♥ GF

Although raised by the same parents and grandparents, each sibling in the family can change recipes. I would say to my sister, Mary, "I still have the written recipes from Mom, Nonna, or Grandma," but Mary would have different versions from the same people. It proves one thing, that recipes continue to change all the time. When you think you have the best and most secret recipe, someone can add new ingredients, and now that is their favorite. Mary has gone to Italy several times, and this is a sauce she had while she was there. She likes it because the vegetables give the sauce a sweeter, milder taste, and I admit I like it, too.

Serves: 4

In a large skillet over medium heat, cook until no longer pink:
1 pound extra lean ground beef
Crumble the **meat**.

In a medium saucepan, sauté:
1 medium white or yellow onion, chopped
¼ cup carrots, chopped
¼ cup celery, chopped
1 teaspoon sweet basil
2 garlic cloves freshly squeezed
¼ teaspoon salt
When **vegetables** are *crisp tender,* place in food processor and puree, then set aside.

Add to **prepared meat:**
pureed vegetables
1 (14.5 ounce) can diced tomatoes
½ cup tomato paste
½ cup water
Bring to a boil, then reduce to simmer until **sauce** slightly thickens. Remove from heat.

While the **sauce** is simmering, prepare **your choice of pasta**: **spaghetti**, **linguine**, **fettuccine**, or **gluten-free pasta**, pages 35 and 40.

To serve: Spread **Bolognese sauce** over drained **pasta**. Sprinkle with freshly grated **Parmesan cheese**. Serve immediately.

Carol Staab, Mary, Fran, and Roni Lewis on The Good Life.

Chicken Florentine

Lemon Parsley Chicken was such a favorite Special of the Week that I put it on the regular menu. Chicken Florentine was its replacement for the Special of the Week and turned out to be a favorite of many of my customers. The chicken breast is prepared the same way, but the sauce is different. I have always been amazed by Asian cuisine: You add or subtract one or two different ingredients, and you have a new entrée. This is also true of Italian cooking: Change the sauce and an ingredient or two, and you have discovered a new dish. This is a good example.

Serves: 4 to 6

Have prepared:
1 recipe Basic Tomato Sauce, page 43

Preparation of the Chicken Breasts

Filet and tenderize **8 (5-ounce) chicken breasts**
Set aside.

In 2 bread pans and 2 (9 × 13-inch) baking pans:

Bread Pan #1
1 cup unbleached flour
1 teaspoon salt
½ teaspoon white pepper
¼ teaspoon tarragon

Both the stems and leaves of parsley can be added to savory dishes, including stews, baked fish, and omelets. The leaves in particular have a strong flavor. Parsley freezes well but does not dry well. Chop parsley finely if sprinkling on dishes as an edible garnish.

Bread Pan #2
1 cup milk

9 × 13 Baking Pan #1
2 to 3 cups bread crumbs, page 3
1 to 2 teaspoons parsley flakes

9 × 13 Baking Pan #2
line with waxed paper

Dip, one at a time, each **chicken breast** in this order: Dredge the **chicken breast** in the seasoned **flour**, then dip the dredged **chicken breast** into the **milk**. Coat both sides with parsley-seasoned **bread crumbs**. Place in 9 × 13 Baking Pan #2 lined with waxed paper. Continue until all **chicken breasts** are coated. Place in refrigerator or freezer until ready to use.

In a Crock-Pot on low, add:
1 cup chicken broth, page 13
Cover with lid.

In a large hot skillet, add:
1/2 to 1 cup canola oil or enough oil to be ¼-inch deep in skillet
1 garlic clove, freshly squeezed

In skillet, place:
3 to 5 breaded chicken breasts
Thoroughly cook and *brown* on *both sides*. Set aside in Crock-Pot.

Or place **chicken breast** in a covered baking pan, add:
1 cup chicken broth
Place in a warm oven at 200 degrees until ready to serve.

When Ready to Serve

In the hot skillet, add:
2 cups Tomato Sauce, page 43
¼ cup dry red wine
Bring the **sauce** to a simmer; add **prepared chicken breasts**, turn one time.

Place in the center of **chicken breast**:
1 tomato slice

In a stainless steel steamer pan over **boiling water**, place;
fresh spinach leaves
Steam until **leaves** are barely wilted, approximately 2 to 3 minutes. Drain excess water.

Arrange the **spinach** on *heated* plates and place a **chicken breast** in the center of the **spinach**. Cover the **chicken breast** and **tomato** with **extra tomato sauce**; garnish with a **single mushroom slice** in the center of **tomato** and **sliced black olives** on each side. Serve immediately.

Work area to prepare chicken breast for Chicken Florentine: chicken, board with meat mallet, flour mixture, milk.

Bread crumbs and flat plastic box lined with waxed paper.

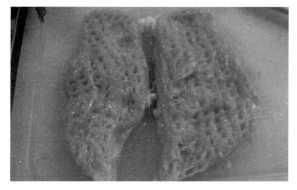

Whole chicken breast pounded and cut into two pieces.

Chicken breast dredged in flour on both sides.

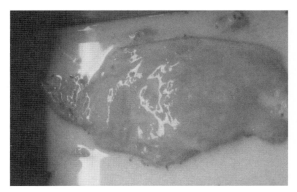

Chicken breast dipped in milk.

Chicken breast coated with bread crumbs.

Prepared chicken breast ready to cook, refrigerate, or freeze.

Linguine and Clam Sauce 🍎 ♥ GF

One of our Specials of the Week was Linguine and Clam Sauce, and it was a regular on the menu during Lent. This recipe was one of my own creations, just sautéing some vegetables, making a white sauce, and adding clams. One of my waitresses, Winnie Fullerton, suggested that I use sea clams rather than ocean clams because they are sweeter and don't have a heavy fish odor. She was right; they taste similar to lobster. With the clams we had left over, we made clam chowder, a recipe that is in *Family Favorites*, page 324.

Serves: 4

Have prepared:
1 recipe Pasta Dough, page 35
Cut into **linguine noodles**. Set aside.

In a large skillet, melt:
4 Tablespoons (½ stick) butter

Add to the **melted butter**:
½ cup celery, finely chopped
¼ cup white or yellow onions, finely chopped
Sauté until the **vegetables** are tender and transparent.

Sprinkle over the **vegetables**:
3 Tablespoons unbleached flour
Stir constantly with a wire whisk until bubbly.

Stir in and cook until smooth and thick:

2 cups clam juice

Add:

1 cup fresh or canned sea clams

salt and white pepper to taste

Continue to cook on low heat until the **sauce** thickens.

In a large pot with **6 to 7 quarts of boiling water**, add:

1 Tablespoon salt

prepared linguine noodles

Cook until *al dente*.

To serve: Place the cooked **pasta** in a large *warmed* bowl or platter and pour the hot **clam sauce** over the **pasta**. Serve immediately.

Helpful Hints

■ If the **clam sauce** is too thick, add **extra hot clam juice**.

■ If the **clam sauce** is too thin, whisk **1 Tablespoon flour** into ¼ **cup clam juice** and add to the **clam sauce**. Continue to cook until **sauce** thickens.

Option

■ **GF** Substitute **1 ½ Tablespoons corn starch** for **unbleached flour** and **gluten-free noodles** for **regular noodles**, page 40–41.

Pasta Carbonara 🍎GF

Because my family always had basic tomato sauce on our pasta, I was not aware of Alfredo sauce until after I was married. While in New Orleans for a school board convention, I got my first taste of the "white sauce" and fell in love with it. Later when I attended the Nebraska Italian Food Festival in Omaha, I was introduced to Spaghetti Carbonara. Yum! Yum! Similar to Asian cuisine, add one ingredient—crisp bacon—change the type of pasta, and the entrée gets a new name, Spaghetti Carbonara. I'm calling this Pasta Carbonara because it can be served with the pasta of your choice, spaghetti, fettuccine, linguine,and other macaroni types. At Nonna's, we used fettuccine.

Serves: 4

Have prepared:
1 quart Alfredo Sauce, page 61
1 recipe Fresh Pasta Dough, regular or white whole wheat, page 34
Cut into the **pasta of your choice**. Set aside.

In an 8-cup Pyrex cup add:
8 slices bacon, nitrate/nitrite free, cut into small strips (bacon bits)
Microwave on high until crisp. Drain on paper towel. Set aside.

In a large pot with an insert/strainer that will hold **4 to 5 quarts of boiling water**, add:
1 Tablespoon salt
1 pound freshly cut pasta
Cook until *al dente*, page 38–39. Place in a warmed pasta serving bowl.

Sprinkle generously over the **pasta**:

4 to 6 ounces freshly grated Parmesan cheese

Toss the hot **pasta** so that the **cheese** is evenly distributed. Add enough hot **Alfredo sauce** to make the **noodles** creamy.

Sprinkle over the top of the **pasta**:

crispy fried bacon bits

Serve immediately.

Options

- If you want fettuccine Alfredo, omit the **bacon.**
- **Whipping cream** can be substituted for **half-and-half.** I recommend half of each.
- GF   Use **gluten-free pasta**, page 40–41.

Helpful Hints

- If the **sauce** is too runny, add more **grated cheese.**
- If the **noodles** are too dry and sticky, add more warm **Alfredo sauce.**
- To keep **pasta** warm until ready to serve, place in a Crock-Pot on *low*, page 50.

Record's Spaghetti (Naked Spaghetti) 🍎♥GF

During the horse-racing season at Fonner Park, John Record, a color commentator for the races, was a regular customer at Nonna's. He would either dine in or order carryout, but his order was always the same. "I want naked spaghetti with olive oil and garlic and maybe some melted butter." When we decided to add this to our menu, I decided to call it "Record's Spaghetti" because I didn't think "naked" sounded "very proper" in this restaurant setting. You can imagine the surprise when John opened the menu the following racing season and saw this listed on the menu. He brought his menu back to the kitchen, asked me if he could have it, then asked me to autograph it. It was the first time anyone had asked me for my autograph.

Record's Spaghetti soon became a popular request, but it was so simple to make I didn't feel anyone who liked it would need a recipe. But I was wrong! A regular customer, Jim Goble, bought *Family Favorites* and went through the entire cookbook looking for this recipe. When he saw me, he said he was upset that I didn't include the recipe. I told him I didn't because I thought most people could figure it out on their own. He said, "I've tried, but it doesn't taste like yours." My question to Jim was, "Did you use homemade egg pasta?" He said he did not. That was the problem. So, to all the Record's Spaghetti (naked spaghetti) fans, here is this simple recipe.

Serves: 4

Have prepared:
1 recipe Fresh Pasta Dough, page 34
Using your pasta machine, roll and cut into **spaghetti**. Set aside.

In a large pot with an insert that will hold 4 to 5 quarts of boiling **water**,* add:

1 Tablespoon salt

prepared spaghetti

After the **pasta** is placed in the **water**, immediately stir the **pasta** to keep it from sticking together. Allow fresh **pasta** to boil for 3 minutes.** At this time you can test the doneness by biting the **noodle**. If it tastes and feels chewy and you can see a tiny bit of raw **noodle** in the center, it is *al dente* and ready to be removed from the water. Drain thoroughly but do not rinse under cold water because the **pasta** gets slippery and can lose some of its flavor. Check the doneness of the **pasta** often: *Most Americans tend to overcook pasta.*

Place **pasta** on a large, *warmed* platter or serving bowl, add:

2 to 3 Tablespoons extra virgin olive oil

1 to 2 garlic cloves, freshly squeezed

Toss **pasta** well and serve immediately.

Options

■ You may also add **butter**, your choice of **pesto sauce** (recipe in *Family Favorites*, page 77), and **grated Parmesan cheese** to taste.

■ **GF** Use **gluten-free pasta**, page 40–41.

*A pan insert is a colander-like insertion that fits inside the pot used for boiling pasta. It allows you to drain pasta from the pot without removing the water.

**Cooking times: fresh spaghetti pasta, 3 to 5 minutes; fresh angel-hair pasta, 2 to 3 minutes.

Sweet Potato (Yam) Gnocchi (Gluten Free or Regular)

While visiting my sister and brother-in-law, Katy and Larry Lingo in Las Vegas, Katy suggested we make gnocchi with sweet potatoes (yams) she had bought at an organic food market. We had just tried gluten-free (rice) flour in a cookie recipe. She had another type of gluten-free (garbanzo bean) flour, and she thought it might be good for gnocchi. Because neither of us had ever made gnocchi with sweet potatoes (yams), we decided to make half of the recipe with gluten-free flour and the other half with unbleached flour. We needed to have a taste test. What we found out was the gnocchi made with the unbleached flour was smoother in texture, but the taste was the same.

Serves: 6

Bake: Preheated 350 degree oven
Time: 20 to 30 minutes

On a baking sheet, place:
1 or 2 large yams cut in halves lengthwise
Brush the skin and surface of **yam** with **olive oil**. Bake until *fork tender*. Cool.

In a mixer bowl with dough hook, measure and place equal amounts:
1 to 2 cups yams or sweet potatoes
1 to 2 cups gluten-free or unbleached flour

Knead the **dough** until smooth, soft, and slightly sticky. Continue to add **additional flour** until you get the right consistency for a *soft* gnocchi.

Place the **dough** on a **floured surface**. Divide **dough** and shape each section into **ropes about as thick as your thumb**, then cut the rope into ¾- to 1-inch sections (we call them *pillows*; see photos below). **Flour and cover with a towel** until ready to use. When you are ready to boil the **gnocchi**, **flour the gnocchi generously**, and with your fingers, make a deep impression in the center of the **gnocchi**. This serves to thin out the middle of the **dumpling** so that it will cook more evenly and also serves as a trap for the **sauce**, making the **dumpling** even tastier.

Into a large kettle with an insert/strainer that will hold **5 quarts boiling water**, add:
1 Tablespoon salt
approximately 2 dozen gnocchi
In a very short time, the **gnocchi** will rise to the top. Cook for 1 to 2 minutes. Remove from water and drain. Place on a large, *warmed* platter. Continue this until all are cooked.

In a small saucepan, melt and slightly brown:
4 Tablespoons (½ stick) butter
Add:
½ teaspoon sage
½ teaspoon cinnamon
Pour over top of the **gnocchi**.
Sprinkle with **Parmesan cheese**. Serve immediately.

Rolling out section of dough into ropes as thick as your thumb, then cutting into ¾- to 1-inch sections.

With your fingers, making a deep impression in the center of the gnocchi.

The Pizza Story

As with many foods, pizza has evolved from ancient times, but the pizza so many Americans know and love originated in Naples, Italy. A dish of the poor people, it was sold in the streets ... a flat bread covered with white sauce.

In June 1869 the Neapolitan chef Faffaele Espostio created the Pizza Margheritta to honor Margheritta, consort queen of Italy. It is reported that the queen, on a visit to Naples, was served his new pizza, which resembled the colors of the Italian flag: red (tomato), white (mozzarella cheese), and green (basil). These ingredients remain the basis for our modern pizzas with their many variations and additions in countries all over the world from Nepal to Israel to Australia.

Italian immigrants had pizzerias in America in the early twentieth century, but they were mostly confined to the eastern United States, particularly New York City, and also in Chicago and San Francisco. But it was the American GIs returning from World War II who brought the pizza craze from Italy to the entire country, making it almost as American as apple pie. In Nebraska in the early 1950s one had to drive to Omaha to find pizza. Today, of course, you find pizza everywhere ... local pizzerias, national chains, and available frozen in supermarkets. There are trendy pizzas in fancy restaurants, some barely recognizable from the original.

Pizza originally was part of the healthy Mediterranean Diet, but today's American pizza is often loaded with high-fat meats and cheeses. These and its other salty ingredients and additives raise new concerns about health issues.

If you make your own pizza, you are in charge of how much fat and salt you choose to use, and you can make a truly healthy and very delicious pizza. My pizza, which won first place in the 2014 Nebraska State Fair, was prepared following my mother's recipe, but now I use white whole-wheat flour for an extra health benefit. Here again you can experiment with ingredients, including spices and herbs to make your own personal pizza.

Meat Pizza 🍎🐞

In the '50s the first pizza restaurant in Grand Island opened across the alley from our house. My mother, a first-generation Italian, was very upset because the owner was German. His last name was Nieman and he put an *O* at the end of his last name, Niemano's Pizza. We never had pizza at our home until it became popular. Niemano's pizzas had a thin crust, but Mom always made her crust with raised yeast bread, so we had a thick crust pizza. Whenever we have our class reunions, my classmates always remember our spaghetti parties and my mother's pizza. My friend Charl Ann Kahrhoff Mitchell would cut my hair for one of Mom's pizzas. Because there were very few Italian families in Grand Island, Mom was well known for her Italian food.

Pizza Crust

Makes: 2 pizza crusts

Bake: Preheated 450 degree oven
Time: 5 minutes

Have prepared:
2 greased pizza pans, set aside
1 recipe Basic Tomato Sauce, page 43

In mixer bowl, with a dough hook, combine:
1 cup warm water
1 Tablespoon honey or sugar
1 ½ teaspoons salt
1 package (1 Tablespoon) dry yeast
Mix together until everything is dissolved. Set aside at room temperature until **mixture**

becomes bubbly, about 10 minutes. If it doesn't become bubbly, the **yeast** is not active; throw the **mixture** out and start over.

Add to the **mixture**:
¼ cup canola or **olive oil**
2 cups white whole-wheat flour
Beat at medium speed until **flour** is thoroughly mixed.

Add to the mixture **enough flour** to make a soft elastic **dough**:
1 to 1 ½ cups unbleached flour
Place on a **floured surface** and knead until **dough** is no longer sticky. Place in large bowl and allow the **dough** to double in size. Divide the **dough** in half; form into balls and roll into 12- to 15-inch circles. Place on 12- to 15-inch pizza pans. Crimp the edge of the **dough** and prick the **dough** inside with a fork. Set aside and allow the **dough** to double. Bake as instructed above. Place on wire rack to cool.

Prepare Seasoned Ground Beef while dough is rising.

Seasoned Ground Beef

In a stainless steel skillet, combine:
1 pound (80/20) ground beef
1 teaspoon sweet basil
½ teaspoon oregano
1 garlic clove, freshly squeezed
salt and pepper to taste
After **meat** is browned, drain off excess grease and set aside to cool.

Putting It All Together

Bake: Preheated 450 degree oven
Time: 10 minutes (total)

Spread evenly over each *cooled* **crust**:
½ to 1 cup Basic Tomato Sauce
Divide evenly the cooled, seasoned **ground beef**.
Bake for 5 minutes.

Sprinkle over the top of each pizza:
½ to 1 cup mozzarella cheese
Bake as instructed for 5 minutes or until **cheese** is slightly *browned* and *melted*. Cut each pizza into desired serving pieces.

Option

■   You can add to the pizza **bell peppers**, **onions**, **olives**, **tomatoes**, **mushrooms**, or any of your favorite toppings.

I received a first-place blue ribbon in the 2014 Nebraska State Fair for this meat pizza.

Appetizers

Zoey

Glossary

crudités. An assortment of raw vegetables, served as an hors d'oeuvre, often with a dip.

ball. To scoop melons or similar fruits into ball shapes using a special round spoon-like tool (melon baller).

blanch. To cook briefly (3 to 5 minutes) in boiling water.

bruschetta. A snack of Italian origin, basically consisting of garlic toasts topped with tomato, garlic, and olive oil. Variations may include meats, cheeses, etc.

chipotle. "Hot chili pepper," usually a dried and smoked jalapeño; used in cooking Mexican dishes.

chop. To cut into coarse or fine pieces with a knife or chopper.

condiment. Something, often a sauce, used to impart certain flavor to some foods or enhance flavors; examples: ketchup, mustard, salsa; also pickles, relishes.

cube. To cut into solids of six equal sides, usually ¼ to ½ inch in size.

garnish. To decorate food with small portions of other colorful foods.

glaze. To cook food or cover food with a thin syrup or jelly, giving a glossy surface.

jalapeño pepper. Small green pepper, moderately hot, popularly used in salsas and other Mexican dishes.

julienne. To cut fruits, vegetables, or cheeses into match-like pieces.

mince. To cut or chop into very small pieces.

pare. To cut off the skin or outer covering of a fruit or vegetable, such as an apple or potato, with a knife.

peel. To remove outer covering by stripping it off; used to prepare foods such as tomatoes, peaches, or bananas.

salsa. Spanish word for "sauce," often tomato based; typical of Mexican cuisine, particularly as a dip and as a condiment.

savory. Appetizing to taste or smell. Piquant, pungent, or salty to the taste; not sweet.

serrano pepper. Small, slender pepper, similar to jalapeño but with fiery heat and sharp flavor.

Watermelon Fruit Basket GF

A fruit tray is always a nice addition as an appetizer, but a watermelon fruit basket can be an edible centerpiece. Yes, it will take some time to prepare, but it is time well spent when everyone raves about how beautiful it is. Most of the preparation can be done the day before, but putting it all together should be done just before the party begins. If you have all your fruits prepared, it is an easy task. Think of this appetizer as a two for one: A centerpiece and a fruit tray, it will be the hit of the party.

Day Before Party

Draw a handle in the center of the **melon**, halfway down. Draw the side of the basket a little above halfway so you can make a zigzag edge.

With a **sharp knife**, cut handle on both sides to the line marking the sides of the basket. Cut each side in quarters for easy removal; cut along the basket line to the handle. Remove pieces and set aside. Hollow out the handle.

With a **melon baller**, make **watermelon balls** until the pink-white rind appears. Place in a large plastic container with a lid. Refrigerate.

Make a zigzag edge, cutting out triangles around the edge of the basket. If you want a scalloped edge, round off the tips of the zigzag. Cover the **watermelon basket** with **plastic wrap** and place in the refrigerator.

Using a melon baller, prepare:
1 cantaloupe
1 honeydew melon

Using a knife, peel and cut in chunks or slices:
1 pineapple
3 kiwi

Store each type of prepared fruit in a separate container with a lid and refrigerate until ready to use.

Day of the Party

Wash and drain:
1 carton blueberries
2 cartons strawberries with caps on; remove caps and slice in halves just before placing in basket
White and red seedless grapes; remove from vines

Place **watermelon basket** on a **large platter** (grandmother's silver platter would be elegant). Add:
above prepared fruits
Mix gently. On the outside of the basket, garnish with **bunches of grapes** and **strawberries with caps attached**, or you can place the **watermelon basket** in a **bed of kale** with a **sprinkling of fresh flowers**. See photo on page 87.

Buying Fruits

- **Cantaloupes** should have a golden glow and sweet fragrance.
- **Watermelons** need to be plugged to see if the flesh is a bright red. The seller will usually do this.
- **Kiwi fruit** should be firm but gentle to pressure and have no signs of bruises.
- **Cherries** should be clean, firm, and dry with a green stem.

How to Choose a Pineapple

- If the shell is golden in color, it indicates a softer **fruit** that is better for desserts.
- A greener color indicates a firmer **fruit**, which is better for savory dishes.
- **Hawaiian pineapples** have a good balance of acid and sugar.
- **Mexican pineapples** are said to be sweeter.
- Avoid **pineapples** with dried-out, brownish leaves.

Helpful Hints

- To preserve fruits such as **bananas** and **apples** from browning, soak them in **lemon water** (**water** to which **1 or 2 Tablespoons of lemon juice** have been added) for 10 minutes just before adding them to the fruit tray.
- How many appetizers per person?

  4 to 6 appetizers if meal follows quickly
  6 to 8 if meal is late
  8 to 12 if no meal

- For total number of appetizers to prepare from each recipe, use this caterer's formula:

  12 pieces × the number of people ÷ the number of different appetizers
  When full meal is being served, halve the total
  For less than 45 people, plan 6 types of appetizers; more than 45, 8 types
  For smaller gatherings, 8 to 10 people, 3 types; 14 to 16 people, 4 to 5

Primary Fruit Tray 🍎 ♥ GF

When my grandson, Justin, had his birthday party, his mother, Maria, asked if I would make a fruit tray. I always like to make something that people will like and is easy to prepare. In *Family Favorites* I suggested a Strawberry Tray, page 87, as it seems that everyone loves strawberries. This tray is not quite as simple, but it has just three fruits. They are of the three primary colors, red, blue, and yellow, so that is where it gets its name, Primary Fruit Tray. This is a great time to use your grandmother's large silver tray, lined with greens of your choice. This makes a wonderful presentation.

Gently wash and thoughly drain:
2 to 4 boxes fresh strawberries, leaving on the caps and stems

In a colander, gently rinse and drain:
1 (16-ounce) carton fresh blueberries

Peel and cut into bite-sized pieces:
1 whole fresh pineapple

Store each **fruit** in *separate covered* containers until ready to use.

Line a large tray with:
kale or leaf lettuce

Place the **strawberries** and **pineapple** on either side of the tray and the **blueberries** in the center. Serve with a **fruit dip**, recipe next page.

Fruit Dip 🍎GF

In a mixer bowl using the wire whip, combine:

1 (8-ounce) package cream cheese

½ cup sour cream

½ cup brown sugar

1 cup pureed fresh strawberries

Beat until smooth, place in your grandmother's crystal dish, and chill.

Watermelon Fruit Basket.

God's Pharmacy

Grapes hang in a cluster that has the shape of the heart. Each grape looks like a blood cell, and all of the research today shows grapes are also profound heart and blood vitalizing food.

Bruschetta ♥

Bruschetta is an antipasto from Italy whose origin dates to at least the fifteenth century. It consists of grilled toast topped with a garlic-olive oil blend. Other toppings include tomatoes, roasted peppers, and cured meats, such as salami and pepperoni. This originally was a way of using bread that was going stale. The early Italian women were so inventive, they knew how to use up leftovers for ravioli filling and old bread for bruschetta. Now bruschetta is a very trendy appetizer, and you can find the bruschetta toppings in jars at the supermarket; but they don't compare to the freshly made toppings, and they are very expensive. Use your creative side and take the time to do these quick recipes.

Classic Bruschetta ♥

In medium bowl, combine:
6 to 8 plum tomatoes, seeded and chopped
1 garlic clove, freshly squeezed
½ cup fresh basil, thinly sliced
Mix well.

Add to above mixture:
1 teaspoon apple-cider vinegar
1 Tablespoon extra virgin olive oil
salt and pepper to taste
Set aside and allow the flavors to combine.

Use basil in soups, tomato sauces, pesto, and salads. A pot of basil in the kitchen will repel flies by its scent.

Serves: 4
Grill: Preheat oven on broil setting

When ready to serve, slice a loaf of **French bread** or **baguette** in 1-inch diangonal cuts.

Place on baking sheet and drizzle with:
extra virgin olive oil
salt and pepper to taste
Grill on both sides until slightly charred, about 30 seconds on each side. Set your timer.

Top toasted **bread slices** with:
prepared tomato-basil topping
sprinkled with grated Parmesan cheese
Serve immediately.

Roasted Pepper Bruschetta 🍎♥

Advance Preparation

Bake: Preheated 400 degree oven
Time: 10 minutes

Cut in half, remove seeds, place on baking sheet:
4 large red bell peppers
Broil **peppers** 4 inches from the heat until skins blister, about 10 minutes. Remove from oven and place in covered bowl to cool. Once cooled, hold over a bowl so you don't lose any **liquids** and carefully remove skins.

In another bowl, cut **peppers** into strips, toss with:

salt and pepper to taste

1 Tablespoon extra virgin olive oil

1 to 2 garlic cloves, freshly squeezed

reserved juices

Cover and place roasted **peppers** in refrigerator. Roasted **peppers** will keep in refrigerator for about 5 days. If you cover them with **olive oil**, they will last a couple of weeks.

Grill: Preheated oven on broiler setting

When ready to serve, slice a **loaf of French bread or baguette** in 1-inch diagonal cuts. Place on baking sheet and drizzle with **extra virgin olive oil**. Grill on both sides until slightly charred, about 30 seconds on each side. Set your timer.

Serves: 4

Bake: Preheated 400 degree oven

Spoon on toasted **bread slices**:

prepared peppers

slice of goat cheese

Cook until **cheese** is softened. Garnish with **fresh basil** and serve immediately.

Mini Pizzas

Pizza Dough

In your mixer bowl, using the dough hook, mix well:

2 cups water

1 package (1 Tablespoon) dry yeast

1 ½ teaspoons salt

2 Tablespoons sugar

Allow the **yeast** to soften in the **water**. To be sure your **yeast** is active or good, wait until the **mixture** becomes bubbly. This is very important.

Add to the **yeast mixture**:

¼ cup canola oil

Mix well with dough hook.

All at once, add:

4 cups white whole wheat or unbleached flour

On low setting, continue to mix with the dough hook.

Add and continue to mix:

1 or 2 cups unbleached flour

Scrape down the sides of the mixer bowl with spatula and cut the **flour** into the **dough**. Continue to mix until **dough** is soft and slightly sticky. Place the **dough** on a **floured surface** and knead until it is no longer sticky to touch. Place the **dough** into a large bowl and allow the **dough** to double in size.

Have prepared:
1 recipe Basic Tomato Sauce, page 43

Makes: 4 to 5 dozen

Bake: Preheated 350 degree oven
Time: 10 minutes

On a **floured surface**, roll out above **dough** to approximately ½-inch thickness and cut with round cutters (2 ½-inch). Place on a **lightly greased baking sheet** and let the **dough** double in size. Bake as directed above or until *lightly browned*. As soon as you remove the **rolls** from the oven, *indent the center with back of a small measuring cup* (I use my ⅓ metal cup, 2-inch diameter). This allows for a surface to place your **sauce**.

Place **rolls** on a baking sheet. On each *indented surface*, place:
1 teaspoon basic tomato sauce
1 slice pepperoni
small amount (1 teaspoon) mozzarella cheese
Return to the oven and bake until **cheese** has melted. Serve on a **platter**.

Options

- Use any topping: **cooked ground beef or sausage, Canadian bacon,** or **cheese.**
- Use any sauces: **tomato** (page 43), **pesto** (recipe in *Family Favorites*, page 77), or **Alfredo** (page 61).

Fresh Salsa 🍎❤GF

Salsa and chips, served before the meal, have become the typical appetizer in Mexican restaurants, and jars of salsa crowd grocer's shelves, actually replacing ketchup as America's condiment of choice. But while visiting Mexico, we were always served delicious fresh salsa from mild to hot, so tasty and healthy that we always looked forward to it. It also inspired me to make my own from this simple recipe.

Makes: 2 cups

In **medium-sized bowl**, add:
5 to 6 Roma tomatoes, seeded and chopped
⅓ cup white or yellow onion, finely diced
2 cloves garlic freshly squeezed
⅓ cup fresh cilantro, finely chopped
Mix well.

Over top of **mixture**, add:
1 teaspoon salt
1 teaspoon black pepper
1 Tablespoon extra virgin olive oil
2 Tablespoons lime juice
Mix well and place in a serving bowl. Refrigerate **salsa** for at least 2 to 4 hours before serving.

Serve with **corn chips**.

Options

- **GF** Substitute **gluten-free corn chips** for **corn chips**.
- If you prefer a salsa with a "kick," add some **bottled hot sauce** or a **finely chopped jalapeño or serrano pepper.*** Be sure to split the **pepper** and remove the **seeds**, then taste frequently until you get the desired flavor.
- In place of **tomatoes**, use **other vegetables** and **fruits** such as **avocados, mangoes, melons, peaches**, or **pineapple**.
- For flavor, color, and texture, add **bell peppers, fresh corn kernels**, or **black beans**.

Helpful Hint

- Dice **onions** by hand; food processors tend to pulverize the **onion**, releasing so much juice that the flavor becomes overpowering.

*Be careful when handling peppers. Wash your hands thoroughly after handling and be especially careful not to touch your eyes.

Use freshly chopped cilantro leaves in salads or with fish, meat, avocado, coconut, and citrus. Use the dried seeds in curries and Asian dishes; they are sweet, spicy, and mildly orange flavored.

Guacamole Dip 🍎 ♥ GF

Guacamole is a dip made with avocados, salt, and lime juice that originated in Mexico. While we were in Mexico, this dip was served as an appetizer along with salsa and corn chips. There are many variations of this dip—you could add tomatoes, onions, jalapeño or serrano peppers, cilantro, or black pepper. I have tried several recipes, and I like this combination the best.

Makes: 2 cups

In a food processor, place:
4 avocados, seeded and peeled
Using *pulse* setting, roughly mash (do not overdo; the **avocados** should be a *little chunky*).

Add to **avocados**:
2 Roma tomatoes with seeds and pulp removed
1 small white or yellow onion, finely minced
2 Tablespoons fresh cilantro leaves, finely chopped
¼ cup lime juice, freshly squeezed
½ teaspoon salt
¼ teaspoon black pepper
Using the pulse setting, blend just enough to get all the **ingredients** mixed together. Place in a serving bowl, cover with plastic wrap, and refrigerate until ready to use.

Serve with **corn chips**.

Options

- **GF** Substitute **gluten-free corn chips** for **corn chips**.
- If you like a hotter version, add a **jalapeño or serrano pepper** to the dip. Start with a half of a pepper, taste, and continue to add to the **guacamole** until you get the desired hotness. *Taste after each addition. You can always add more, but once added, you can't remove it.*
- To make a quick **guacamole**, add ¼ **cup of Fresh Salsa**, page 93, to your mashed **avocados**.
- Sweet **bacon** dip: To the basic guacamole, add some **sugared bacon**.
  In a **4-cup Pyrex bowl**, add **6 to 8 slices nitrate/nitrite-free bacon**, cut in small strips. Microwave until **bacon** becomes crispy. Drain **bacon** grease. Then add **2 to 3 Tablespoons brown sugar** to **bacon**. Mix well and set aside to cool. Add ¾ **of the sugar bacon** to the basic dip. Place in a serving bowl and use the remaining **bacon** as a garnish over the top of the **dip**.

God's Pharmacy

Avocados, eggplant, and pears target the health and function of the womb and cervix of the female—they look just like these organs. Today's research shows that when a woman eats one avocado a week, it balances hormones, sheds unwanted birth weight, and prevents cervical cancers. And how profound is this? It takes exactly nine months to grow an avocado from blossom to ripened fruit. There are over 14,000 photolytic chemical constitutents of nutrition in each one of these foods (modern science has only studied and named about 141 of them).

Smoked Fish Spread 🍎 GF

For holiday parties, this is an impressive hors d'oeuvre that you could spoon into miniature cream puffs (page 227 in *Family Favorites*) or serve with crackers.

Makes: 3 cups

Remove skin and bones from:
1 pound flaked, smoked fish
Set aside.

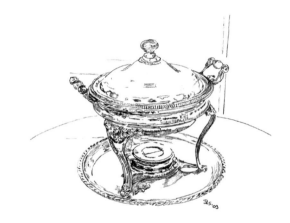

In a mixer bowl, using flat beater, combine:
1 package (8-ounce) cream cheese
1 Tablespoon sour cream
2 Tablespoons mayonnaise
2 to 3 green onions, finely sliced
juice of 1 lemon
1 teaspoon hot sauce (Tabasco)
½ teaspoon pepper
1 teaspoon dill
dash paprika
Mix well.

Add to the **above mixture** and mix well:
prepared fish
Transfer to a serving dish, cover, and refrigerate for at *least one hour* before serving.

GF Serve with **gluten-free rice crackers** or **corn chips**.

Deviled Eggs 🍎 GF

At potluck suppers or family gatherings, it seems one of the traditional foods is deviled eggs. The lady that brings this dish doesn't have to worry about bringing home any leftovers. Deviled eggs are loved by almost everyone. The original recipe is very basic, but over the years, cooks have added their special touches. However, we always remember how our grandmothers and mother made them, and that is often the best recipe for us. Here is our family recipe.

Serves: 12

In a large pan, place and cover with **cold water**:
12 large eggs
Bring to a rapid boil; at once reduce the heat to keep the water just below simmer. Cook for 15 to 20 minutes. Remove from water and *cool immediately* in **cold water**. This makes **eggs** easier to handle, prevents a dark surface on the yolk, makes peeling easier,* and instantly stops the cooking.

Peel and slice the **eggs** into halves lengthwise, and scoop **egg yolks** into a medium-sized bowl. Set **egg whites** aside.

In bowl with **egg yolks**, combine:
½ cup salad dressing or mayonnaise
1 Tablespoon mustard

*When boiling eggs, older eggs seem to peel easier.

½ teaspoon salt

½ teaspoon white pepper

Mix until thoroughly combined. Taste and adjust **seasonings**.

Spoon **yolk mixture** back into **egg white halves** and garnish with **sprinkles of paprika**. Place in on a **serving plate** and refrigerate until ready to serve.

Options

- Add: **1 Tablespoon chipotle, finely chopped**, and **½ teaspoon apple-cider vinegar**, then garnish with **cilantro, finely chopped**.
- Add: **1 ½ Tablespoons sweet pickle relish** and garnish with **thin sweet pickle** or **pimento slices**.
- Add: **2 Tablespoons cheddar cheese, finely grated**, and garnish with **bacon crumbles**.
- Add: **2 Tablespoons pesto** and **1 teaspoon lemon juice**, then garnish with **bacon crumbles**.
- Add: **1 teaspoon curry powder** and **1 teaspoon lemon juice**, then garnish with **sliced almonds** and **chopped chives**.

Deviled eggs.

Larry and Sandy Younger with the deviled eggs. Sandy let me use her deviled egg dish.

Beverages

Skyhler

Glossary

apple cider. Unfiltered, unsweetened beverage made from apples; may be opaque due to fine apple particles in suspension and may be tangier than apple juice.

apple juice. Juice from apples that has undergone a filtration process to remove coarse particles, pulp, and sediment. Clear in appearance, it may be pasteurized to stay fresh longer.

black tea. Made from leaves that have been fermented, heated, and dried.

café au lait. Equal parts hot coffee and hot milk.

chill. To allow to become very cold without freezing.

demitasse. French for half a cup of strong after-dinner coffee served in small cups.

dissolve. To cause a powdered substance to pass into a liquid substance.

Greek yogurt. Yogurt that has been strained of whey, resulting in less sugar, fewer carbohydrates, and more protein. Can be plain or flavored.

green tea. Leaves are not fermented; usually from China or Japan.

infusion. To steep (as in tea) or soak without boiling to extract elements or flavors of leaves, herbs, fruits, etc.

mocha. A mixture of coffee, milk, and chocolate.

mulled cider. Cider heated with spices and citrus fruit.

oolong tea. Made from tea leaves that have been fermented only briefly.

smoothie. A creamy drink of fruit or vegetables, blended with any or all of the following: milk, juice, yogurt, crushed ice, etc.

steep. To allow herbs, tea, or fruits to stand in hot water to extract the flavor.

yogurt. Semisolid food made when certain bacteria is added to milk. Sometimes sweetened and flavored.

wassail. Hot beverage made of mulled cider, additional spices, and citrus fruits; associated with the Yuletide.

whey. Liquid remaining after milk has been curdled; a by-product of cheese and Greek yogurt making.

Beverages

Beverages are liquids specifically prepared for human consumption, and the lists and variations of beverages are endless: coffees, teas, sodas, chocolate, dairy, soy, rice, sweetened, diet, hot or cold, alcoholic, nonalcoholic, and on and on. But the most important liquid we should be drinking is plain water. It wasn't too long ago it was recommended that we drink eight glasses of water daily, and you couldn't count other liquids such as coffee, soda, or liquors—just "water."

In our daily life, we may want to drink something more exciting than water, and our choices are never ending. Nothing is more refreshing than a tall glass of iced tea or lemonade on a hot summer day or more warming in the winter than to have hot chocolate or coffee after you have shoveled the snow or gone sledding. But the difficulty is in deciding which variety you want to drink. We have so many choices; we have syrups, powders, extracts, liquors, and spices to change the taste of our classic teas, coffee, sodas, and other beverages.

The latest trend in beverages are smoothies, a blended and sweetened beverage made with fresh fruit. They often have crushed ice, milk, yogurt, or ice cream; for the health conscious, you can add soy milk, green tea, and herbal and protein supplements. If you are really health conscious, you can make a vegetable smoothie using kale, broccoli, spinach, or parsley. Yum? Yum? I guess it is a matter of taste.

Then there are the holiday beverages we sing about. Wassail … what is it and do we have a familiar substitute for it? Did you ever hear your grandparents talk about "Tom and Jerrys?" No, I'm not talking about the cartoon. This was a very popular toddy; many families had a Tom and Jerry bowl and cups to match that were decorated with a colorful Christmas design.

This all said, what it gets down to is what the majority of people really like the most are the ancient beverages of years ago—tea, coffee, and plain old water. You will find these recipes and more in this section. *Drink up!*

Coffee Culture   GF

The earliest evidence of either coffee drinking or coffee trees was in the middle of the 15th century in the monasteries of Yemen. Coffee spread to Egypt and North Africa, and by the 16th century it had reached the rest of the Middle East. From the Middle East, coffee drinking spread to Europe during the vibrant trade between Venice and Egypt, as well as the countries of the Middle East and North Africa, when they brought a large variety of goods, including coffee, to this leading European port. Venetian merchants introduced coffee drinking to the wealthy in Venice, charging them heavily for the beverage. Coffee was widely accepted after the controversy over whether it was acceptable for Catholics to consume it was settled in its favor by Pope Clement VIII in 1600, despite appeals to ban it. The first European coffeehouse was opened in Venice in 1645.

In the Americas coffee spread to the Caribbean in 1720. In 1727 coffee was introduced to Brazil, and massive tracts of rain forest were cleared in the vicinity of Rio de Janeiro and Sao Paulo for coffee plantations. By the 1930s Brazil was the major producer of coffee in the Americas. Arabica coffee dominates both Brazil and the world with 70% of the production. Once coffee came to the New World, it was inevitable that it would find its way to the North American colonies, on its way to becoming America's most popular beverage.

The Importance of Coffee

Coffee is both refreshment and relaxation. Even those who drink decaffeinated coffee find it is a good "pick me up." How often do we say, "Come over and have a cup" ... "Let's go out for coffee." The coffee break or after-dinner coffee has become part of our daily lives. It is simply our way of expressing hospitality. So making good coffee really is an important part of cooking skills.

Selecting coffee ... it's the type, not the brand. When I opened Nonna's in 1983, I had many food representatives trying to sell me their products. One company offered me a coffee machine if I would purchase all my coffee supplies from them. The coffee machine had three warming plates, and it seemed perfect for my business. The salesman also emphasized that if you want to be successful, you need to provide a good cup of coffee. He said, "Coffee is one of the cheapest products you buy for your business, and your return on coffee is one of the highest, so buy a good coffee." I took his advice and always bought Colombian or Arabica and made it strong. We always got compliments on our coffee and were often asked what brand we used. I always told them, "It's not the brand, it's the type." To this day, I only purchase Colombian or Arabica in coffee grinds or instant. If I want flavored coffees, I use my own spices and extracts; it's easier and less expensive.

Coffee roasting transforms the chemical and physical properties of green coffee beans into roasted coffee products. The roasting process produces the flavor of coffee and also changes the color, taste, and smell, depending on how long the coffee beans are roasted. Light or mild roast is the point when the coffee bean first emits a cracking sound. The frequency of the cracking sound and the louder the sound, the darker the roast. Different levels of roasting are mild, medium, medium dark, and dark. There are also coffee roasts associated with the area, such as American roast (medium), French roast (dark), Italian (very dark), espresso, and Spanish roast (extremely dark).

So, how do you make a good cup of coffee? It is very easy, but there are a few rules. There are different types of coffees and coffeemakers, but these rules generally fit the most popular ones.

Brewing Coffee

1. Use fresh coffee and always keep the coffee tightly covered. Those who don't drink coffee often keep their coffee in the freezer to have on hand for company.
2. Use the right grind for your coffeemaker.
3. Clean your coffeemaker after each use. Oils can ruin the taste.
4. Always start with **cold water** and don't use softened water.
5. Use enough coffee for the desired strength. I usually use 1/2 cup coffee grounds for 8 to 10 cups.
6. I prefer Colombian and/or Arabica coffee; I feel they have the richest flavor.
7. Make the coffee right before needed and serve as soon as possible.

Tea Legends and Lore   GF

The history and legends of tea are long and complex, spanning over thousands of years. A popular legend tells of a Chinese emperor who was drinking a bowl of boiled water when a few leaves were blown from a nearby tree into the water, changing the color. The emperor took a sip of the water and was pleasantly surprised by its flavor and restorative properties. Tea is a name given to a lot of brews. They are all derived from a shrub native to China and India and contain unique antioxidants called flavonoids. Tea also has caffeine, which seems to heighten mental alertness. When ill, especially with gastrointestinal problems or flu-like symptoms, tea has long been the beverage of choice.

Common Types of Teas

Black Tea: Made with fermented tea leaves, this tea has a high caffeine content. It is usually the basis for flavored teas, like chai, along with instant teas.

Oolong Tea: The leaves are fermented only a short time.

Green Tea: Made with steamed tea leaves.

Pu-erh Tea: Made with fermented and aged leaves and pressed into cakes.

It is the process of making the tea that is more important than the type of tea you use. The type of tea is usually an individual's choice since there are so many types and flavors.

The Teapot

The teapot should be made of china, glass, or ceramic pottery. Metal pots will impair the taste of the tea. The teapot should be spotlessly clean and washed with soap and hot water after each use. The teapot should be heated by filling the pot with boiling water, letting it stand for a few minutes, then pouring the water out. It is then that you put the tea leaves into the bottom of the pot.

The Making of the Tea

Measure the **tea** into the heated pot—usually **1 teaspoon per cup** if you are using loose tea (loose teas give the richest flavors). Pour the **boiling water** into the pot. Stir well. Place the lid on the pot and allow the tea to steep for 3 to 5 minutes. To prevent the tea from becoming bitter, it is *the correct time rather than the color* that should be your guide. If your tea steeps too long, it will release the tannin in the tea that makes it bitter.

To serve, strain the **tea** into cups or in a special serving teapot.

The English enjoy their **tea** with **cold milk**, never cream, which is thought to make the **tea** *cloudy*. The **milk** is added first, then the hot tea. **Sweeteners** and **lemon** are optional.

Iced Tea

This tea is popular year-round, especially in the summer when it can be made in a fun way called **sun tea**.

In a **gallon jar filled with water**, add:
6 regular tea bags (any flavor)
Set outside in the sun for several hours. When the **water** turns the color of the **tea** used, bring into the house, remove tea bags, and refrigerate or serve over ice. **Sweeteners** and **lemons** are optional.

Brewed Ice Tea

In the basket of your coffeemaker, place:
6 regular tea bags (any flavor)
Fill a large pitcher with **ice** (be careful not to use a glass pitcher; it may crack). Brew the tea in the coffeemaker as you would coffee (**8 to 10 cups cold water**), then pour brewed **tea** over the **ice**. **Sweeteners** and **lemons** are optional.

Fruit-Flavored Iced Teas

In an **8-cup Pyrex glass bowl**, add:
1 cup fruit (strawberries, raspberries, etc.)
4 cups water
Microwave or cook on high for about 4 to 5 minutes. Then add:
4 regular tea bags
Allow the **tea** and **fruit** to steep for 1/2 to 1 hour, then strain.

Fill a pitcher with **ice** and pour the **tea-fruit mixture** over the ice. **Sweeteners** and **lemons** are optional.

Herbal Teas

Herbal tea isn't really made from tea, which is a specific plant. Herbal tea is an infusion of leaves, seeds, roots, or barks extracted in hot water. It is made from peppermint, spearmint, ginger, chamomile, lemon, orange, rosehips, or a combination. Each has different benefits, from soothing a tummy ache to relieving insomnia or calming a mind. Herbs have all sorts of healing powers and are a good source of vitamins and minerals. You can make herbal iced or hot teas in any of the above ways. Herbal teas are especially nice because they are usually without caffeine, which you may prefer to avoid.

Green Tea and Its Benefits

Green tea is made from *Camellia sinensis* leaves that have undergone minimal oxidation during its processing. It originated in China but recently became more widespread in the West. You constantly hear about the wonders of green tea; it is brimming with antioxidants and wipes away germs that cause bad breath (that's important). It has cancer-fighting antioxidants called cathechins, considered one of the most beneficial compounds found in green tea. It also has the amino acid L-theanine, which gives green tea a calming effect and its unique flavor. But it is this unique flavor that I'm not fond of. Now, I want all the benefits of this beverage, so in order for me to drink it, I need to add some other natural flavors. Here are some of my suggestions.

Pineapple Lemon Iced Tea

Makes: 8 to 10 servings

In an **8-cup Pyrex pitcher**, add:
8 cups water
Microwave for 10 minutes until **water** is simmering or boiling.

Remove pitcher from microwave and add to **water**:
6 green tea bags
Steep until **water** changes color, about 3 to 5 minutes. Squeeze tea bags, then discard the bags.

Add to brewed tea:
⅓ to ½ can unsweetened frozen pineapple juice concentrate
⅓ cup lemon juice
¼ cup sugar
Stir until **sugar** is dissolved. Refrigerate overnight for the flavors to blend. Serve over **ice**.

Strawberry Iced Tea

Makes: 8 to 10 servings

In a large pitcher, combine:
⅓ to ½ can unsweetened frozen strawberry concentrate*
⅔ cup sugar
¼ cup water
Let stand 20 minutes.

Add and stir to combine:
8 cups brewed green tea
Refrigerate until cold. Serve over **ice**.

*Old Orchard has a nice selection of frozen and regular
juices with natural colors, flavors, and sweeteners.
Products are ever changing, so ... ALWAYS read the
labels before purchasing any juice.

Orange Julius 🍎 ♥ GF

Orange Julius is a fruit beverage that is a mixture of orange juice, milk, sugar, vanilla extract, and ice. The drink grew out of an orange juice stand in 1926 operated by Julius Freed in Los Angeles. People would line up at the store and shout, "Give me an orange, Julius," and eventually it was called "Orange Julius." In the late 1970s, when our sons, Tony and Chris, took the seventh-grade home economics class (a required subject) at Centura School, their teacher, Annette Davis, made Orange Julius in their classes. Recently, Chris asked me to contact Mrs. Davis to get this recipe.

Makes: 6 servings

In a blender combine:
1 (6-ounce) can frozen orange juice concentrate
1 cup milk
1 cup water
¼ cup sugar
1 teaspoon vanilla extract
Blend on high speed for 15 to 30 seconds or until sugar is dissolved.

Add to **above mixture**:
10 to 12 ice cubes
Blend until ice is mostly crushed yet still a bit coarse.

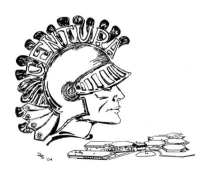

Smoothies 🍎♥GF

Smoothies, yum, yum. Everyone has their favorite! You drink them for health, to diet, or because they are cool and taste good. Because of all of the above, there are many recipes, but they are very similar, so it is just an exchange of ingredients to mix in your blender. You can use fruits, vegetables, milk (your choice), juices, yogurt, ice, and some sweeteners, such as honey, agave, or any other natural sweeteners. If you are using a smoothie to diet, you should know that eating fresh, raw vegetables and unpeeled fruits uses up more calories to digest the food than it does if the food is blended. The whole food also stays in the stomach longer, reducing the feeling of hunger. But either way, this is a good source of the vitamins, fiber, and antioxidants we need to stay healthy. I'm going to give you a couple examples of each, fruit and vegetable, then you use your imagination and experiment with your favorite fruits and veggies.

Fruit Smoothies

Blueberry-Pomegranate Smoothie

Makes: 2 cups

In a blender, combine:
⅔ cup frozen blueberries, unthawed
½ cup yogurt, your choice
½ cup milk, your choice
¼ cup pomegranate juice
1 cup crushed ice
Blend on high speed until smooth. Pour into tall glasses and serve immediately.

Strawberry-Banana Smoothie

Makes: 4 cups

In a blender, combine:
1 ½ cups frozen strawberries, cut in halves if necessary
1 banana, sliced
1 cup juice (orange, apple, or other)
1 cup yogurt, your choice
1 cup crushed ice
Blend on high speed until smooth. Pour in tall glasses and serve immediately.

Vegetable Smoothies

Green Julius Smoothies 🪲

> I wonder what Julius Freed would think? See page 111.

Makes: 4 to 6 servings

In a blender, combine:
1 (6-ounce) can orange juice
2 large mangoes
2 cups spinach, parsley, or kale
2 cups crushed ice
honey to taste
Blend on high until smooth. Pour in tall glass and serve immediately.

Green Coconut Smoothie

Makes: 6 cups

In a blender, combine:

2 frozen bananas

2 handfuls spinach, parsley, or kale

1 cup milk (your choice)

¼ teaspoon cinnamon

1 teaspoon vanilla extract

1 Tablespoon coconut oil

2 cups crushed ice

Blend on high speed until smooth. Pour in **tall glasses** and serve immediately.

Options

- Use **frozen peaches**, **berries of all kinds**, **grapes**, **apples**, **pears**; the list is endless.
- Use any kind of **yogurt**, regular or Greek, plain or flavored.
- Use any kind of **milk** (whole, 2%, skimmed, almond, coconut, soy).
- Use any kind of green vegetable (**parsley**, **kale**, **spinach**, **broccoli**, etc.).
- Use any natural sweetener (**honey**, **agave**, **raw sugar**, **stevia**, etc.).

Party Slush Punch 🍎 ♥ GF

Starting in the spring there are many family events when a hostess is looking for a good punch recipe that is easy and most people will like. Many parents are concerned about unhealthy additives that are in our beverages. Most powdered drinks and sodas are made with artificial colors and flavorings, touting it is a diet drink that has no calories. But now we have available many unsweetened juices that are all natural or organic, such as cranberry, strawberry, cherry, raspberry, Concord grape, white grape, peach, pineapple, apple, lemon, lime, and orange. This allows us to make a refreshing beverage that is also healthy. I will give you a sample recipe, then you choose the flavors and colors of the punch you want, mix them together, and freeze. I used this recipe for our grandson Jordan's graduation party. I made it a week before using raspberry juice. It was a hit!

Makes: 30 to 40 servings

In **1 (5-quart) container**, combine:*
2 packages Knox unflavored gelatin
1 ½ cups sugar

Stir into the **above mixture**:
1 ½ cups boiling water to dissolve the sugar-gelatin mixture

*I use a 5-quart ice cream bucket.

Add:

5 cups of your choice of unsweetened juices: cranberry, cherry, raspberry, strawberry, Concord grape, or blueberry

1 cup lemon or lime juice

1 (46-ounce) can unsweetened pineapple juice

Mix well, cover with a lid, and place on a **cookie sheet** when carrying it to the freezer. Place on a flat surface so the **punch** will freeze evenly and to prevent spilling. Freeze until **punch** is slightly firm, then make a design using the **fruits** of the juices of the **punch**. Allow the **fruit** to set for about 1 hour. Cover the **fruit** with the **soda** you are using for the **punch** and let it freeze for at least 2 days.

Remove from the freezer 3 to 5 hours before serving.

When thawed enough to unmold, place in punch bowl *fruit side up*:

frozen punch

About 1 hour before serving, add to the **punch**:

2 (2-liter) bottles lemon-lime soda or ginger ale

With a fork or small knife break up frozen **punch** to make a slush. Serve in small **punch cups**.

Ice Ring for the Punch Bowl

If you prefer to have cold punch with an ice ring, make your punch several days ahead. Use some of the punch to make the ice ring and refrigerate the remainder of the punch until ready to use.

Fill a **ring mold ⅔ full of punch**; allow it to partially freeze until it is firm enough to place **fruit** on the top. Make a design using the **fruits** of the **juices** of the **punch**. Allow the **fruit** to set about 1 hour, then cover the **fruit** with the **soda** you are using in the **punch**. Freeze. Unmold and place *fruit side up* in the punch bowl. Add **prepared punch**.

Top: Beverage table with punch, coffee, and mints. Left: Ice ring for punch. Right: Mints, page 190.

Bloody Mary Mix 🍎 ♥ GF

Whenever we travel by air, Dave and I like to drink Bloody Mary mix in the can; not a Bloody Mary, just the tomato mix. I found several recipes, and many of them have "trendy" ingredients that are not found in most cupboards. This can make the recipe costly. I formulated a generic recipe that I really like. You can taste it, and if you find something lacking, you can add other ingredients to give the juice more zing.

Makes: 6 servings

In a large glass pitcher, combine:
1 (46-ounce) can tomato juice
⅓ cup lemon juice
1 teaspoon brown sugar
1 Tablespoon Worcestershire sauce
1 Tablespoon horseradish (not horseradish sauce)
1 teaspoon tabasco sauce
¼ teaspoon celery seeds
½ teaspoon salt
Stir ingredients until combined.

The freshly grated root of the horseradish works well mixed with cream to make a sauce. Serve with smoked fish or beef.

Options

■ To make mix have more zing, add any of these ingredients:

1 ½ Tablespoons Angostura Bitters
1 ½ Tablespoons Old Bay seasonings
1 teaspoon black pepper

or

Increase these ingredients to:
1 ½ Tablespoons horseradish
1 ½ Tablespoons Worcestershire sauce
1 ½ teaspoons Tabasco sauce

There is a mixture to fit everyone's taste; just experiment until it is right for you.

Bloody Mary

Moisten the rim of an **8-ounce glass** with:
lemon juice

On a small plate, pour small amount:
salt
Press the moistened rim of glass into **salt**.

In salted glass, combine:
1 cup ice cubes
1 jigger (1 ½ ounces) vodka
enough Bloody Mary Mix to fill glass
Mix well. Garnish with a **giant spear of celery** and **two green stuffed olives**.

Tom and Jerrys ♥ GF

In *Family Favorites*, I have the recipe for egg nog (pages 114–115), and several people asked me if I knew the recipe for Tom and Jerrys … I admitted that I didn't. I remember my parents going to the Liederkranz (a German social club) every Christmas and New Year's for Tom and Jerrys. If they entertained at our home during the holidays, they would get out the Tom and Jerry bowl and cups, then Mom would make the batter. My brothers, sisters, and I always liked egg nog better, so I was never interested in the recipe. But I had so many people ask me about it, I got curious and looked it up. I would call it a form of egg nog or a hot toddy but with more "spirits" added. No wonder Mom only made us egg nog!

Makes: 12 to 15 servings

Separate into different **bowls**:
12 (large) eggs

Place in mixer bowl with wire attachment:
egg yolks*
Beat well.

To egg yolks, gradually add:
2 cups sugar
½ teaspoon cloves

*When using raw eggs, be sure the eggs are fresh and not cracked (Healthful Hits, page 234–235).

Mom and Dad's Tom and Jerry bowl.

½ teaspoon nutmeg
½ teaspoon ground allspice
Mix well and place batter into Tom and Jerry bowl or large glass bowl.

Clean mixer bowl so there is no trace of **egg yolk** and dry the bowl thoroughly, then add:
egg whites
Beat **egg whites** until stiff.

Fold egg whites into **batter** and place it into refrigerator until ready to use.

To serve:

For each drink, using an **8-ounce glass cup**, mix:
¼ cup batter
1 ounce brandy
1 ounce rum
Fill the cup with equal parts **hot milk** and **boiling water**, then sprinkle the top with **nutmeg**.

Wassail 🍎 ♥ GF

During the Christmas Season, we hear the song, "Here We Come A-wassailing." This is a traditional Christmas carol and New Year's song. Bands of beggars and orphans used to dance their way through England's snowy streets to sing good cheer in hopes the people of the house would let them in and give them a drink from their wassail bowl or a penny or allow them to stand a few minutes by the warmth of the fireplace. Wassail is a combination of hot apple cider, spices, citrus fruit, and maybe enough "spirits" to give the singers some warmth. Today this drink is commonly called hot apple cider, and the ingredients are very similar.

"Love and joy come to you / And to you your wassail, too / And God bless you a happy New Year"

Makes: 20 to 25 servings

In a large stainless steel pot with a pasta insert/strainer, mix:
2 quarts apple cider
1 quart cranberry juice
2 cinnamon sticks
1 teaspoon allspice
1 orange studded with whole cloves
Heat on stove on low heat for 1 hour; reduce heat just enough to keep it warm, 2 to 6 hours.

When you are ready to serve, remove the pasta insert with the **orange** and the **spices** and add:
1 cup rum, sherry or brandy (optional)
Serve in small cups.

Options

- Large electric coffee urn: Place your **juices** in the urn. Place your **spices** and **orange slices** in the coffee grounds tray. Process as you would coffee.
- Crock-Pot: Place **juices**, **orange slices**, and **cinnamon sticks** in Crock-Pot. In a cheese cloth place **loose spices (cloves and allspice)** and tie firmly at the top; add to the **juices** and cook on low for 4 hours.
- If not sweet enough, you can add **½ to 1 cup sugar** to the recipe.

Here we come a-wassailing!

Breads

Roslin

Glossary

baker's dozen. The custom of adding an extra item when customer purchases a dozen of a particular item for a total of thirteen. Good public relations and no chance of accidentally shorting the customer.

bleached flour. Refined flour that has had the germ and bran removed and a whitening agent added. It is aged by using a bleaching agent, maturing agent, or both. The four most common additives are potassium bromates, benzoyl peroxide, ascorbic acid, and chlorine gas. All bleaching agents (with the exception of ascorbic acid) are banned in the United Kingdom.

flour. Powder made from grinding grains, seeds, beans, roots. Basic ingredient of bread, pasta, and most baked doughs and batters. Wheat is most common in this country. Also a thickener for gravies, soups, other liquids.

glaze. To cook food with or cover with a thin syrup or jelly, giving it a glossy coating.

gluten free. Any product, but particularly flour, that does not contain wheat, barley, rye, or spelt, made up of one or a combination of alternative grains, roots, beans, or other plant products for cooking or baking. Important for those suffering from celiac disease or other sensitivity to gluten-containing products.

knead. To mix and work into a uniform mass by folding, pressing, and stretching dough with hands; can also be done with an electric mixer using a dough hook.

preheat. To heat to the desired temperature, as in an oven, before placing food in it.

quick bread. Breads that are leavened with baking powder or soda instead of yeast; they require no kneading or rising before baking. Usually baked in a loaf, but also includes muffins, biscuits, coffee cakes, pancakes, etc.

raw sugar. Also called Turbinado. Partially refined sugar in which two-thirds of the molasses is removed.

sponge. A batter made from yeast.

unbleached flour. All-purpose flour that is not chemically bleached.

yeast breads. Breads that require yeast as a leavening; kneaded either by hand or by the dough hook of a heavy-duty mixer and allowed to rise at least once before baking.

white whole-wheat flour. Flour milled from hard white spring wheat rather than traditional red. Contains same nutrients, bran, germ endosperm as regular whole wheat. Milder flavored. Use as regular whole wheat.

whole-wheat flour. Made from whole grains of the wheat, including bran.

History of Breads

Bread is a staple food prepared by baking a dough of flour and water. It is one of the oldest prepared foods. The history of bread started with the Neolithic Age and the dawn of agriculture and marched through time according to the ingredients available. The earliest breads were unleavened and varied in grains, thickness, shape, and texture; breads also varied from culture to culture. Leavened bread was available in Egypt as early as 4000 BC, as was the practice of using yeast as a leavening agent, which was also used for brewing ale. The Egyptians used bread as money, paying laborers who built the pyramids three loaves of bread and two jugs of beer for a day's work. The art of making bread soon spread to Rome, Spain, and Britain. The early European bakers used a brewer's yeast, a thick scum strained from the surface of fermenting wine, to leaven bread. The class system of the medieval world made dark rye bread the staple of the working class while the rich enjoyed fine white bread.

Bleached white flour, which comes from the center core of the wheat called the endosperm, is widely used today. But consumers are beginning to become wary of all the additives in our packaged foods, and unbleached flour is becoming a popular replacement. But we are still not getting the nutrients of whole-wheat flour because we are missing the bran and wheat germ. Many people avoid eating whole-wheat bread or pastas because they don't like the bitter taste of whole-wheat flour. But now we have an alternative, white whole-wheat flour.

White whole-wheat flour is flour milled from hard white spring wheat rather than traditional red wheat. In England, whole-wheat flour is more commonly made from white whole-wheat instead of red as in the United States. White whole wheat has all of the nutrients (bran, germ, and endosperm) of red whole wheat but is lighter in color and milder in flavor, requiring less added sweetner. The reason for its milder taste is it does not contain the strongly flavored phenolic acid and tannins that are in red wheat. I have found that you can use it to make noodles, bread, cake, pie crust, and cookies, and I discovered little difference when I used unbleached flour for these products. The big plus is you have all the nutrition of whole-wheat flour and the taste and texture of white flour. Now, this is my choice of flour.

White Whole-Wheat Bread

Makes: 4 loaves
Bake: Preheated 350 degree oven
Time: 35 minutes

Bake, boil or microwave:
1 medium to large potato
Set aside to cool, then peel.

In mixer bowl using the dough hook, mix well:
1 quart warm water
2 packages (2 Tablespoons) dry yeast
1 Tablespoon salt
¼ cup honey
1 Tablespoon unsulfured molasses
Allow the **yeast** to soften in **water** until it appears bubbly.

In food processor, puree:
½ cup canola oil
prepared potato, cut into pieces
2 large eggs
Add to the **yeast mixture**.

Add to **above mixture** to make a sponge:
4 cups white whole-wheat flour
Mix well and allow the **sponge mixture** to rise about 1 hour or until sponge *doubles*. Mix, if needed, every 20 minutes. *Set timer.*

Add to the **sponge mixture**:
3 cups unbleached flour
Mix well.

On a **floured board**, knead until no longer sticky. Place in a large bowl and allow the **dough** to rise *twice* before shaping. Then divide into 4 equal parts, shape into **loaves**, and place into **greased 9 × 5 ×3-inch loaf pans**. Allow the **bread** to again *double* in size. Bake as instructed above or until crust is brown.

Helpful Hints

- The additions of fats, such as **butter** or **oils** and **milk**, can greatly assist the rise.
- **1 scant Tablespoon bulk yeast** equals 1 package of **yeast**.
- Hot **water** kills **yeast**. If you cannot feel hot or cool, the **water** is just right.
- Substitute **leftover mashed potatoes**, approximately 1 to 2 cups, **reserved potato water**, and enough **warm water** to make **1 quart**.

Convection Ovens

Convection ovens circulate hot air inside the oven cavity using a built-in fan, cooking more quickly and evenly than conventional ovens. One advantage to this type of oven is that more food can be baked at once because of the movement of air, but it does make a difference in how you cook. If you are used to a conventional oven, you can achieve the same results by following these general rules: Lower the temperature by 25 to 50 degrees and reduce baking time by 25%.

Coffee Cake Ring

In 2014, I entered a coffee cake in open class at the Nebraska State Fair using my potato recipe. I used a sweet potato (yam) rather than a white potato and a blend of white whole-wheat and unbleached flours. It was a pleasant surprise. First, the bread had a wonderful yellow-orange hue, and second, it gave the bread a sweeter taste. I decorated this coffee cake with all-natural colored and flavored cream cheese frosting. I won a second-place ribbon. This is a recipe I will use frequently because the taste is wonderful and it has a beautiful presentation... Two pluses!

Have prepared:
1 (12- or 14-inch) round pizza baking sheet
1 (5-inch) stainless steel bowl

Makes: 1 ring
Bake: Preheated 350 degree oven
Time: 25 minutes

Boil, bake, or microwave:
1 small yam
Peel and set aside.

In food processor, add and puree:
prepared yam
¼ cup canola oil
1 large egg
Set aside.

In mixer bowl using dough hook, combine:

2 cups warm water

1 ½ teaspoons salt

1 Tablespoon honey

1 Tablespoon unsulphured molasses

1 package (1 Tablespoon) dry yeast

3 cups white whole-wheat flour

Mix well and allow the **sponge mixture** to rise, about 1 hour.

Add to **sponge mixture**:

2 cups unbleached flour

Mix well, place on a **floured surface**, and knead **dough** until the **dough** is no longer sticky. Place the **dough** in a large bowl and let it *double* in size.

Remove the **dough** from the bowl and divide it into three equal pieces; roll each piece of **dough** into 12- to 15-inch lengths, tapering the ends.

In a flour sifter, mix:

1 cup sugar

1 Tablespoon cinnamon

Brush each of the pieces with **melted butter** and **sprinkle with sugar-and-cinnamon mixture**.

To braid: Follow instructions on the next page.

Grease a 12- to 14-inch round baking (pizza) sheet. **Grease** the outside of a 5-inch stainless steel bowl and place in the center of the baking sheet.

Place **braid** around bowl and connect the edges of the **braid**. Allow the braid to *double* in size, approximately 1 hour.

Bake as instructed on page 130. Decorate with **natural frostings**, pages 154–155.

Line up the ropes 1 inch apart.

Starting with the center rope, loosely bring left rope underneath center rope and lay it down.

Bring right rope underneath the new center rope and lay it down.

Repeat to the end.

Place braid around bowl and connect edges of braid.

Potato Rolls (White Whole-Wheat Flour)

We always want "the best of both worlds," bread with whole grain nutrition and the texture and taste of white bread. The potato roll recipe in *Family Favorites* was a favorite of anyone who ever ate these rolls. I had made rolls using only white whole-wheat flour, but they were not as soft as the rolls with unbleached. Sooo, I compromised and made them with a combination of both. Problem solved.

Make: 2 to 3 dozen

In mixer bowl, using dough hook, combine:
1 ½ cups water or **potato water**
1 package (1 Tablespoon) dry yeast
⅔ cup sugar
1 ½ teaspoons salt
Mix well and allow to stand until the **yeast** mixture becomes bubbly. *This is a very important step because it tells you if your yeast is good.*

Add to **yeast mixture** :
⅔ cup canola oil
2 large eggs or 4 egg yolks (*use egg yolks for a rich golden color*)
1 to 2 cups mashed potatoes
3 cups white whole wheat flour
Mix well and allow the **sponge mixture** to rise, about 1 hour.

Add to **sponge mixture:**
2 cups unbleached flour
Mix well and place on a **floured surface** and knead **dough** until no longer sticky. Place **dough** in a large bowl and let it *double* in size. Shape the **dough** into the dinner rolls of your choice.

Options

■ **Cocktail Sandwich Rolls**

Makes: 2 to 3 dozen
Bake: Preheated 350 degree oven
Time: 15 to 20 minutes

On a **floured surface**, roll out **potato dough** to approximately ½-inch thick and cut with round cutters the size you desire. Place on a **greased cookie sheet** and let double in size. Bake until slightly brown.

■ **Cloverleaf Rolls**

Makes: 2 dozen
Bake: Preheated 350 degree oven
Time: 15 minutes

After the **potato dough** has risen, shape into 3 small balls so they half fill a **greased muffin tin**. Let double in size and bake.

■ **Crescent Rolls**

Makes: 4 dozen
Bake: Preheated 350 degree oven
Time: 15 minutes

Divide **dough** into 4 parts. Roll **dough** into a 12-inch circle, ¼- to ½-inch thick. Using a pizza cutter, cut the **dough** into 12 wedges. Starting at the side opposite the point, roll up each wedge. Repeat with **remaining dough**. Place on **greased baking sheets**, point edge up. Let the dough double in size. A mini option for these **rolls** is brushing with an **egg glaze** (**1 egg yolk and 1 cup water**, beaten together). Sprinkle tops with **sesame**, **flax**, or **poppy seeds**.

Cutting out the Cocktail Sandwich Rolls.

Preparing the Cloverleaf Rolls.

The Crescent Roll circle with wedges.

Rolling the Crescent Rolls.

Helpful Hint

■ Frozen **rolls** tend to form ice crystals if left in the freezer for an extended period of time. When thawing the **rolls**, remove any noticeable ice crystals, turn the **rolls** upside down on a cooling rack, and allow them to thaw. Place the thawed **rolls** in a clean plastic bag until ready to use.

Gluten-Free Bread 🍎 ♥ 🐝GF

I searched the Internet for a gluten-free bread recipe. First you need to understand that gluten-free all-purpose flour is made from some or a combination of these ingredients: corn (maize), buckwheat, quinoa, brown rice, corn starch, arrowroot, amaranth, tapioca, potato starch, xanthan gum, ground flax seeds. I found a gluten-free flour blend that has 13 of the above ingredients. I added the amounts in the recipe of the individual ingredients, which equaled 3 cups, then substituted 3 cups of this blended flour. This bread recipe also called for ½ cup of potato starch, so I boiled a medium-sized potato, using the potato water for the water in the recipe. I substituted honey for sugar and increased the yeast from 1 Tablespoon to 1 ½ Tablespoons. I was pleased with the results. My suggestion to cooks who are using gluten-free flours, always continue to look for new and improved flours. You'll never know when you might find the right combination. This recipe won a second-place ribbon at the 2014 Nebraska State Fair.

Makes: 2 loaves
Bake: Preheated 385 degree oven
Time: 25 minutes
Turn oven off
Time: 10 minutes *(see Helpful Hints on next page)*

Have prepared:
2 **greased** 7 × 4 × 2-inch loaf pans

In small saucepan, add:
2 cups water
1 medium potato, peeled and cut into chucks
Cook until **potato** is tender. Cool and drain **water** into a small bowl, set aside. Save or freeze **potato** for use in another recipe, such as **gnocchi**, pages 74–75.

In 4-cup Pyrex cup, combine:

1 ¼ cup reserved potato water

1 ½ Tablespoons (1 ½ packages) yeast

⅓ cup honey

1 ½ teaspoons salt

Let stand until **yeast** softens and becomes bubbly.

In a small bowl using a wire whisk, combine:

3 large eggs

⅓ cup olive oil

Mix well and add to **yeast mixture.**

In mixer bowl with dough hook, add:

3 cups gluten-free flour

1 teaspoon baking powder

½ cup pecans, finely chopped

Mix well with dough hook and make a well in the middle of the **flour.**

Gradually pour into the well (center) of **flour:**

yeast and egg mixture

Mix for about 2 minutes until **flour** is completely moistened. Spoon or pour **dough mixture** into prepared loaf pans. Smooth the top with the back of a spoon moistened with **water.** Loosely cover the **loaves** with a kitchen towel or waxed paper; place in a warm area to rise, about 1 hour. Bake as instructed above.

Helpful Hints

■ Since gluten-free flour lacks gluten, it is difficult for bread to retain its shape. Other ingredients such as **xanthan** and **guar gums, corn starch** and **eggs** are used to compensate for the lack of gluten. Your finished product will be a rather dense and moist **bread.** I prefer it toasted and like the addition of **nuts** and **seeds** for added taste and texture.

- When I made my first two loaves of gluten-free bread, the bottom crust was too moist and soft. I remedied this problem by increasing the temperature of the oven. After baking, turn off oven and cover **bread** with a loose foil tent (prevents further browning of the top crust). Allow the **bread** to stay in the oven an extra 10 minutes or more. Cool on wire rack.
- Check internal temperature with a pocket thermometer. If the temperature is 210 to 220 degrees, the bread is done.
- No matter how tempting, allow the **bread** to *cool completely* before slicing.

Options

- Add your choice of finely chopped **nuts**—**walnut**, **pecan**, **almond**, etc.
- Add your choice of **seeds**—**sesame**, **flax**, **poppy**, etc.

Serving the gluten-free bread.

History of Quick Breads

Quick bread is any bread leavened with leavening agents other than yeast; this includes a variety of baked goods, fruit breads, biscuits, muffins, pancakes, scones, cakes, and cookies. Quick breads were widely used in the United States at the end of the 18th century. Before that time, baked goods were leavened by yeast. During the Civil War (1861–1865), the demand for food was so high, bread had to be made faster and was leavened by using baking soda. In 1846 commercial baking soda (one component) was introduced in Indiana, and in 1856 baking powder (two components) was introduced in New York. During the chemical leavening process, these leavening agents, usually a weak acid and a weak base, are added to the dough mixture. These agents undergo a chemical reaction to produce carbon dioxide, increasing the baked good's volume and producing a change in shape and texture. Because the category of "quick breads" includes so many types of baked goods, you will find other recipes in different sections of this cookbook, such as Cookies and Cakes.

During the holidays, it is nice and easy to do quick breads for your guests or to give as gifts. They can be made early and frozen for use as needed during the holidays.

Helpful Hints

- As you probably will notice, I don't sift my dry ingredients together. I let my mixer do that—just one more step that can be eliminated.
- Recipes are for basic 9 × 5 × 3-inch loaf pans, but you may want to use smaller sizes to make more than one loaf. Just be sure to watch your oven temperature and time very carefully.
- If your quick breads are tough, try mixing eggs and milk (if called for) together before adding to other ingredients.
- Your bread is done when it shrinks slightly from the sides of the pan and a toothpick inserted in the center comes out clean.
- Be sure bread is completely cooled before slicing or storing.

Banana-Nut Bread (White Whole-Wheat Flour)

When changing from unbleached flour to white whole-wheat flour, I noticed the volume of my batter to be larger. By using two smaller loaf pans (7 × 4 × 2) rather than one large loaf pan (9 × 5 × 3), I seemed to have better results and less baking time.

Makes: 2 loaves

Bake: Preheated 350 degree oven
Time: 45 minutes

Have prepared:
2 medium-sized 7 ×4 × 2-inch **well-greased** loaf pans

In mixer bowl, combine and mix well with flat beater:
2 cups white whole-wheat flour
1 cup sugar
2 teaspoons baking powder
½ teaspoon baking soda
½ teaspoon salt

Add to **flour mixture** all at once:
2 large eggs
½ cup canola oil
3 ripe bananas
1 teaspoon lemon juice
½ cup milk
Mix just until **dry ingredients** are moistened.

Fold in with mixer on *low* or stir by hand:

1 cup chopped walnuts or pecans

Pour into prepared loaf pans. When baked, let cool 10 minutes before removing from pan. Cool completely on wire rack.

Option

- **GF**   To make gluten free, substitute **gluten-free flour** for **white whole-wheat flour**.

Serving the Banana-Nut Bread.

Raspberry-Lemon Muffins ♥ GF

It is difficult for me to give up on gluten-free recipes. I'm always looking for new cooking ideas and tips to make these recipes more palatable. While in Omaha, I found a new gluten-free flour. The ingredients included a blend of nutritious grains selected for taste and all allergen-free. The blend consists of brown rice, golden flaxseed, quinoa, buckwheat, and amaranth. The label read, "Gluten-Free, Flax and Ancient Grains." This specialty flour is a wonderful replacement for all-purpose whole-wheat flour. This recipe received a first-place and Best of Division ribbons at the 2014 Nebraska State Fair.

Have prepared:
12-cup muffin tin with white paper liners. Set aside.

Makes: 12
Bake: Preheated 375 degree oven
Time: 22 to 25 minutes

In 1-cup Pyrex cup, combine:
1 cup milk
1 teaspoon apple-cider vinegar
Mix well and set aside for 20 to 30 minutes.

In medium bowl, combine:
¼ cup gluten-free flour
2 cups frozen raspberries
Stir gently to coat **berries**; this prevents **raspberry** drop. Set aside in refrigerator or freezer.

In large bowl, combine and set aside:
1 ¾ cups gluten-free flour

Serving gluten-free Raspberry-Lemon Muffins.

1 Tablespoon baking powder
1 teaspoon soda
½ teaspoon salt

In medium-sized bowl, mix with wire whisk:
4 Tablespoons (½ stick) butter, melted and cooled
½ cup honey
prepared milk
2 large eggs
1 teaspoon lemon zest, freshly grated
1 teaspoon vanilla extract
Add above mixture to **flour mixture** and give about 10 stirs: You want to just *barely* get things lightly combined. The **batter** will be slightly thick.

Add and fold gently into **batter** with about 5 stirs:
prepared raspberries
Just enough to evenly distribute the **berries** throughout the **batter**.

Divide the **batter** between the 12 cups. Bake as instructed above or until the tops are golden brown. Cool on wire rack. Serve immediately or store for later.

Frost with **Confectioner's Icing**, page 168. Add to the frosting **2 teaspoons lemon juice**.

Cranberry-Walnut Muffins 🍎 ❤ GF

At the first Thanksgiving feast, the Indians are believed to have brought gifts of cranberries as a symbol of peace. The Pilgrims named them "crane berries" because the cranberry blossoms looked like the heads of cranes.* Wild cranberries became very popular with the colonists. To control the picking of cranberries, some settlements passed laws imposing a penalty for picking more than a quart before September 20. Cranberries are one way of making a dessert healthy because they are a good source of vitamin C and fiber. And even better, walnuts not only give the muffins a crunchy taste, they score the highest in the omega-3s that protect against heart disease. It's a win-win muffin.

Makes: 12
Bake: Preheated 375 degree oven
Time: 22 minutes

Have prepared:
12-cup muffin pan with white paper liners. Set aside.

In a large bowl, add:
1 cup white whole wheat flour
½ cup unbleached flour
¾ cup sugar
2 teaspoons baking powder
¼ teaspoon salt
Mix well and set aside.

The cranberry blossom looks similar to the head and beak of a crane. (Rob Routledge, Sault College, Bugwood.org/Wikimedia Commons)

*In Grand Island, we have "Wings over the Platte," which celebrates the migration of the sandhill cranes.

In a medium bowl using wire whisk, combine:

1 large egg

½ cup milk

4 Tablespoons butter, melted

1 teaspoon vanilla extract

Mix well. Add **liquid ingredients** to **dry ingredients**, then stir just until **batter** forms.

Fold gently into **batter**:

1 ⅔ cups cranberries, halved

½ cup walnuts, coarsely chopped

Fill each muffin cup ¾ full.

Mix together:

1 Tablespoon raw sugar

¼ teaspoon cinnamon

Sprinkle over top of each muffin and bake as instructed above or until tops are golden brown. Cool on a wire rack. Serve immediately or store for later.

Options

- Substitute **unbleached flour** for **white whole wheat**.
- **GF** Substitute **gluten-free flour** for **white whole-wheat and unbleached flours**.

God's Pharmacy

A walnut looks like a little brain, a left and right hemisphere, upper cerebrums, and lower cerebrums. Even the wrinkles or folds on the nut are just like the neocortex. We now know walnuts help develop more than three dozen neuron transmitters for brain function.

Frannie's Scones 🍎

Scones baked at home are usually made from a family recipe, since often it is a family member who holds the "best and most treasured recipe." My sister-in-law Fran Seymour is a wonderful cook: She bakes, cans, fixes wonderful dinners of turkey, ham, chicken and duck for Dave, plus all the side dishes. While she was recovering from surgery, I spent a week with her, and we had fun swapping recipes and cooking together. She made these wonderful scones.

Makes: 8
Bake: Preheated 375 degree oven
Time: 20 minutes

In small bowl, combine:
2 large eggs
¾ cup whipping cream
Stir slightly. Set aside.

In mixer bowl with wire whip attachment, combine:
2 ½ cups unbleached flour
¼ cup sugar
1 Tablespoon baking powder
¼ teaspoon salt
With mixer on *stir or low* setting, mix just enough to *blend* ingredients.

Add to **dry ingredients**:
½ cup (1 stick) cold butter, cut into small pieces
Mix on *stir* or *low* setting until well distributed into **flour mixture**; it should resemble a coarse meal. *Do not over mix.*

Using a fork, add *slowly* to the **butter-and-flour mixture**:

prepared egg-and-cream mixture

Mix only until **flour** is *moistened*.

Gently stir in:

½ cup raisins or craisins

¼ cup nuts

1 teaspoon grated orange zest

Turn **dough** out on a slightly **floured** surface. Quickly knead **dough** by gently folding and pressing **dough** for 6 to 8 strokes or until **dough** is nearly smooth. Place **dough** on a baking sheet and lightly roll out into an 8-inch circle. Using a sharp knife or a pizza cutter, cut the circle into 8 wedges. *Do not separate the wedges.*

Brush the tops with **milk** and sprinkle with **raw sugar**. Bake as instructed above.

To serve: After baking, cool the **scones** on a wire rack for 5 minutes, break **scone's circle** apart into wedges. Serve *warm*.

Helpful Hints

- If your **scones** are too heavy: Be sure you are not cutting **fat** into the **dry mixture** beyond coarse stage. When adding **egg-and-cream mixture**, stir just until moistened; *do not overmix*.
- If **scones** are dry and crumbly: Handle the **dough** more gently and knead the **dough** for the number of strokes indicated in the recipe.
- If your **scones** have a hard crust: Check temperature of your oven. If it is too high or low, adjust it to the proper temperature. Check **scones** at the *minimum time*; **scones** are done when the top and bottom **crusts** are an even golden brown.

Cakes & Frostings

Jared

Glossary

bake. To cook using dry heat in an oven.

batter. A mixture of flour and liquid (usually in combination with other ingredients) that is thin enough to pour. Cake is usually a batter as opposed to cookie or bread dough, which is stiffer and usually not pourable.

beat. To mix with vigorous, over-and-over motion with spoon, wire whip, or electric mixer.

blend. To mix very thoroughly one or more ingredients.

Bundt pan. A deep cake pan with a tube in the center, having a curved bottom and fluted sides.

cake flour. Especially soft wheat flour, formulated to give cakes high volume, fine texture, and delicate tenderness.

combine. To mix unlike ingredients.

confectioners' sugar. Same as powdered sugar (see below).

cream. To soften fat by rubbing it against the bowl with a spoon or beating it with an electric mixer until it is light and fluffy.

cream together. To blend two ingredients together until the mixture is light and fluffy, e.g., butter and sugar.

fold in. To incorporate a delicate substance, such as whipped cream or egg whites, into another substance without releasing air bubbles. A spatula or wooden spoon is used to gently bring part of the mixture up from the bottom, fold it over the top of the two substances, and cut them down in, repeating the process as the bowl is slowly rotated.

frost. To cover cake with frosting.

funnel. A cone-shaped utensil with tube for directing food from one container to another; also used to invert angel-food cake pan if your pan does not have legs.

icing. Same as frosting.

powdered sugar. Confectioners' sugar. Granulated sugar mixed with small portion of corn starch to give a fine, powdery effect. Most often used in frostings or for dusting desserts.

preheat. To heat oven to desired temperature before putting food in.

sift. To pass through a sieve or flour sifter.

tube pan. A deep (4 inches) cake pan with a tube in the center, usually used for angel-food cake.

Celebrate with Cake

"If I knew you were comin', I'd've baked a cake." So goes that 1940s oldie, reminding us that cake just means hospitality and celebration. Most often, baking cake is to celebrate an event … birthdays, graduations, weddings, baptisms … the list goes on and on. Luckily, it is one of the easiest desserts to make. Make one to fit the occasion, a small one for a birthday, a large one for a wedding or graduation. Cake can be plain or made with fruits (apples, bananas, cherries, etc.) or even vegetables (carrots and beets). Many times the cake is the centerpiece of the table and the actual event. When the children were little, I made a castle cake, pumpkin cake, bunny cake for Easter, and a treasure chest cake. And, it is the frosting that makes the cake, completing it and turning even the simplest ones into beautiful creations. The recipes for frostings in this book are made with all-natural ingredients, including the colorings and flavorings. Since the Nebraska State Fair moved from Lincoln to Grand Island, I have entered several of my cakes in Open Class and won several ribbons. I was especially pleased when my Beet Cake won Best of Division! This was the first time I had entered a layered and decorated cake, and, yes, it was all natural from the cake to the frosting to the decorations.

Helpful Hints

For perfect cakes:

- Fill pans about ⅔ full. Leave a slight hollow in the center.
- Cake is done when it shrinks away from the sides of the pan or it springs back when lightly touched with a finger.
- Place cake on wire rack after removing from oven. Let cool in pan for about 5 minutes. Then loosen sides with a knife and turn on rack to finish cooling (exception: angel-food cakes should be completely cooled in pan).
- Cakes should be completely cooled before frosting.
- Sprinkle some powdered sugar on cake to keep frosting or icing in place.

Beet Layer Cake 🍎 ♥

I call this cake "THE ALL-NATURAL RED VELVET CAKE." Because of the red beets, the cake has a natural red hue (you don't have to ingest 2 vials of red food coloring) and it taste better. You can compare this cake to a carrot cake because it is moist and stays moist for a long time. The recipe provides you with a big cake (6 cups of batter), so I made a four-layer cake using 1 ½ cups of batter for each layer. This was my first four-tier layer cake, so I was nervous about the outcome. I entered it into the 2013 Nebraska State Fair in open class and won first-place and Best of Division ribbons. On the back of the entry ticket, the judge wrote, "Lovely unique decorations and ingredients! Very moist, flavorful and nice texture. Best of Division."

Have prepared:
In a medium saucepan, cook until tender:
3 medium beets
Allow to cool, then peel **beets**. Set aside. Reserve **peelings** for food coloring, page 154.

Four 8-inch round pans, lined with parchment paper; **greased** and **floured**

Serves: 8 to 12
Bake: Preheated 350 degrees oven
Time: 19 to 25 minutes

In a mixer bowl, with wire whisk attachment, combine:
2 cups unbleached flour
1 ⅓ cups sugar
½ cup cocoa
1 ½ teaspoons baking soda
½ teaspoon salt

Mix well and set aside.

In food processor with metal blade, combine:
3 large eggs
1 ¼ cups canola oil
2 teaspoons vanilla extract
prepared beets, cut into medium-sized chunks
Blend on *high* until mixed well.

In the mixer bowl, using the flat paddle attachment, add slowly, combining the **egg/beet mixture** into:
prepared dry ingredients
Mix until **dry ingredients** are moistened.

Pour **1 ½ cups of batter** in each prepared pan and bake as instructed above.

Remove from oven and allow the layers to cool in pans completely before frosting.

This beet cake was entered into the 2013 Nebraska State Fair in open class and won first place and Best of Division.

Cream Cheese Frosting 🍎GF*

The frosting is an all-natural cream cheese frosting, and the decorations on the cake are also all-natural, using **beet juice** for the red and sweet **green peas** for the green.

In mixer bowl with flat beater, combine:
1 (8-ounce) package cream cheese, room temperature
½ (1 stick) cup butter, softened
2 teaspoons vanilla extract
Cream together.
Gradually add:
4 cups powdered sugar
Beat until smooth.

Red Frosting

In a 4-cup Pyrex glass cup, combine:
reserved peelings from beets
¼ cup water
Cover the top of the cup with a paper towel; microwave for 3 minutes and allow to steep for 1 hour. Strain liquid through a sieve, lined with a coffee filter, and squeeze the peelings to remove as much liquid as possible. Pour into a (snack) resealable plastic bag until ready to use. Freeze the remaining juice for later use.

Add to **¼ to ½ cup above frosting**:
 juice from the beet peels, drop by drop, until you get the color you want
⅛ teaspoon almond extract
extra powdered sugar to get the correct consistency

*You may have to double this recipe for a layered cake.

Green Frosting

In a 4-cup Pyrex cup combine:

¼ cup water

25 to 30 frozen sweet green peas

Cover the top of the cup with a paper towel; microwave for 3 minutes or until tender, then allow to steep for 1 hour. Drain off excess water, set aside, and reserve. If you want a *smooth* green **frosting**, strain the **peas** through a sieve or use **whole peas** to get a leaf-like appearance.

In a food processor and add:

1 cup powdered sugar

prepared peas

Process until it reaches the right consistency. Add more **powdered sugar** or **liquid from the peas** if needed.

Add, *drop by drop*, to your own taste:

mint extract

Mix well.

See more **colored frostings**, pages 165–167.

A bundt beet cake.

Options

- You can make a two- or three-layer cake; increase baking time to 25 to 35 minutes.
- For a single-layer cake, **grease** and **flour** a 9 × 13 × 2-inch pan; increase baking time to 25 to 35 minutes.
- For graduations and weddings, **extra sheet cakes** can be easily made. **Grease** and **flour** the sides and bottom of a 9 × 13-inch or larger pan. Line the pan with waxed paper. Pour the **batter** directly onto the waxed paper. After the **cake** is baked, cool for 15 to 30 minutes. Turn onto a foil-covered cardboard sheet: carefully remove the waxed paper. Allow the **cake**

to air about 1 hour before **frosting** the top and sides of the cake. Decorate in the colors of the event.

- For a **bundt cake**, increase baking time to 50 to 60 minutes.
- Kids love this moist **cake**, and it is a good recipe for **cupcakes**. Place white paper liners in muffin pans; fill ½ full. Increase baking time to 20 minutes or until done. Makes: 24.

Helpful Hints

Since this was my first time frosting a multilayered cake, I checked with the experts: "my mother's old cookbooks." Here is what I learned.

- Make **flowers** and **leaf** decorations a day or two ahead to allow them to harden.
- If you need to cut a layer in half horizontally, cut a notch in the edge. This helps you realign the top and bottom layers to make **cake** level.
- Before frosting, lightly brush off the **crumbs** of each layer with a pastry brush.
- Keep the cake plate clean while frosting by sliding 6-inch strips of waxed paper under each side of the cake, then transfer the first layer, placing the topside down. Once the **cake** is frosted and the **frosting** is set, pull the strips away, leaving a clean plate.
- Spread about ½ **cup frosting** on top of the layer and spreading to the edges of the layer. Repeat for the second and third layers.
- Place the **top layer**, topside up, on the **frosted layer**. Spread a thin coat of **frosting** around the sides of the cake to seal in any crumbs, so they won't show up in the final coating.
- Add a thicker coating of **frosting** to the sides of the **cake** and swirl upward to the top edge about ¼ inch above the top of the cake.
- Spread the **remaining frosting** on top of cake, blending the **frosting** at the edges.

Oatmeal Cake

Our church, St. Mary's Cathedral, had a monthly breakfast after the Masses on Sunday. At one of these breakfasts, I had a piece of cake that was so delicious, I went into the kitchen and asked who had made it. It was Pat Donner, one of the faithful workers who always helped with this event. This cake is healthy and has two of my favorite ingredients, oatmeal and coconut. This can be served as a coffee cake or a dessert cake.

Serves: 12
Bake; Preheated 350 degree oven
Time: 35 to 45 minutes

Have prepared:
9 × 13-inch pan, **greased** and **floured**. Set aside.

In a medium bowl, pour **1 ½ cups** boiling **water** over:
1 cup old-fashioned oatmeal
½ cup white whole-wheat flour
Mix well, set aside, and allow it to stand for 20 minutes.

In a bowl, using a wire whisk, combine:
1 cup unbleached flour
1 teaspoon baking soda
1 teaspoon cinnamon
½ teaspoon salt
Mix well and set aside.

In a mixer bowl with flat beater, combine:

2 large eggs
1 cup sugar
½ cup canola oil

Mix well.

Add:

Prepared oatmeal/white whole-wheat flour mixture
prepared dry ingredients

Mix well, pour into prepared cake pan.

In a small mixing bowl, combine:

⅔ cup brown sugar
½ cup shredded coconut
½ cup walnuts, coarsely chopped
3 Tablespoons melted butter

Mix together and sprinkle on the top of the cake batter. Bake as instructed above.

Cappuccino Chocolate Angel-Food Cake GF

Mom always made us a chocolate angel-food cake for our birthdays, and I continued the tradition with our family. When I had Nonna's, I made many angel-food cakes for my customers, and sometimes I would get requests for different flavors. Because mocha and cappuccino were popular new flavors, this cake was an experiment for a different flavor of angel-food cake to enter into the Nebraska State Fair. I received a first-place ribbon, Best of Division rosette in 2014.

Serves: 12
Bake: Preheated 375 degree oven
Time: 35 minutes

Sift together 3 to 4 times and set aside:
2 Tablespoons instant coffee
1 ½ Tablespoons cocoa
¾ cup cake flour
1 ¼ cups powdered sugar

In mixer bowl with whip attachment, beat together until **egg whites** form soft peaks:
1 ½ cups egg whites (10 to 12 large eggs)
1 ½ teaspoons cream of tartar
¼ teaspoon salt
1 teaspoon vanilla extract
¼ teaspoon almond extract

Beat in, **2 Tablespoons at a time**, on medium to high speed:
1 cup sugar
Continue to beat until the **meringue** holds stiff peaks.

Then put mixer on lowest speed or "stir" and sprinkle over the **meringue, 2 Tablespoons at a time**, until all is used:

prepared flour mixture

At this point, the **flour** will not be completely incorporated. Remove mixer bowl and finish incorporating **flour** by carefully folding the **meringue** with a wooden spoon. Distribute the **batter** into an ungreased 10-inch tube pan. With a table knife, slice through the **batter** from center to edge of the pan all the way around, about eight slices. Bake as instructed.

After baking, immediately invert **cake** in pan and let cool completely. Frost with **Confectioner's Icing**, page 168.

Options

- Chocolate Angel-Food Cake: Increase **cocoa** to ¼ **cup**, omit **instant coffee**.
- White Angel-Food Cake: Increase **cake flour** to **1 cup**, omit **cocoa and coffee**.
- GF   Substitute **gluten-free rice flour** for **cake flour**; increase **egg whites to 2 cups (14 egg whites)** and increase **sugar to 1 ¼ cups**.

Helpful Hints

- For high-altitude baking, add **2 Tablespoons corn starch** to **dry ingredients**.
- Do not use **egg white** that has even a trace of **egg yolk**. It will undersize your **cake**.
- In my experience, **cold eggs** separate better than those at room temperature ... but **egg whites** beat better at room temperature.
- Try not to underbeat or overbeat your **egg whites**. The peaks should stand straight up when the beater is lifted out of the **mixture**.
- I am not usually one to quibble over exact measurements; however, the amount of **sugar** and **flour** are particularly critical to the tenderness of **angel-food cake**, so be sure to measure these items accurately.

- It is said that **angel-food cakes** don't rise well on rainy or very cloudy days, but I have never had this problem.
- Fold in **ingredients** until just combined; avoid overmixing.
- Upon removing from oven, immediately invert **cake** in pan to cool. If you do not have a tube pan with legs, place pan on a funnel or long-necked bottle.
- If you freeze **cake**, leave in tube pan and place in a large, tightly sealed freezer bag. Remove from pan when slightly thawed. **Cake** can be frozen up to 3 months.
- To remove from pan, loosen **cake** by running a knife along the edge of the pan and around the tube. Remove from pan and run knife along pan bottom.

For my sister Mary and her husband Laurel's 20th wedding anniversary, I made five angel-food cakes. Pictured are the cappuccino chocolate (left), white (right), and chocolate (center).

Poppy Seed Cake 🍎

With Bob and Judy Eversoll, we spent many wonderful times together, driving to Colorado for a Nebraska football game, having picnics on the Fourth of July at Stuhr Museum and in their backyard, having holiday dinners together when none of our children were coming home. Bob's father and my father were Prudential Insurance agents in Grand Island, and Bob and I graduated the same year from Grand Island Senior High. Bob had a wonderful and humorous personality. He prided himself on being a good cook and would often fix a wonderful meal, but this recipe is Judy's. I have had poppy seed cake before, but her cake is special because it has a delicious topping.

Have prepared:
In a small bowl, combine:
1 cup milk
2 Tablespoons poppy seeds
Allow the **seeds** to soak for 2 hours.

Greased and lightly **floured** 9 × 13 pan and set aside.

Serves: 10
Bake: Preheated 350 degrees oven
Time: 35 minutes

In a medium bowl, using a wire whisk, combine:
2 ¼ cups unbleached flour
1 Tablespoon baking powder
1 teaspoon salt
Mix well and set aside.

In two small bowls, separate:

5 (large) eggs

Reserve **egg yolks**.

In a mixer bowl, using wire whip attachment, add:

egg whites

Beat on medium to high setting until stiff peaks form. Gently place in a medium bowl and set aside in refrigerator until ready to use.

In the same mixer bowl (no need to wash it), using paddle attachment, combine:

¾ cup shortening

1 ½ cups sugar

1 ½ teaspoons vanilla extract

Mix well and cream until light and fluffy.

Add **flour mixture** into **creamed mixture**, alternating with **milk and poppy seed mixture**, beating after each addition.

Gently fold into the **batter**:

prepared egg whites

Gently pour the batter *evenly* into **prepared pan**. Bake as instructed above. After **cake** is baked, cool on a wire rack. Cool thoroughly before adding the **topping**.

Cake Topping

In an 8-cup Pyrex bowl, melt:

½ cup (1 stick) butter

Using a wire whisk, add to **melted butter**:

1 cup sugar

1 cup evaporated milk

Mix well and microwave on high for 2 minutes.

Using a wire whisk, temper a small amount of **hot milk mixture** in:
3 of the egg yolks
Mix well.

With wire whisk, combine:
prepared hot milk mixture
prepared egg mixture
Mix well and microwave on *high* until **mixture** thickens. Set aside to cool, approximately 15 minutes. Gently pour over **cooled cake**. Allow the **topping** to set before serving.

To serve: Cut into serving pieces and add a dollop of **whipped cream,** page 230, on the top of each piece of **cake**.

Left: Bob and Judy Eversoll. Right: Bob Eversoll barbecuing.

Naturally Colored and Flavored Frostings GF

Presentation, presentation, presentation. That's all you hear when making cakes and cookies … how beautifully they can be decorated. Very often a cake is the centerpiece on your table. But are all the artificial colorings, flavorings, and preservatives causing problems with our children's learning and health?

It has been 40 years since I first heard of Dr. Feingold, a pediatrician and allergist, and his diet for hyperactivity. Learning and behavioral problems continue to increase and so do the additives in our food—10% in the 1950s to the current 63%. Is there a correlation? In the 1970s Dr. Feingold warned about these additives, and it is these same additives the European Union has banned from its foods because those countries believe the additives cause these problems. But the United States continues to use them. Are we not seeing the forest for the trees?

My motto about food is, number one, it has to taste good. No matter how beautifully it is decorated, if the food is not tasty, people won't eat it. Number two, it has to be healthy. And finally, it has to look good, not beautiful. I love to decorate cookies for the holidays and have found many ways to color my frostings for cookies, cakes, and gelatins. The colors may not be as vivid, but the presentations were good enough to win Best of Division at the Nebraska State Fair. Here is my list of colorings and flavorings that taste good, are healthy, and have a nice presentation.

Dark Pink Frosting

In a 1-cup Pyrex cup, add:
¼ cup water
15 blueberries
Microwave on *high* for 2 to 3 minutes. Allow the **berries** to steep for ½ hour. Drain and reserve **liquid**; set aside.

Mix in food processor and puree:

1 cup powdered sugar

cooked blueberries

If **frosting** is too runny, add more **powdered sugar**. If too dry, add **small amounts of reserved liquid** until you reach the right consistency.

Yellow Frosting

In food processor, combine:

1 cup powdered sugar

1 or 2 pinches of turmeric (a little goes a long way)

lemon extract, drop by drop, according to taste

enough milk to make a smooth frosting

If too runny, add more **powdered sugar**.

Orange Frosting

In 2-cup Pyrex cup, add:

1 small carrot, thinly sliced

¼ cup water

Microwave on *high* for 2 minutes or until **carrots** are soft. Drain and reserve **liquid**; set aside.

Mix in food processor and puree:

1 cup powdered sugar

prepared carrots

⅛ teaspoon orange extract

If frosting is too runny, add more **powdered sugar**. If too dry, add **small amounts of liquid** until you reach the right consistency.

Brown Frosting

In food processor, combine:
1 cup powdered sugar
2 to 3 Tablespoons cocoa
¼ teaspoon vanilla extract
enough milk to make a smooth frosting
If too runny, add more **powdered sugar**.

Basic Butter Frosting 🍎

In a mixer bowl, using a wire whip, combine:
⅓ cup butter
¼ cup milk
1 teaspoon vanilla extract
dash of salt
Beat until light and fluffy.

Gradually add:
2 cups powdered sugar

Then beat until you reach the desired consistency:
up to 2 ½ cups additional powdered sugar
Add **milk** if needed to make the frosting thinner.
Add **more powdered sugar** to make the frosting thicker.

Confectioner's Icing 🍎GF

This is the thin icing you use on an angel-food cake or Bundt cake and to decorate cookies.

Combine in mixing bowl:
2 cups powdered sugar
dash of salt

Stir in:
enough half-and-half to make pourable but not too runny
Add:
1 teaspoon vanilla extract

Pour around the edges of the **angel-food cake** and allow to drip down the side of the **cake**. Use a slightly thicker version to decorate **cookies** or a **Bundt cake**. Pour over top of the **Bundt cake** and let drizzle down the sides.

Fall holiday cookies with all-natural frostings.

Candies

Gavin

Glossary

blanche. To remove skin from nuts or fruits by placing them briefly in boiling water.

condensed milk. Milk with sugar added, reduced to thick consistency by evaporation. Usually found in cans and not to be confused with evaporated milk, which is thinner and has no added sugar.

confection. Candy; also, a fancy dish or sweet.

confectioners' sugar. Same as powdered sugar (see below).

corn syrup. A sweetener made from corn and often used in candy. Can be light or dark (see "A Word about Corn Syrup").

nougat. A confection of nuts or fruit pieces in a sugar paste.

powdered sugar. Same as confectioners' sugar. Granulated sugar with a small amount of corn starch added to give a soft, powdery texture.

sliver. To cut or shred into long, slender pieces.

A Word about Corn Syrup

Since corn syrup is used in so many candies, I thought I should share what I have learned about it. Corn syrup is food syrup that is made from the starch of maize (corn) and composed mainly of glucose. It is used in foods to soften texture, add volume, prevent crystallization of sugar, and enhance flavor.

High-fructose corn syrup is distinct from corn syrup, created when corn syrup undergoes enzyme processing that produces a sweeter compound containing high levels of fructose and becoming an undesirable, highly concentrated sugar that can raise blood sugar levels. High-fructose syrup is commonly found in many commercially processed foods, such as canned fruits, soups, salad dressings, spaghetti sauces, and other sauces. I use **Karo Light Corn Syrup**, which is *not* high-fructose. There are now some house brands that are not high-fructose, but you should check labels carefully to make sure they are not. The more general term glucose syrup is sometimes used synonymously with corn syrup since glucose syrup is most commonly made from corn starch.

Since other Karo syrups, the darker varieties, are high-fructose, you may want to combine **Karo Light Corn Syrup with molasses** to make a pancake syrup or for other recipes calling for dark syrup.

Candies

You may wonder why I am including candy recipes in this cookbook. When our son was on the Feingold diet, he could not have candy bars and other commercial candy because some of the ingredients were not all natural, such as imitation vanilla (vanillin) instead of vanilla extract. But everyone deserves a treat once in a while, and I found a recipe for everything. I began gathering a variety of recipes, many of which produced candies similar to brand-name candy bars, so our children didn't have to feel deprived of the kinds of candy everyone else could have. I found candy making to be fun and creative, almost as tasty and healthy as I could make other foods. Candy is nice to have around the holidays and also makes especially nice gifts.

When I was originally making candies for my children, I didn't' have a microwave, so most of the recipes had to be done on the stove using a pan or double boiler. By using the microwave, I have cut the time I spend making these candies by half or more. Candy can be made in your microwave without worry of scorching because cooking occurs on all sides rather than just the bottom.

Helpful Hints

- Select a cooking bowl that is heavy enough to withstand very hot temperatures and is large enough to allow sufficient boiling space to prevent spilling over during cooking. I use an 8-cup Pyrex glass bowl, never plastic because the syrup gets too hot.
- Since candy is very hot when removing it from the microwave, be sure to have hot pads handy.
- The purchase of a candy thermometer is invaluable if you are a serious candy maker. Never leave the thermometer in the candy while microwaving.
- When melting chocolate to use in candy making, check page 173 for hints.

Candy Testing

The use of a candy thermometer is the easiest way to determine if your candy has reached the proper temperature. When making candy in the microwave, it is important to **remember not to use the thermometer or a temperature probe in the microwave**.

Always remove the candy from the microwave and clip the thermometer to the side of the bowl; allow it to stay there until it quits moving. The temperature and firmness will be noted on the indicator column.

The firmness of the candy can also be tested by **cold-water testing**. Have ready a **cup with very cold water** (*not* ice water). Remove the candy from the stove or microwave. Immediately drop a **few drops of syrup** into the water; it will form into a ball. Compare the firmness of the candy to the chart below.

Cold-Water Testing	Temperature
Soft-ball stage: The candy will roll into a soft ball that quickly loses its shape when removed from the water.	234–238 degrees
Medium-ball stage: Preferred for marshmallows.	238–244 degrees
Firm-ball stage: The candy will roll into a firm but not a hard ball. It will flatten out a few minutes after being removed from the water.	244–248 degrees
Hard-ball stage: The candy will roll into a hard ball that has lost most of its plasticity and will roll around the plate on removal from the water.	248–254 degrees
Very-hard-ball stage: Similar to hard-ball stage, the candy will roll into a hard ball that has lost most of its plasticity and will roll around the plate on removal from the water.	254–265 degrees

Light-crack stage: The candy will form brittle threads in the water that will soften on removal from the water.

265–285 degrees

Hard-crack stage: The candy will form brittle threads in the water that will remain brittle after being removed from the water.

290–300 degrees

Coating Candies

Using a glass pie plate, spread evenly and melt in the microwave on 70% power:

6 ounces chocolate chips—milk, semisweet, or bittersweet

Microwave for 1 minute; stir well and continue to microwave in 10- to 15-second intervals. Stir the **morsels** after each cooking, since semisweet and milk chocolate hold their shapes while melting. Using two forks, dip and roll the **candy** into the **chocolate** and place on waxed paper. Allow the **chocolate** to air dry, then cut off the excess with a knife or pizza cutter. Continue this process until all pieces are coated. See illustrations on the following page.

Using a glass pie plate, melt chocolate chips. Using two forks, dip and roll each piece of candy.

Roll candy on all sides and place on wax paper.

Coconut Peanut Brittle 🍎 GF

Making candy at Christmastime was always a tradition in our family; fudge, penuche, divinity, and peanut brittle were the favorites. I liked all the above, but my favorite is coconut peanut brittle. It is very easy to make in the microwave, but you need to keep a close eye on your candy thermometer when the syrup gets to the light-crack stage because it can burn easily. Read Candy Testing, page 172, before starting. Always use an 8-cup Pyrex bowl and a wooden spoon to stir. Have your hot pads close at hand. Good luck!

Have prepared:
lightly buttered baking sheet with edges; set aside.

Microwave on high for 1 minute:
1 cup raw Spanish peanuts

In an 8-cup Pyrex glass bowl, using a wooden spoon, combine:
1 cup sugar
½ cup light Karo syrup*
dash of salt
Cook on high for 5 minutes. Stir and cook for 2 more minutes. Stir.

Add:
prepared Spanish peanuts
Stir and cook an additional 1 to 2 minutes or until **mixture** begins to turn a light brown color.

*Light Karo corn syrup has no high-fructose corn syrup
and real vanilla extract.

Use a candy thermometer with this candy. The temperature should be 265 to 285 degrees or at *light-crack stage*. I have experienced overcooking this **candy** if I go to the hard-crack stage because a few degrees can burn the **syrup**, ruining the **candy**.

After it reaches a *light-crack stage*, add:
2 teaspoons butter
1 teaspoon soda
1/2 cup Gurley's natural raw chip coconut*
Stir until light and fluffy. Pour onto the prepared baking sheet; spread as thin as possible. Cool and break into pieces.

Option

■ If you want **plain peanut brittle**, omit the **coconut**.

*Do not use sweetened flaked coconut.

Honey Chocolate Caramel 🍎🐝GF

In 2010 the Nebraska State Fair moved to Grand Island. I had entered cakes and pies in the Hall County Fair but never considered entering the Nebraska State Fair; but with the fair being just a mile from our house, I thought I would give it a try. I was amazed at all the categories, and one that interested me was the honey category. In Family Favorites, I had a recipe for chocolate caramels as an option for vanilla caramel, so I thought I would use that recipe and substitute honey for the white Karo syrup and molasses for the sugar. I received a second-place ribbon, but on the back of the entry ticket, the judge wrote, "Tasty but quite sticky." To put this recipe in this cookbook, I wanted to correct that problem, and I think I did.

Makes: 24 (1-inch squares)

Have prepared:
lightly buttered 8 × 8-inch glass pan; set aside.

In an 8-cup Pyrex glass bowl, melt in microwave:
½ cup (1 stick) butter

Add to **butter** and, with a wooden spoon, mix well:
½ cup sugar
¾ cup honey
½ cup half-and-half
Microwave on high for 8 minutes.

Add to the **caramel mixture** an additional:
½ cup half-and-half
Mix well and microwave on high for 3 minutes; stir well. Continue to microwave in 3-minute

intervals, stirring each time, until mixture reaches a *soft-ball stage* (234 degrees on the candy thermometer).

Add to the **caramel mixture**:

1 cup bittersweet chocolate chips

1 teaspoon vanilla extract

Pour into prepared pan. Cool, cut into squares, and enjoy.

Welcoming Rocco: Leslie, Brian, and Jordan.

Chocolate Easter Nests 🍎 ♥ GF

When I became interested in candy making, I would put shredded coconut into the leftover chocolate chips, mixing until the coconut was completely covered with the chocolate. Then I divided the mixture into small paper cups: These were called Ting-a-Lings by a local candy company. Then I noticed this company made candy nests during the Easter season. This gave me the idea to do chocolate candy nests for our Easter baskets. So, with some waxed paper and my thumb, I started a new Easter tradition for our children and continue it for our grandchildren.

Makes: 12

Have prepared:
as eggs for the nests, **white chocolate-covered dried blueberries** (prepared the night before)

Using a glass pie plate, spread evenly and melt in the microwave on chocolate setting or 70% power:
white chocolate chips
Microwave for 1 minute. Continue to microwave until **chocolate** is melted. Stir the **morsels** after each cooking since the **chocolate** holds its shape while melting.

Add to **melted white chocolate**:
¼ cup dried blueberries or ¼ cup shelled pistachio nuts
With a fork, cover the entire **berry or nut** and place on waxed paper. Continue until all are covered. Allow the **berries or nuts** to dry overnight.

Using a glass pie plate, spread evenly and melt in the microwave on chocolate setting or 70% power:
6 ounces chocolate chips—milk, semisweet, or bittersweet

Microwave for 1 ½ minutes and stir well. Continue to microwave until the **chips** are melted. Stir the **morsels** after each cooking since **chocolate chips** retain their shape while melting.

Add to the **melted chocolate chips**:
1 ½ cups sweetened coconut
Mix well until **coconut** is completely covered with **chocolate**.

Place evenly on waxed paper:
(12) 1 Tablespoon coconut/chocolate mixture
Make an indentation in the center with your thumb, forming a **candy** "Easter nest."

Place in the center:
3 to 4 blueberries *or* pistachio nuts
Allow the **candy** to air dry. Place each **nest** in a small cellophane bag and seal the bag with an Easter sticker.

Easter nest. Top row: semisweet chocolate chips with sweetened coconut. Middle row: milk chocolate with sliced almonds. Bottom row: bittersweet chocolate with raw chip coconut. Eggs are made of dried blueberries dipped in white chocolate chips.

Chocolate-Covered Marshmallow Rabbits GF

While our son was on the Feingold diet, I would make these marshmallow rabbits for the children's Easter baskets. People are always amazed when you tell them that you make your own marshmallows. It is your grandmother's recipe for 7-minute frosting plus 2 packages of Knox gelatin added. Simple! These rabbits won second place in the 2014 Nebraska State Fair.

Marshmallow

Have prepared:
10 × 15-inch baking sheet with sides lined with a brown paper sack or parchment paper

In a small bowl, combine:
½ cup cold water
2 packages Knox unflavored gelatin
Sprinkle the **gelatin** over **cold water**.

In an 8-cup Pyrex glass bowl, using a wooden spoon, mix well:
1 cup sugar
1 cup Karo light corn syrup
⅓ cup water
Microwave on high 10 minutes, stirring once, and then at 2-minute intervals until the **syrup** reaches the *soft-ball stage* or 240 degrees on your candy thermometer. Stir well between cookings.

Remove from the microwave, stir in:
softened gelatin
Mix well until dissolved. Set aside and allow it to cool for about 10 minutes.

In a mixer bowl with the wire whip attachment, beat until *stiff* peaks form:

1 egg white

Slowly add **cooled syrup** and beat on high until candy forms *soft* peaks; this could take 7 to 10 minutes. Set your timer.

Add:

1 teaspoon vanilla extract

Pour **mixture** into prepared baking sheet and spread *evenly* over the paper. Allow it to set overnight.

Next morning, sift **powdered sugar** lightly over the **marshmallow** and turn over onto waxed paper. Peel the paper off the **marshmallow** using a rubber spatula. Dust the bottom with more **powdered sugar**. Cut into rabbits with a metal cookie cutter. Set aside for one day to allow the marshmallow rabbits to dry.

Chocolate Coating

Using a pastry brush, remove any excess **powdered sugar**.

Using a glass pie plate, spread evenly and melt in the microwave on chocolate setting or 70% power:

1 cup bittersweet chocolate chips

1 cup white chocolate chips

Microwave for 1 minute; stir well. Continue to microwave in 10- to 15-second intervals. Stir the morsels after each cooking, since the **chocolate** holds its shape while melting. On the smooth, back side of the rabbit, spread the **chocolate** over the rabbit with a knife. Dip the other side of each rabbit into the **chocolate**, then take a knife and spread the **chocolate** around the edges. Using two forks or a small spatula, place rabbits on waxed or parchment paper. Allow the **chocolate** to set. If the **chocolate** spreads, cut off any excess with a knife. (I have experienced that this combination of **chips** allows the **rabbits' chocolate covering** to set harder without being sticky.)

Cutting out bunnies with metal cookie cutter.

Serving the Chocolate-covered Marshmallow Rabbits.

Frosting the smooth side with melted chocolate chips.

Rabbit's eye decoration:

¼ **cup powdered sugar**
⅛ **teaspoon vanilla extract**
**enough raspberry, cherry, or beet juice to
make it spreadable**
With a frosting decorator with the small
round tip, make a small, round pink eye on
each rabbit.

Option

- Use a **dried cranberry** or **cherry** and cut
  it into the shape of an eye.

*With two forks, placing bunnies on waxed paper to
air dry.*

Salted Nut Roll   🍎 GF

It is always exciting to find a recipe for a store-bought candy bar that is one of your favorites. A high school classmate and good friend, Elsie Spiehs Hansen, brought salted nut rolls to our morning coffee group. Our group tries to solve most of the world's problems, and we also exchange recipes. You can make this recipe with store-bought marshmallow creme and caramels, but making these two easy recipes will not only save money, the taste is "heavenly." I entered this candy bar in the Nebraska State Fair in 2012 and received a first-place ribbon.

Makes: 25 (2-inch pieces)

Marshmallow Creme

In a 1-cup measure, soften:
½ **cup water**
2 packages Knox unflavored gelatin
Sprinkle **gelatin** over **cold water.**

In an 8-cup Pyrex glass bowl, mix well:
1 cup sugar
1 cup Karo light corn syrup*
⅓ **cup water**
Microwave on high 5 minutes and then at 2-minute intervals until the **syrup** reaches the

Elsie (Spiehs) Hansen.

*Karo light corn syrup does not contain any high-
fructose corn syrup and uses real vanilla, not vanillin.

soft-ball stage or 240 degrees on your candy thermometer. Stir well with a wooden spoon between cookings.

Remove from the microwave, stir in:

softened gelatin

Mix well until dissolved. Set aside and allow it to cool for about 10 minutes.

In a mixer bowl with the wire whip attachment, beat:

1 egg white

Slowly add cooled **syrup** and beat on high until candy forms soft peaks; this could take 7 to 10 minutes.

Add:

1 teaspoon vanilla extract

Divide the **creme** into two parts. *Each part equals a 7 ½-ounce jar of commercial marshmallow creme.*

In a mixer bowl, with the dough hook, combine:

1 part marshmallow creme

3 ½ cups (1 pound) powdered sugar

1 Tablespoon butter

Knead until the **powdered sugar** blends *thoroughly* with the **marshmallow creme**.

Divide into eight equal parts. On a board, sprinkled generously with **sifted powdered sugar**, roll out *each* **part** into *small, long rope-like* **rolls** about the *diameter* of your little finger. Wrap each **roll** in plastic wrap, place on a cookie sheet, and *freeze until firm*.

Caramel Coating

In an 8-cup Pyrex glass bowl, *melt*:

½ cup (1 stick) butter

Add to the **butter** and mix well using a wooden spoon:

1 cup sugar

⅔ cup Karo light syrup*

1 Tablespoon unsulfured molasses*

½ cup half-and-half

Microwave on *high* for 8 minutes.

Add to the **caramel mixture** an *additional*:

½ cup half-and-half

Mix well and microwave on high for 3 minutes; stir well. Continue to microwave in 2-minute intervals, *stirring* each time, until **mixture** reaches just *under* a softball stage (230 degrees on the candy thermometer). You want the **caramel** to be *soft* and *spreadable to coat* the **marshmallow center**. Allow the **caramel** to *cool* for about *10 minutes* before using.

Putting It All Together

In a food processor, using the *pulse setting, coarsely* chop:

16 ounces (1 pound can) party peanuts

Place a 16-inch piece of waxed paper on the counter and in the *middle* of the paper, add and spread *evenly* across the length of the waxed paper:

1 cup of chopped peanuts

Place below the **peanuts**:

1 *rope-like* marshmallow center

*Use the combination of Karo light syrup and
unsulfured molasses to create dark corn syrup.

Spread to cover the top of the *exposed* **marshmallow center**:
soft **caramel coating**

Take the *bottom* of the waxed paper, lift the paper up, and *roll* the **marshmallow center** *into* the **peanuts.** *Firmly* press the **peanuts** into the **caramel coating**. Repeat until the **marshmallow center i**s *completely* covered with **caramel** and **peanuts**. Continue until all the **marshmallow centers** are covered. Wrap *each* roll in plastic wrap and store in a *cool* place or *freeze*. Cut the **salted nut rolls** into 2-inch pieces.

Rolling out the marshmallow center in powdered sugar.

Spreading caramel over the marshmallow center.

Lifting the waxed paper and rolling the caramel-covered center into the chopped peanuts.

Rolling the nut roll in plastic wrap.

Snickter Bars 🍎 GF

What does this taste like? What is a Snickter Bar and where did it get its name? Once you make this candy bar and eat it, you will get the answer to the first part of the question, but the name of the bar is rather unique. Dave's mother's (Clara) maiden name was Vandersnickt. His sister Franie had a dachshund named "Snicker." Due to trademark infringement, we couldn't call this candy treat by its trade name, so we added the "t" to the name in honor of Dave's family that immigrated from Germany. I entered these candy bars in the 2014 Nebraska State Fair and they received a second-place ribbon.

Makes: 18 to 20 bars

Have prepared:
9 × 13-inch pan, lined with aluminum foil

Marshmallow Creme, page 183–184

In glass pie plate , melt and add:
1 cup bittersweet chocolate chips
1 cup white chocolate chips
Mix well and continue to microwave until melted. Spread *evenly* on bottom of prepared pan. Place in refrigerator or freezer for **chocolate** to harden.

Nougat Filling

In a mixer bowl, combine:
prepared 2 cups marshmallow creme
2 cups powdered sugar

½ cup creamy peanut butter

2 Tablespoons butter

¼ to ½ cup half-and-half (enough to make the nougat spreadable)

Mix well and pour over *hardened* **chocolate layer**; *spread evenly.*

Spread evenly over **nougat**:

1 ½ to 2 cups party or cocktail peanuts

Place in refrigerator to set up.

Caramel Coating

In an 8-cup Pyrex glass bowl, melt:

½ cup (1 stick) butter

Add to the **butter** and mix well using a wooden spoon:

1 cup sugar

⅔ cup Karo light syrup*

1 Tablespoon unsulfured molasses*

½ cup half-and-half

Microwave on *high* for 8 minutes.

Add to the **caramel mixture** an *additional*:

½ cup half-and-half

Mix well and microwave on high for 3 minutes; stir well. Continue to microwave in 2-minute intervals, *stirring* each time, until **mixture** reaches just *under* a soft-ball stage (230 degrees on the candy thermometer). You want the **caramel** to be *soft* and *spreadable* to coat the **peanuts.** Allow the **caramel** to *cool* for about 10 minutes before spreading over the **peanuts.**

*Use the combination of Karo light syrup and
unsulfured molasses to create dark corn syrup.

Place in refrigerator to set up. Cut into 3 ½-inch by 1 ½-inch pieces. Set aside in refrigerator until ready to coat.

Chocolate Coating

Using a glass pie plate, spread evenly and melt in the microwave on chocolate setting of 70% power:

1 cup bittersweet chocolate chips

1 cup white chocolate chips

Microwave for 1 minute; stir well. Continue to microwave in 10- to 15-second intervals. Stir the morsels after each cooking since the **chocolate** holds its shape while melting. Use two forks, dip each candy bar on both sides, then take a knife and spread the **chocolate** around the edges. Using both forks or a small spatula, place candy bars on waxed or parchment paper. Allow the **chocolate** to set. If the **chocolate spreads**, cut off any excess with a knife or pizza cutter. Repeat this recipe until all bars are coated.

Grandpa Frank and Grandma Rose Vandersnickt's wedding photo.

All-Natural Cream Cheese Mints 🍎 GF

I entered these all-natural colored and flavored Cream Cheese Mints into the 2014 Nebraska State Fair, and they won a second-place ribbon.

In a food processor, combine:

3 cups powdered sugar
1 Tablespoon *softened* **butter**
1 (3-ounce) package cream cheese
1 or 2 Tablespoons jam (your choice—I used blueberry jam)
2 drops mint extract
Process, using *on* and *off* pulses, until **mixture** comes together into a **ball**.

Using a knife or spatula, place the **mint dough** in a Mirro frosting decorator with the star tip. For best results, fill the tube only *half full*, then screw on the plunger and make **mints** on a sheet of waxed paper.

Sprinkle **sugar** over the top of **mints**; allow the **mints** to dry overnight. Next day, remove the **mints** and place on a different piece of **sugared** waxed paper to cover the bottom part of the **mints**.

Store **mints** in refrigerator or freezer in a covered container for up to 2 or 3 months. See **mints** photo on page 117.

Cookies

Justin

Glossary

bake. To cook using dry heat in an oven.

baking sheet. Also cookie sheet or jelly-roll pan. A large, rectangular pan with no sides or very shallow sides about ½-inch high.

beat. To mix with vigorous over-and-over motions with spoon, wire whip, or electric mixer.

blend. To mix very thoroughly two or more ingredients.

condensed milk. Milk with sugar added, reduced to thick consistency by evaporation. Usually found in cans; not to be confused with evaporated milk, which is thinner and has no sugar.

cream. To soften fat by pressing against bowl or beating with an electric mixer until light and fluffy.

chill. To allow to become thoroughly cold but not frozen.

gluten. Protein composite found in foods processed with wheat, barley, rye, and spelt. It gives dough elasticity, helping it raise and keep its shape, often giving the final product its chewy texture.

gluten free. Any product, but particularly flour, that *does not* contain wheat, barley, rye, or spelt, made up of one or a combination of alternative grains, roots, beans, or other plant products for cooking or baking. Important for those suffering from Celiac disease or sensitivity to products containing gluten.

lard. Solid cooking fat rendered from pork, softer and more oily than butter, margarine, or shortening. Also has more shortening power when used in baked products.

preheat. To heat oven to desired temperature before placing food inside.

roll out. To place on a board and spread out with a rolling pin.

shortening. Specifically in this book, the word shortening is used for the all-natural, partially hydrogenated vegetable oils (plain with no artificial coloring or preservatives).

unbleached flour. Regular all-purpose flour that has not been chemically bleached.

vegetable oil. Fat pressed from plants. May be in either a liquid state or partially hydrogenated (solid or semisolid state). Examples include corn, cottonseed, canola, soy, flax, and olive.

white whole-wheat flour. Flour milled from hard white spring wheat rather than traditional red. Contains same nutrients, bran, germ, and endosperm as regular whole wheat. Milder flavored. Use as regular whole wheat.

zest. The grated, colored outside portion of citrus peel used as a flavoring.

Cookies

The word *cookie* comes from the Dutch word for cake, *koekje*. These little "cakes" were baked to make sure that the oven temperature was correct for the big cakes.

Cookies are one of the most expensive foods we buy. To make a batch of sugar cookies, it only costs approximately two dollars and you get five dozen. Often, it was one of the first recipes your mom allowed you to make because they were the easiest, fun to make, tasted good, and created the least mess. An organization to which I belong was selling cookie dough for a fundraiser for our club. The first year I was one of the best sellers thanks to my husband, Dave, who took my list and sold many boxes to his coworkers. While on television, I always try to emphasize how much money you save by cooking from scratch, so when I was demonstrating Christmas cookies, I figured out the cost of making sugar cookies. First, I weighed a box of the purchased cookie dough and then of my homemade dough. They weighed the same. Each box is one batch of cookie dough. Then I figured out the cost of ingredients, since most cookie recipes have similar ingredients ... flour, sugar, oil or shortening, butter, flavorings (vanilla/vanillin), soda, and salt.

Here are the results:

2 cups unbleached flour, $.30
½ teaspoon cream of tartar, $.20
½ teaspoon soda, N/A
pinch of salt, N/A
1 cup sugar, $.30
½ cup canola oil, $.25
½ cup butter, $.66
1 teaspoon vanilla extract, $.18

Total = $1.89

A box of cookie dough costs $13.50. You save $11.63 by making your own dough, and either way you have to bake the cookies. Other cookies call for other ingredients, such as chocolate chips, oatmeal, peanut butter, etc., so add $.50 to $1.50 to cover that cost. Their label listed all-purpose flour (bleached), vanillin (artificial flavoring), and shortening. The ingredients in my cookies were all natural: no artificial colors, flavors, or preservatives and unbleached flour, canola oil, whole eggs, butter, and pure vanilla extract. Since most cookie recipes contain similar basic ingredients, it makes sense to make several batches at once. Wrap in waxed paper, place in a Styrofoam carryout container, and freeze. When cookies are needed, all you have to do is take them out of the freezer and bake just as you do the expensive purchased cookie dough.

Continue to read my other shortcuts on the following pages on how to make most cookies as easy as one-two-three. Good luck!

Types of Cookies

Drop Cookies. Drop dough by rounded heaping teaspoonfuls. Push the dough onto the cookie sheet with another spoon.

Refrigerator or Sliced Cookies. Press and mold dough with hands into a long roll as big around as you want the cookies to be, usually 1 to 1 ½ inches. Wrap in waxed paper. Refrigerate. Cut into ¼- to ½-inch slices before baking.

Bar Cookies. Spread dough into a greased pan and bake as directed. Cut into squares or bars when slightly cooled.

Rolled-Out, Cut-Out Cookies. Dough is rolled to ⅛- to ¼-inch thickness and cut with your favorite cookie cutters.

Helpful Hints

Know your oven:

- All baking times are approximate, so watch your oven temperature carefully.
- In a conventional oven, bake on one rack at a time. Don't overload.
- In a convection oven, you can use 1 to 3 racks at a time.
- Electric ovens bake faster than gas ovens because the former holds its temperature longer.

If your cookies are doughy:

- Bake your next batch 1 to 2 minutes longer to avoid underbaking.
- If your cookies spread too much, use a *lighter* coating of shortening on your cookie sheets or add an extra tablespoon of flour to the dough.
- When recipe calls for packed brown sugar, fill correct size cup, then use the back side of one cup smaller (example: ½ or ¾ cup) to pack down the brown sugar into the cup.
- Refrigerate your cookie dough until it is cool to the touch.
- Allow cookie sheets to cool before reusing.
- Be sure your oven temperature is correct.

If your cookies are dry and hard:

- You may be overbaking; try baking the next batch 1 to 2 minutes shorter.
- You may be overmixing; after adding flour, mix just until combined.

Storing cookies (if you have any left!):

- To keep baked cookies from sticking to one another, do not stack or store until thoroughly cooled.
- Store cookies in tightly covered containers or resealable plastic bags. This will prevent humidity from softening crisp cookies or air from drying out soft cookies.

For a change:

- Coat a roll of cookie dough in finely chopped nuts or flaked coconut, pressing to make it stick. Wrap in waxed paper and chill before cutting and baking.

For roll-out and cut-out cookies:

- Roll out dough on a slightly floured board. To prevent sticking, sprinkle a little flour on top of dough before you roll it.
- Use ¼ to ½ of the dough at a time, keeping the rest refrigerated until needed.
- Dip your cookie cutter in flour between uses.
- To get the greatest number of cookies from the rolled-out dough: Use several cutters, leaving very little, if any, space between cut outs. Reroll scraps to make additional cookies and use all your dough, handling as little as possible.
- Some cookies need indentations on top to fill with jam or chocolate. Use the rounded end of a honey dipper.

Making Cookies as Easy as One-Two-Three

Here are some of my suggestions.

First of all, I use the same bowl for all the cookies I am baking. And I never wash the bowl between recipes. I make the lightest cookies, such as plain sugar cookies, first and proceed through the various kinds to the darker, stronger-flavored cookies, like ginger or chocolate.

Then I use my three-step quick-trick method of assembling the cookie dough. The first step consists of placing flour, baking powder and/or soda, and salt in a large bowl all at once and mixing with a wire whisk. This eliminates the step of sifting flour.

The second step consists of adding the fat (shortening, coconut or canola oil, or butter), sugar, eggs, flavorings, and any other liquid ingredients to the mixing bowl and creaming them all at once instead of each item individually. A heavy-duty mixer allows you to do this.

In the third step I put the two mixtures together and mix well. Time is saved, and the cookies are no less delicious. Most of the cookies in this book can be made this way.

If you are adding fruits, nuts, or chips, you will have a fourth step, mixing them in by hand or on low, stirring with the mixer.

Coconut and Its Benefits

The scientific name for coconut is *Cocos nucifera*. Early Spanish explorers called it *coco*, which means "monkey face," because the three indentations (eyes) on the hairy nut resemble the head and face of a monkey. *Nucifera* means "nut bearing."

Coconut provides a nutritious source of meat, juice, milk, and oil; it is a staple in the Asian and Pacific populations. The Pacific islanders consider coconut oil to be the cure for many illnesses. The coconut palm is so highly valued that it is called "The Tree of Life."

Only recently has modern medical science unlocked the secret to coconut's nutritional and healing powers. When I think back on the warnings against using palm oils, I think coconut oil is the "prodigal son" of oils. For years it was mistakenly believed unhealthy because of its high saturated fat content. Now it is touted to possess many health benefits due to its fiber and nutritional content.*

How can this be?

Well, we were told coffee wasn't good for us; now it is. Eggs were another villain; now they're back in favor. Lard was a "no no," but now it is safer than shortening because shortening has trans fatty acids and all kinds of additives and preservatives to give it shelf life.

The difference between coconut oil and other vegetable oils is in the fat molecule. Coconut has a *medium* chain fatty acid (MCFA). It is very different from the *long* chain fatty acid (LCFA) found in most all vegetable oils. MCFA is very different from LCFA because MCFA does not have a negative effect on cholesterol and helps to protect *against* heart disease. Now coconut oil has been described as "the healthiest oil on earth."

*To see a list of health benefits, go to http://www.coconutresearchcenter.org/.

Chocolate Chip Cookies 🍎GF

Chocolate chip cookies are the most popular cookies made, and there are many recipes for them. If your mother made these cookies, you always felt that hers was the best recipe of all chocolate chip cookie recipes. Now, with white whole-wheat flour plus bittersweet chocolate chips, this recipe and its gluten-free option can not only be the best but can be healthier too.

Bake: Preheated 350 degree oven
Time: 10 to 12 minutes
Makes: 4 dozen

In a medium bowl, combine:
2 cups white whole-wheat flour
1 teaspoon soda
½ teaspoon salt
Mix well with a wire whisk and set aside.

In mixer bowl with flat paddle, combine:
½ cup (1 stick) butter, room temperature
½ cup coconut oil
¾ cup brown sugar, packed
¾ cup sugar
2 large eggs
1 ½ teaspoons vanilla extract
Mix well on *medium* speed until all ingredients are *creamy*.

Gradually add to **creamed ingredients**:

prepared flour mixture

Continue to beat until all the **flour** is combined.

Add to **cookie dough** with mixer on low or stir:

2 cups bittersweet chocolate chips

Use a small cookie scoop or drop by teaspoonfuls onto a baking sheet. Bake as directed above or until *lightly* browned.

Remove **cookies** from baking sheet to wire rack and allow to cool completely before storing.

Options

- ■ **GF** For gluten-free cookies, substitute **2 cups gluten-free all-purpose flour** for **white whole-wheat flour**.
- ■ For original cookies, substitute **unbleached flour** for **white whole-wheat flour** and **semisweet chocolate chips** for **bittersweet chocolate chips**.
- ■ Substitute **shortening** for **butter** and **coconut oil**.

Grate the ginger root to add a refreshing tang to stir-fries, curries, cookies, cakes, desserts, chocolate, and teas. Freeze the roots first and use them straight from the freezer.

Cappuccino Coconut Macaroons
(Gluten Free) 🍎 ♥ GF

My love for coconut is very apparent in this book. This is another recipe I had never made, but when I saw it in the paper, I had to try it. They were delicious, but I didn't like the way they looked because part of the batter mixture oozed out, making a ring around the cookie rather than a nice, fluffy ball. Because there was no flour in the recipe, I decided to add ¼ cup brown rice gluten-free flour to get the desired presentation. I received first place, Best of Division in the 2014 Nebraska State Fair.

Have prepared:
2 baking sheets lined with parchment paper. Set aside.

Makes: 22 to 24
Bake: Preheated 350 degree oven
Time: 20 to 25 minutes

In a large mixing bowl, combine:
1 (14-ounce) package sweetened shredded coconut
1 teaspoon vanilla extract
¼ cup gluten-free brown rice flour

Sprinkle over top:
2 teaspoons instant coffee
1 teaspoon cocoa

Add:

1 (14-ounce) can sweetened condensed milk

Mix well.

In mixer bowl with wire whip attachment, add:

2 large egg whites

¼ teaspoon salt

Beat until *stiff* peaks form.

Gently fold the **egg whites** into the **coconut mixture**.

Using a *medium-sized* cookie scoop, form **mixture** into balls, slightly smaller than a golf ball. *Do not compact the **mixture***.

Bake as instructed above. Cool on baking sheet, then place on wire rack.

Presentation of the Cappuccino Coconut Macaroons.

Oatmeal Coconut Lace (Gluten Free) GF

While visiting my sister and brother-in-law, Katy and Larry Lingo, I offered to make my oatmeal coconut cookies. Katy had some gluten-free flour, so we thought it would be fun to use it and see what would happen. The dough's appearance seemed normal but when we baked the cookies, the dough spread out over the baking sheet and stuck to the sheet, making the cookies difficult to remove. It appeared to be another cooking disaster. We all tried the disastrous cookies and were surprised that we liked the taste and texture. Katy said, "They look like lace." So the next day we made the cookies again and changed some of our methods, and this time we made delicious and beautiful cookies. I entered these cookies into the 2013 Nebraska State Fair and they received a second-place ribbon.

Have prepared:
2 baking sheets, lined with parchment paper

Makes: 5 dozen
Bake: Preheated 350 degree oven
Time: 10 to 12 minutes

Place in a bowl and blend together with a wire whisk:
1 ½ cups (brown rice) gluten-free flour
1 teaspoon salt
1 teaspoon soda

In mixer bowl, using the flat beater *cream* together all at once until *light* and *fluffy*:
1 cup (2 sticks) butter
1 cup sugar
1 cup brown or raw sugar
2 large eggs

1 teaspoon vanilla extract

Add the **flour mixture** to the **creamed mixture**.

Fold in by hand or with the mixer on *stir* or *low* setting:

2 cups gluten-free oatmeal

1 cup shredded coconut

½ cup walnuts, coarsely chopped

Mix well just until combined. Use a small cookie scoop, or drop by teaspoonfuls, to place **mixture** on prepared baking sheets; allow *3 inches* between **cookies** (**cookies** will spread). Bake until **cookies** are flat and *slightly* firm. Place baking sheets on wire racks, allowing **cookies** to cool on baking sheets before removing.

Options

- Spread **melted bittersweet chocolate chips** on the bottom of each *cookie*. Turn **cookies** face down and allow the **chocolate** to air dry.
- Spread **melted bittersweet chocolate chips** on the bottom of one **cookie** and place another **cookie** on top of the **chocolate**, making a cookie sandwich.

Larry and Katy Lingo.

Ginger Crisps (Gluten Free) 🍎 GF

During my visit with my sister Katy, I picked up a Farmer's Almanac and found this recipe for Ginger Crisps. After reading the recipe, it reminded me of the problems we had with making the oatmeal coconut lace cookies, page 202: They spread all over the baking sheet. Their suggestion was to use parchment paper and to be sure to give the dough plenty of room to spread. The words, "They are delicious and you can't eat just one" also echoed in the article. I immediately got a pencil and pad, wrote down the recipe, then made them using my previous experiences. Everything they said about these cookies is true … "You can't eat just one."

Have prepared:
2 baking sheets lined with parchment paper.

Makes: 5 dozen
Bake: Preheated 350 degree oven
Time: 10 to 12 minutes

In a medium bowl, using a wire whisk, combine:
1 ½ cups gluten-free flour*
½ teaspoon soda
¾ teaspoon cinnamon
¾ teaspoon ginger
½ teaspoon cloves
¼ teaspoon salt
Mix well and set aside.

*For this recipe I used a gluten-free all-purpose flour blend of 13 allergen-free ingredients selected for taste. If you use brown rice or other gluten-free flours, chances are your cookies will spread more. They are still delicious but have a different texture. It is important for cooks to look for new and improved gluten-free flours. They change constantly.

In mixer bowl with flat paddle on *low* speed, cream for 1 minute:

¾ cup (1 ½ sticks) butter, room temperature

1 cup brown sugar

Add and beat just until *fluffy*:

1 large egg

Add *gradually*, beating until incorporated:

¼ cup unsulfured molasses

Place mixer on *low* speed and *gradually* blend:

prepared dry ingredients

Mix just until combined. With a small cookie scoop, place **dough** on prepared baking sheets, *allowing 3 inches* between cookies (cookies will spread). Bake until cookies are flat and *slightly browned* around the edges. Place baking sheets on wire racks, allowing cookies to cool on paper-lined baking sheet before removing.

Options

- Use **white whole-wheat or unbleached flours** instead of gluten free.
- Use **granulated sugar** instead of **brown sugar**.
- For a firmer cookie, substitute **¼ cup coconut oil** for **½ stick butter**.

Helpful Hints

- Always line your baking sheet with parchment paper and space your **cookie dough** far enough apart that the cookies don't spread into one another.
- After the **cookies** are removed from the oven, allow them to cool on the parchment paper; this prevents them from breaking.

Gluten-Free Brownies

In my effort to bake with gluten-free flour, I have found it to be quite a challenge. My muffins won't rise, my cookies spread; so needless to say, I was disappointed. But then I had an idea—try a bar cookie such as a brownie—and I had fairly good results. One thing I have noticed after using this flour, baked items seem to need a day or two to reach the right texture. The first day the brownies were crumbly, but by the third day they seemed to have a more chewy texture. Am I right or wrong? I received a first-place ribbon at the 2014 Nebraska State Fair for these brownies.

Have prepared:
an 8 × 8 glass baking dish sprayed with gluten-free spray; set aside

Makes: 9
Bake: Preheated 350 degree oven
Time: 25 minutes

In small bowl combine:
½ cup gluten-free flour
½ cup cocoa
¼ teaspoon baking powder
Mix well and set aside.

In mixer bowl with flat paddle, combine:
½ cup (1 stick) butter
1 cup sugar
2 large eggs or 4 egg yolks
1 teaspoon vanilla extract
Beat until well blended.

Add to **above mixture**:

prepared flour mixture

Mix until **flour** is just moistened. The **batter** will be thick.

Add to **batter**:

½ cup finely chopped walnuts (optional)

Mix well and spread in prepared glass baking dish. Bake as instructed above.

Option

■ Exchange **gluten-free flour** for **white whole-wheat or unbleached flour**.

*A gluten-free medley: Brownies, Ginger Crisps, and Oatmeal
Coconut Lace.*

A Honey of a Fruit and Nut Bar 🍎 ♥ 🐝 GF

Because this energy bar's sweetener was honey, this recipe qualified for two divisions in the 2012 Nebraska State Fair; "Food Made With Honey" and "Cookies-Health." I used nuts, dried fruits, and chocolate chips, giving these cookies a distinctly different look and taste. This bar received a first-place blue ribbon, plus Best of Division.

Makes: 12 to 14
Bake: Preheated 300 degree oven
Time: 45 to 60 minutes

Have prepared:
foil-lined 9 × 9-inch pan, **oiled** and **floured**; set aside

In large bowl, combine:
2 cups old-fashioned rolled oats
¾ cup walnut, coarsely chopped
¾ cup (5 ounces) dried apricots, coarsely chopped
¼ teaspoon salt
2 Tablespoons white whole-wheat flour
Mix well.

In a small bowl using a wire whisk, combine:
½ cup honey
¼ teaspoon salt
¼ cup egg whites
¼ teaspoon almond extract
Pour above **mixture** into **dry ingredients** and stir to combine. Press into the prepared pan with

Energy bars: Apricot/walnut with semisweet chocolate, followed by cranberry/almond with dark chocolate, followed by raspberry/pecan with white chocolate.

moist hands or with waxed paper or plastic wrap. Smooth the top with double dough roller, page xvii.

Bake as instructed above until **bars** are dry to touch. Cool completely, remove foil, and then cut into 12 to 14 bars with a pizza cutter dipped in hot water.

In a glass pie plate, melt:
1 cup semisweet chocolate chips
Dip the top of each **bar** into the **melted chocolate** and place on waxed paper. Decorate the top of the bar with **dried apricots** and **walnuts**.

Options

- ■   **GF**   Substitute **gluten-free flour and rolled oats** for **white whole-wheat flour**.
- ■   For sugar free **bars**, substitute **2–3 Tablespoons stevia** for **honey**.
- ■   Make your favorite **bars** by using your choice of ingredients:

  GF   Gluten-Free Bars: Substitute **gluten-free flour and cereals (rolled oats)** for **white whole-wheat flour and wheat cereals**.

  Cereals: Granola, puffed rice, puffed corn, puffed wheat, or **wheat flakes**.

  Dried Fruits: Apricots, blueberries, cherries, dates, figs, raisins, pineapple, or **strawberries**.

  Nuts: Cashews, hazelnuts, peanuts, pecans, walnuts, or **shredded coconut**.

  Seeds: Poppy, sesame, flaxseed, or **wheat germ**.

  Baking Chips: Cover the **bars** with any of these **baking chips: bittersweet, semisweet, milk** or **white chocolate**.

Chocolate

The story of how chocolate grew from the knowledge of only ancient cultures in Mexico and Central America into a "global sweet" includes many cultures and continents. Legend has it that Montezuma, the Aztec emperor of Mexico, served "chocolate" to his guests in a golden goblet.

The Spanish conquistador Hernán Cortés was the first European to taste chocolate. He learned that the cacao beans were used as money among the Indians. Cortés was the one who introduced the beans to Europe. Shortly thereafter, the English, French, Italians, and Dutch were experimenting with these beans.

In the 17th century a notice in a London newspaper announced that a French man was offering a West Indies drink called "jacolatte." Soon chocolate was considered a new delicacy drink and was served by the English colonists in America.

Types of Chocolate

Chocolate and cocoa products are available in several forms. Because they are different in flavor and consistency when they are melted, always use the type called for in a recipe.

- **Bittersweet chocolate** is 60% cacao with some sugar and no flavorings added; it does not have any fat removed.
- **Semisweet chocolate** is chocolate made with enough sweetening added to give a partially sweet taste and has added butter fat. Most popular use is for chocolate chip cookies.
- **Milk chocolate** is chocolate with extra cocoa butter, sugar, and milk solids.
- **White chocolate** is composed of cocoa butter, sugar, dry milk solids, and vanilla. It is not considered a chocolate per se because it lacks pure chocolate.

Desserts

Jack

Glossary

corn starch. A thin, flour-like powder, processed from corn and used to thicken juices, gravies, puddings, soups, sauces, and other liquids. A component of confectioner's sugar, it has twice the thickening power of flour.

cream. To soften a fat by beating it at room temperature. Butter and sugar are often creamed together, making a smooth, soft paste.

cream cheese. A smooth, mild-flavored, unaged white cheese, often used as a base for fillings (cheese cake), spreads, and dips; easily accepts and enhances other flavors.

dust. To sprinkle lightly with flour or sugar.

fold. To incorporate a delicate substance, such as whipped cream or egg whites, into another substance without releasing air bubbles. A spatula or wooden spoon is used to gently bring part of the mixture from the bottom to the top. The process is repeated while slowly rotating the bowl until the ingredients are thoroughly blended.

Greek yogurt. Yogurt that has been strained of whey, resulting in less sugar, fewer carbohydrates, and more protein. Can be plain or flavored.
half-and-half. Mixture of equal parts milk and cream.

parfait. A dessert of French origin with various ingredients layered in a specially shaped tall, slender glass parfait dish. May contain such varied ingredients as ice cream if frozen or if chilled, may include gelatin, pudding, whipped cream, yogurt, fruit, or granola.

puree. To mash or strain food into a paste or semiliquid suspension. Most easily and successfully done using a blender or food processor.

steep. To allow fruits, teas, and herbs to stand in hot water to extract their flavor.

temper. To add a small amount of a cooked mixture to eggs, mixing them together before returning them to the rest of the cooked mixture.

whey. Liquid remaining after milk has been curdled; a byproduct of cheese and Greek yogurt making.

whip. To beat rapidly in order to incorporate air and produce expansion, as in heavy cream or eggs.

whipped cream. Heavy cream (or whipping cream) that has been whipped, thus incorporating air into the mixture.

whipping cream. Top or heavy cream with at least 18% butterfat; when whipped, used for topping desserts.

yogurt. Semisolid food made when certain bacteria is added to milk. Sometimes sweetened and flavored.

zest. The grated, colored outside portion of citrus peel used as a flavoring.

Easy Cheesecake Pie

When I closed my restaurant, Nonna's, in 2005, it wasn't too long before people were asking me to help with benefits. While I was working, I didn't have time to volunteer, so I thought it was my time to give back to a community that had given so much to me and my family. Volunteering was common in our family. Dad was the president of the Lion's Club and headed the Lion's Eye Bank. We were the first family in Grand Island to sign up to donate our eyes. Mom volunteered at both the Veteran's and St. Francis hospitals and at our church. A friend and classmate from high school, Karen Koenig Mayer, was trying to find ways to make money for a mission trip to the Dominion Republic sponsored by the Episcopal Church. I offered to do a spaghetti dinner. I did the Italian part of the dinner, and the rest of the congregation provided the dessert. This was their recipe. After our third dinner for their next mission trip, Dave Stoddard asked my husband, Dave, and me to go on the trip with their group; it was one of the most memorable trips of our lives.

As for the dessert, it was a good choice with an Italian meal, satisfying, not too rich; fast and easy to make.

Have prepared:
Basic Graham Cracker Crust, page 293

Serves: 6 to 8
Bake: 350 degrees oven
Time: 25 to 30 minutes

In a mixer bowl, mix well:
1 (8-ounce) package cream cheese
½ cup sugar
1 Tablespoon lemon juice

dash of salt

2 large eggs

Pour into **prepared crust** and bake as instructed above.

Can Cream Cheese Be Frozen?

I wouldn't stock up and freeze cream cheese just because it's on sale or you want to have a supply on hand. However, you can *safely* freeze cream cheese if you didn't get to make that cheesecake you were planning or found you had more than you needed for a recipe. It will be fine in baked goods, though it may not be as smooth as it was originally in dips and spreads. But you may or may not notice much difference. It's best to use within two months after freezing.

This is the mission team that went to the Dominican Republic. Front row, left to right: Jared Hansen, Rich Webb, Karen Mayer, Fran Schaffer. Back row, left to right: Dave Stoddard, Dave Schaffer, Lisa and Dennis Reisinger.

Raspberry Cheesecake

Each month I have to think of a recipe that I can make in 15 minutes on live TV. February is usually an easy month because of Valentine's Day. Candies and desserts with raspberries, cherries, or strawberries are the easiest. My choice was raspberry cheesecake. This was a combination of three recipes in *Family Favorites*: The crust was from the cappuccino cheesecake recipe (page 212), the filling was from the basic cheesecake recipe (page 210), and the topping was the filling of the raspberry pie recipe (page 280). This is a good example of how you can use a combination of recipes to make a new dessert.

Crust

Bake: Preheated 350 degree oven
Time: 10 minutes

Combine in medium bowl, using a fork, and mix well:
2 cups chocolate sandwich cookie crumbs
¼ cup (½ stick) butter, melted
Press into a 9- or 10-inch spring-form pan. Bake as instructed above and set aside.

Filling

Serves: 12
Bake: Preheated 350 degree oven
Time: 45 minutes

In mixer bowl, using flat beater, thoroughly cream together:

4 (8-ounce) packages softened cream cheese

1 cup sugar

1 Tablespoon unbleached flour

dash of salt

Stop the mixer several times during the mixing process to scrape down the sides of the bowl and beater. Be sure there are *no large lumps.*

With beater on *low* speed, add:

4 large eggs, one at a time

Mix until **batter** is smooth.

Add and mix well:

juice and zest of 1 lemon

Pour into the prepared spring-form pan. Place in oven and bake according to above instructions. When done, the center should be *soft but not wobbly.* Turn off oven, leave the oven door ajar, and allow the **cake** to cool in the oven for 2 hours. Be sure to set your timer. Leave in pan and chill in the refrigerator for at least 2 hours or overnight.

Raspberry Topping

In an 8-cup Pyrex glass bowl, combine:

2 cups water

½ cup IQF raspberries*

Microwave on high for 5 minutes. Stir, set aside, and allow to steep for 15 minutes or more.

*IQF berries: Berries are Individually Quick Frozen,

then packaged. Not usually sweetened.

In a medium bowl covered with a sieve, strain:

prepared raspberries and water

Set aside **raspberry solution** until ready to use.

In an 8-cup Pyrex glass bowl, using a wire whisk, combine:

1 cup sugar

⅓ cup corn starch

pinch of salt

Mix well.

Add slowly:

steeped raspberry solution

Mix until all **ingredients** are dissolved. Place in microwave and cook on *high* for 3 ½ minutes. Stir and return to microwave for an additional 3 ½ minutes. If the **topping** appears thick and clear, *it is ready*; if not, return to the microwave for 1 ½ minutes or until the **topping** is thick and clear. Allow the **topping** to cool slightly.

Spread over the top of the **cheesecake**:

prepared topping

Evenly arrange over the **topping**:

2 to 3 cups IQF raspberries, stem side down

Place in refrigerator to allow the **raspberry topping** to set for at least 1 hour before serving.

Serving and Storing Cheesecake

■ Chill cheesecake overnight without removing sides of spring-form pan. Remove sides when ready to serve, but leave cake on pan bottom unless selling or giving away the whole cake. If you are presenting the whole cheesecake to your guests before cutting, do not bother to remove from pan bottom; just place on a serving plate and garnish. Generally, I prefer to cut the cake into individual servings before presenting. Be sure

Raspberry Cheesecake.

the cake is thoroughly chilled or even partially frozen before cutting. Cheesecakes will cut better if slightly frozen.

■ Shallow cracks may occur in spite of your best efforts. These will not impair the quality of the cheesecake. By cutting into individual servings and topping with fresh fruit, fruit sauces, nuts, etc., you can still make a picture-perfect presentation.

Before slicing through the cheesecake, put the fork tines over the knife blade against the back of the crust and pull the knife through the tines to protect the outer crust from crumbling.

Frozen Yogurt 🍎 ♥ GF

Frozen yogurts and sorbets... are they friend or foe? It appears they have all the right ingredients, fruit and low-fat content, but do they have artificial sweeteners (aspartame), colors ("the rainbow of risk," Blue 1 and 2, Citrus Red 2, Green 3, Orange B, Red 3 and 40, or Yellow 5 and 6), and artificial flavors that match the fruits? It is wise to check the fine print. I recently checked the yogurts at the local stores and found that most of the diet (low-fat and sugarless) yogurts had artificial additives, sweeteners such as aspartame, colors from the "rainbow of risk," and flavors, like imitation raspberry, strawberry, blueberry, etc., that resembled the fruits in the yogurts. The way to ensure you have healthy ingredients is to make your own version, using your food processor. You can use plain (unflavored) or Greek yogurt and any fruit of your choice. For sweeteners you can use sugar, honey, agave, or a host of other natural sweeteners (page 11). Because I like a tart taste, I usually cut the amount of sweetener in half.

In *Family Favorites*, our recipes for sorbets were well received because you were able to make sorbet without using an ice cream freezer; a regular (not a small-sized) food processor is all you need. Because of its popularity, I tried the same method for yogurt, and it worked!

Berry Frozen Yogurt

Makes: 6 cups

Use your choice of **IQF* strawberries**, **raspberries**, or **blueberries**.

*IQF berries: Berries are Individually Quick Frozen,
then packaged. Not usually sweetened.

In food processor, using the metal blade, combine:

3 cups IQF berries (strawberries, blueberries, raspberries)

½ to 1 cup sugar

2 cups Greek or plain yogurt

Process until smooth.

Add:

additional 2 cups Greek or plain yogurt

2 Tablespoons schnapps (flavor of fruit you are using)*

Process until mixed well. Pour into a covered container and place in the freezer. Every hour, for 2 to 4 hours, stir mixture with a wire whisk; then allow the yogurt to freeze overnight.

To serve: Place 1 or 2 scoops in a sherbet dish.

Option

- Spoon into a popsicle mold or a small Dixie cup. After **yogurt** is partially frozen, insert a wooden stick in the center of the **yogurt**. Easy, healthy treats.

*If you cannot find the flavor of your schnapps

uncolored, use any uncolored fruit schnapps available.

I don't notice any change in the taste.

Peach or Apricot Frozen Yogurt 🍎♥GF

Makes: 6 cups

Have prepared:
larger fresh fruit (**peaches**) peeled, cut into the size of a *medium strawberry*, then IQF (page 19) before making Frozen Yogurt.

In food processor, using the metal blade, combine:
3 cups prepared apricots or (3 to 4 medium) peaches
½ to 1 cup sugar
2 cups Greek or plain yogurt
Process until smooth.

Add:
additional 2 cups Greek or plain yogurt
2 Tablespoons schnapps (flavor of fruit you are using)*
¼ teaspoon almond extract
Process as instructed in Berry Frozen Yogurt.

Helpful Hints

- If the **yogurt or sorbet** is too firm, increase the **schnapps** to 3 Tablespoons.
- If your **fruit** is frozen, defrost approximately 2 pounds of **fruit** in the microwave using the *fish* or *poultry* setting for 3 to 4 minutes. This is good for **peaches** or **strawberries**. Smaller **berries** can be processed frozen.

*If you cannot find the flavor of your schnapps
uncolored, use any uncolored fruit schnapps available.
I don't notice any change in the taste.

American Parfait (Saint or Sinner) 🍎♥GF

Any recipe that has the colors red, white, and blue reminds us of the American flag, the Fourth of July, or Presidents' Day. Serve this recipe for breakfast with yogurt, you are a saint; serve it as a dessert with whipped cream, you are a sinner. Either way, it is delicious and has a beautiful presentation.

Have prepared:
1 recipe Granola, page 240
1 package (12 ounces) IQF raspberries
1 package (12 ounces) IQF blueberries
1 (24-ounce) carton Greek Yogurt ... or:
In a mixer bowl, using a wire whip, whip until *soft* peaks form:
1 cup whipping cream
1 Tablespoon sugar

Makes: 4 parfait

In 4 parfait glasses, layer times 3:
2 to 3 Tablespoons yogurt or whipped cream
2 Tablespoons granola
Then *evenly distribute* **raspberries** and **blueberries**.

Top **parfait** with:
1 dollop yogurt or whipped cream

Garnish with
raspberries and blueberries
Refrigerate until ready to serve.

Sorbet 🍎♥GF

Because the sorbet ingredients and methods in Family Favorites are part of making frozen yogurt, I have included this recipe below.

Makes: ½ gallon

In food processor, using metal blade, process half of the following until smooth:

5 cups IQF fruit

½ cup sugar

2 Tablespoons schnapps (flavor of fruit you are using)*

1 (12-ounce) can frozen fruit juice concentrate, thawed but still very cold

    (a flavor the same or similar to the fruit you are using)

Place first half into ½ gallon container; set aside in freezer. Then process the second half the same way. Add to the first **mixture** and stir well. Every hour, for 3 to 4 times, stir **mixture**; then allow the **sorbet** to freeze overnight. Scoop into sherbert dishes.

*If you cannot find the flavor of your schnapps

uncolored, use any uncolored fruit schnapps available.

I don't notice any change in the taste.

Gelato (Ice Cream) 🍎GF

Creamy Italian Raspberry Gelato   GF

Makes: ½ gallon

In mixer bowl with wire whip attachment, combine:
2 cups whipping cream
1 cup sugar
Beat well until **sugar** is dissolved and **cream** forms *soft* peaks. Set aside in refrigerator.

In food processor, using metal blade, process until smooth:
3 cups IQF raspberries
3 Tablespoons raspberry schnapps*
1 cup sugar
Fold **fruit mixture** into **cream mixture** and mix until blended. Place into a half-gallon container; set aside in freezer. Stir with a wire whip every hour about 4 times.

Serve individually in sherbet dishes or make a gelato pie. See recipe on the next page.

*If you cannot find the flavor of your schnapps
uncolored, use any uncolored fruit schnapps available.
I don't notice any change in the taste.

Creamy Italian Peach Gelato   GF

In a mixer bowl with wire whip attachment, combine:

2 cups whipping cream

1 ½ cups sugar

Beat well until **sugar** is dissolved and **cream** forms *soft* peaks. Set aside in refrigerator.

In food processor, using the metal blade, process until smooth:

3 cups IQF peaches, slightly thawed

2 Tablespoons peach schnapps

2 Tablespoons lime juice

¼ teaspoon lime zest

¼ teaspoon almond extract

Gently fold processed **fruit mixture** into **cream mixture**. Mix until blended. Pour into a half-gallon container and set aside in freezer, stirring with wire whip every hour about 5 times.

Serve individually in sherbet dishes or make into a **peach gelato pie** (recipe below). Garnish with a dollop of **whipped cream** and a **peach slice**.

Quick Raspberry or Peach Gelato Pie

Serves: 8

Have prepared:

1 Graham Cracker Crust, page 293

Pour into **prepared graham cracker crust**:

4 to 5 cups slightly softened raspberry or peach gelato, pages 224–225

Smooth the top of the **pie**. Place in freezer until **pie** is frozen.

Serve with a dollop of **whipped cream**, page 230, and garnish with a **raspberry or peach slice**.

Puddings 🍎 GF

Our grandson, Justin, asked Dave and me to come and visit his second-grade class. Dave was to show them his artwork in the cookbook, and I was to demonstrate some recipes. I made chocolate pudding without using a pudding mix and grape gelatin without using Jell-O. Most teachers, children, and their parents find it hard to believe that puddings can easily be made from scratch by using the microwave and gelatins by using Knox unflavored gelatin. Not only are they easy, but they are more nutritious (egg yolks and milk), void of additives such as artificial colors and flavors (Concord Grape and orange juice), and cost less. But most important of all, they taste better.

Chocolate Pudding

Makes: 8 (4-ounce) servings

In an 8-cup Pyrex glass bowl, combine and mix well:
1 cup sugar
¼ to ⅓ cup cocoa
¼ to ⅓ cup corn starch
dash of salt

Gradually add, mixing well:
1 ½ cups milk
Microwave on high for 3 ½ minutes. Stir. Return the **mixture** to microwave and continue cooking on high in 1-minute intervals until **mixture** thickens .

Separate into 2 small bowls:
4 large eggs
Reserve **egg whites** for another recipe and refrigerate.

In the other small bowl, combine:

4 egg yolks

½ cup milk*

Mix well with wire whisk. Add **egg yolk mixture** to the **pudding**, mixing well. Microwave for 2 to 3 minutes on high; stir well.

Stir in:

2 Tablespoons butter

1 teaspoon vanilla extract

Mix well and pour into sherbet dishes.

Top with a dollop of **whipped cream**, page 230. Store in refrigerator until ready to serve.

Vanilla Pudding

Variations of vanilla pudding are the basis for many cream pies; add cocoa (chocolate pie), brown sugar (butterscotch pie), coconut (coconut cream pie), bananas (banana cream pie). Once you master making vanilla pudding, making any one of these pies or puddings is easy.

Makes: 8 (4 ounce) servings

In an 8-cup Pyrex glass bowl, combine and mix well:

1 cup sugar

¼ to ⅓ cup corn starch

dash of salt

*You can temper egg yolks with cold milk.

Fran showing the pudding to Justin's second-grade class.

Gradually add, mixing well:

1 ½ cups milk

Microwave on high for 3 ½ minutes. Stir. Return the **mixture** to microwave and continue cooking on high in 1-minute intervals until **mixture** thickens .

Separate into 2 small bowls:

4 large eggs

Reserve **egg whites** for another recipe and refrigerate.

In the other small bowl, combine:

4 egg yolks

½ cup milk*

Mix well with wire whisk. Add **egg yolk mixture** to the **pudding**, mixing well. Microwave for 2 to 3 minutes on high; stir well.

Stir in:

2 Tablespoons butter

1 teaspoon vanilla extract

Mix well and pour into sherbet dishes.

Top with a dollop of **whipped cream**, page 230. Store in refrigerator until ready to serve.

Option

■ **Butterscotch Pudding:** Substitute ¾ **cup brown sugar** for **granulated sugar**.

*You can temper egg yolks with cold milk.

Bev Harvey helped by editing the cookbook. She was a family and consumer science teacher at Grand Island Senior High.

Stabilized Whipped Cream 🍎

In a 1-cup measuring cup, combine:
1 Tablespoon cold water
¼ teaspoon unflavored gelatin
Stir well and let stand for 2 minutes.

Place in mixer bowl using wire whip:
1 cup whipping cream
Beat on *high* speed until *soft* peaks are formed. Gradually drizzle the dissolved **gelatin** over it.

Add:
2 Tablespoons sugar
Sprinkle over the top of the **gelatin-cream mixture** and beat until *stiff* peaks form. Store covered in refrigerator for up to 48 hours.

Fat. The five basic tastes may soon be joined by fat. A growing body of research suggests the tongue has receptors that can detect fatty acids, and the luxurious appeal of high-fat foods such as ice cream and butter is more than just a matter of texture.

Eggs & Breakfast Entrées

Rise and shine!

Rocco

Glossary

boil. To cook in boiling (212 degree Fahrenheit) water or other liquid to the point at which bubbles are breaking on surface and steam is given off.

frittata. Italian-style flat (not folded or rolled) omelet, consisting of beaten eggs incorporated with vegetables, meats, cheeses, herbs, and seasonings, sometimes pasta and rice, and finished by baking in oven.

fry. To cook in hot fat.

granola. Breakfast or snack food … a baked combination of rolled oats and other ingredients, such as nuts, honey, or coconut with dried fruits added after baking.

groat. Groats are the hulled kernels of various cereal grains, such as oats, wheat, and rye. Groats are whole grains that include cereal germ, bran, and endosperm.

hard-cooked or hard-boiled eggs. Eggs cooked or simmered in shell until both yolks and whites are solid.

Hollandaise sauce. An emulsion of egg and butter seasoned with lemon juice. French in origin but so named because it was created in honor of the visit of the king of the Netherlands to France.

omelet. A dish in which whites and yolks are mixed together, then cooked and folded, often around a filling.

over easy. Eggs fried on one side, then flipped over to finish cooking without breaking yolk; whites become firm but yolks remain liquid.

poached eggs. To cook eggs gently in hot (not boiling) water or other liquid; whites become firm and yolks remain liquid.

scrambled eggs. Eggs fried with yolks and whites mixed together.

soft-cooked or soft-boiled eggs. Eggs boiled briefly in shell to cook whites firmly while yolks remain liquid. Usually boiled for three minutes.

strata. A layered dish of bread, cheese, eggs, and milk, most often with vegetables or meat added.

sunny-side up. Eggs fried without turning or breaking yolk until white is firm; yolk remains liquid.

Eggs Are Back!

For many years, eggs were often the center of the American breakfast. Then we were told they were not good for us because they had too much cholesterol. Times change, and the "incredible, edible egg" is once again a part of a healthy diet. It was found there is 14% less cholesterol in eggs than was first measured, and they are high in protein and vitamin D. They may also help prevent memory and vision loss.

When buying eggs, check them for cleanliness and uniform size. Make sure they are unbroken and have no cracks. If harvesting your own eggs, be sure to wipe them clean with a soft, dampened cloth. Do not soak or immerse them in water. Eggs, as wonderful as they are, are subject to bacterial infection (salmonella) and can cause serious food poisoning if not handled correctly, but should not be a problem if proper precautions are taken in purchasing, handling, storing, and cooking.

Store eggs in the refrigerator, preferably in the carton in which they were sold. This will better protect them from bacteria and odors found in the refrigerator and cushion them from breakage. Uncooked eggs will keep at least four weeks. Hard-cooked eggs will keep at least a week in the shell. Never leave eggs, cooked or uncooked, at room temperature for more than an hour.

When cooking poached, over-easy, and sunny-side up eggs, be sure the whites are cooked firm, fully coagulated, and the yolks have begun to thicken (not runny). Omelets, scrambled eggs, and casseroles should be cooked until firm throughout with no visible liquid remaining. Eggs in casseroles and sauces should be cooked to an internal temperature of 160 degrees. If using uncooked eggs in a dish, buy pasteurized eggs. It is always a good idea to break the egg into a smaller bowl and then add it to the mixing bowl or pan to prevent getting shells in with other ingredients or, in the rare case, you get a bad egg that would contaminate those other ingredients.

In this special breakfast section I have included two more egg dishes to the ones I had in *Family Favorites*. Eggs are becoming a gourmet food among chefs, but we knew they were gourmet all along. So enjoy eggs in many ways, and if you miss them at breakfast the versatile egg is good at any meal.

Know Your Eggs

When we go to the supermarket, we notice that eggs come in different sizes, thus the costs vary. In cooking, it is important to use the size of egg the recipe calls for, especially in desserts such as cakes, cheesecakes, ice cream, etc. It is my experience that the large egg is most frequently used in most recipes. In researching this book, I have found the equivalents for different sizes of eggs.

Large egg (2 ounces) = ¼ cup
Medium egg (1 ¾ ounces) = ⅕ cup
Small egg (1 ½ ounces) = ⅙ cup

You can see with these different measurements that the wrong size of egg could cause your recipe to fail, especially if the recipe calls for several eggs.

Healthful Hints

- Always keep **eggs** refrigerated at 45 degrees or below, but do not freeze.
- Use only **clean, uncracked eggs**.
- Hold **cold egg** dishes below 40 degrees.
- Hold **hot egg** dishes above 140 degrees.
- It is easier to separate **eggs** when the **eggs** are cold.
- For the highest volume, let the **egg whites** stand at room temperature before beating.
- Use **2 egg yolks** for **1 whole egg**, especially in pie fillings, cheesecakes, salad dressings, and mayonnaise.
- Use **2 egg yolks plus 1 Tablespoon water** for **1 whole egg** in bread and cookies. This will give your bread and cookies a natural yellow hue, eliminating the use of artificial coloring.
- To store an extra **egg yolk**, cover it with **water** and store in a tightly covered container in the refrigerator.

- **Egg whites** will keep for weeks in a tightly covered jar in the refrigerator. I use the **egg whites** that are clear of any **egg yolk** in my angel-food cakes and chantillys. If they have a streak of **egg yolk**, I use them in my pasta.
- It is important to temper your **eggs** before adding them to a **hot mixture**. This is done by gradually stirring a small amount of **hot mixture** into the beaten **eggs**, mixing well, then returning to the **hot, prepared mixture**. Stir and cook the **mixture** until you get the desired consistency. This is common when making puddings and ice cream.
- If you are going to use **eggs** for the garnish, a convenient gadget is an egg slicer. The fine wires cut the egg into even slices.
- If you add a little **vinegar** to the **water**, **egg whites** will not run while poaching.
- To determine whether an **egg** is hard-boiled, spin it. If it spins, it is hard-boiled; if it wobbles and will not spin, it is raw.

Hard-Cooked Eggs

When cooking eggs for salads or garnish, I found some important hints on the proper way to boil an egg. Sometimes we cook a certain way because that is how we were shown but don't know the reason behind it. Such is the case with a hard-cooked egg.

In a medium to large pan, place and cover with **cold water**:

6 to 8 eggs

Bring to a rapid boil; at once reduce the heat to keep the **water** just below simmer. Cook for 15 to 20 minutes. Remove **water** and cool immediately in **cold water**. This makes **eggs** easier to handle, helps prevent a dark surface on the **yolk**, makes peeling easier, and instantly stops the cooking.

Oatmeal 🍎♥GF

Before cold, sugared, dry cereal became popular, oatmeal was a breakfast staple in many families. It was often topped with brown sugar, cinnamon, and milk or cream... It was good and warmed our tummies. The popularity of oatmeal has increased in recent years because of the discovery of its many health benefits. The complex carbohydrates digest more slowly, keeping you energized longer with soluble fiber that may help prevent heart disease, lower cholesterol, and possibly help control weight. Over the years, I continued to serve oatmeal to my children and now do so for my grandchildren. Though oatmeal comes in many forms today, I always use and recommend either old-fashioned or steel-cut oats because they have the most fiber and keep you feeling full longer, plus I prefer the taste and texture.

Oatmeal begins as the whole grain groat, which is husked then roasted at a low temperature to give it a nutty, toasty flavor and make it shelf stable. While whole oat groats are available in some places, oats are usually processed into these familiar but sometimes confusing types.

Rolled oats. These are the most common varieties. The whole grain is steamed to make it pliable, then pressed between rollers and dried. There are three different forms of rolled oats.

Old-fashioned rolled oats have been steamed and then rolled and flattened and are the thickest. They remain whole and, though flattened, retain their shape and texture. They are best for making cookies and hot cereal.

Quick-cooking oats also have been steamed and rolled but are rolled much thinner for quicker cooking. They break into flakes and lack the firm texture of old-fashioned rolled oats.

Instant oats are made from rolled oats but are pressed even thinner than quick oats and often break up into a coarse powder. They usually come in individual packets and cook the quickest of all oats. Instant oats usually have added sugar and sodium, which makes them less desirable for healthy eating. They tend to be mushy.

Steel-cut, Irish, or Scotch oats are not rolled but cut with steel blades and look more like chopped brown rice than oats. They have firm texture and require longer cooking than any of the rolled oats. I personally feel they have the nuttiest flavor.

Gluten-free oats. Oats themselves are gluten free, but the problem lies in the fact that most oats can become contaminated with wheat during transportation and processing. To be safe, it is best to buy gluten-free oats at a health-food store.

Options

Serve oatmeal with any of the following:

- **Dried fruits: raisins, craisins**, or any other **dried fruits.**
- **Fresh fruits: blueberries, strawberries, raspberries**, or **blackberries.**
- **Jellies, jams, preserves**, or **marmalades.**

Microwave Oatmeal 🍎❤GF

While writing about oatmeal, I got so hungry I had to stop and make this recipe. Topped with brown sugar, a dab of butter, and milk, it was heavenly. The remainder I will microwave tomorrow or freeze and add to my next batch of bread dough. Quick, easy, and delicious!

Makes: 2 servings

In a 4-cup Pyrex bowl, add:

1 ¾ cup water

⅛ teaspoon salt

Microwave on high for 1 minute or until **water** comes to a boil.

Add to **hot water** and stir:

1 cup old-fashioned oats

Microwave on *high* for 1 to 2 minutes. Remove, stir, and allow the **oats** to absorb the **water**. Pour into a bowl and top with **brown sugar** and **milk**.

If you want to make several servings, follow the instructions on the oatmeal box.

Options

- ■ GF   Substitute **gluten-free oatmeal** for **regular oatmeal**.
- ■ If you prefer to cook on the stove, follow the instructions on the box.

Crock-Pot Oatmeal 🍎♥GF

Early on when our family was on the Feingold diet, I bought steel-cut oats at the local health-food store. It would take between 20 to 30 minutes to cook, but it was worth the time because I liked the texture and taste of steel-cut oats. The oats have more texture because they have not been steamed or rolled to soften. Now, with a Crock-Pot, you can cook the oats overnight and have a hot and healthy breakfast waiting for you when you wake up in the morning.

Serves: 4

Lightly **grease** a small (1 ½ quart) or medium (3 ½ quart) slow cooker.

In the slow cooker, combine and stir well:
4 cups water
½ teaspoon salt
1 cup steel-cut oats
Place a clean tea towel folded in half over the top of the pot to absorb the moisture. Cover and cook on low for 8 hours or overnight. After cooking, stir well and serve with the Options below.

Reheat any leftovers the next day with a little **milk** or **water** in the microwave.

Options

■ Top **oatmeal** with one or more of these choices:
   Sugars: raw, brown, honey
   Milk, cream, or **butter**, any type
   Spices: cinnamon, ginger, nutmeg
■ Use **gluten-free oatmeal** for **regular oatmeal**.

Granola 🍎♥🐝GF

Dave's sister, Fran Seymour, is a wonderful cook, and we often exchange recipes. This is her recipe for granola, but I have made a few changes to make the recipe healthier: using extra virgin olive oil for vegetable oil and raw coconut for shredded coconut. Either way, this recipe makes a wonderful and tasty granola. Adding granola to Greek yogurt gives it a great texture, then top it off with fresh berries. YUMMY!

Have prepared:
baking sheet with sides sprayed with **cooking oil**; set aside

Serves: 12 (½ cup)
Bake: Preheated 250 degree oven
Time: 60 minutes

In a large mixing bowl, combine:
3 cups old-fashioned rolled oats (*do not use quick oats*)
1 cup almonds, sliced
1 cup coconut, raw
1 teaspoon cinnamon
pinch of salt

In a 4-cup Pyrex cup, combine and microwave on 70% power:
½ cup honey
⅓ cup extra virgin olive oil
Pour over **dry ingredients**, mix well, and spread *evenly* over baking sheet. Bake as instructed above. Stir the **granola** every 20 minutes *times 3*. Turn off oven and leave **granola** to dry until it cools. Store in closed container and place in a cool area.

Options

- ■ **GF** Substitute **gluten-free oatmeal** for **regular oatmeal**.
- ■ After **granola** cools, add **1 cup raisins** or any **dried fruit**.
- ■ **Shredded coconut** can be substituted for **raw coconut**.

Dave with his sisters (from left, Frannie and Alice).

Bacon and Vegetable Frittata 🍎 ♥ GF

At Christmastime in 2012, Dave and I went to Wisconsin to spend the holidays with Tony and his family. Before we went, Dave found this recipe in a Mayo Clinic flyer he received and thought we should try it. It reminded me of a breakfast casserole but appeared to be easier and faster to prepare. I tried the recipe on the Wisconsin family and got a negative response. "TOO HEALTHY!" Because I thought the method was good, I revised the recipe by adding bacon and whole eggs and got a more positive response. Years ago when all the children were home, I would fry the potatoes this way when we had our breakfast with eggs. I like this recipe because it is a fast and easy breakfast that feeds several people.

Serves: 6
Bake: Preheated 400 degree oven
Time: 8 to 10 minutes

Place on stove top an oven-proof 10- to 12-inch skillet on low to medium heat and add:
3 to 4 nitrate/nitrite-free bacon slices, cut in small strips
1 to 2 Tablespoons white or yellow onions, finely chopped
Fry until **bacon** just begins to crisp.

Add to **bacon/onion mixture:**
2 to 3 cups (2 to 3 medium) red or Yukon gold potatoes, peeled, thinly sliced
Cover and cook for about 8 minutes until **potatoes** are *crisp tender.*
(If pan becomes too dry, add **2 Tablespoons water.**)

Add to **potatoes:**
1 red bell pepper, diced
1 clove garlic, freshly squeezed

Cook for an additional 3 minutes or until **potatoes** are *fork tender*.

In a medium-sized bowl with a wire whisk, combine:
8 large eggs
⅓ cup milk
¼ teaspoon thyme
¼ teaspoon oregano
¼ teaspoon black pepper
When **potatoes** are tender, pour **egg mixture** evenly over **potatoes**. Jiggle the pan slightly so the **eggs** run down between the **potatoes**.

Over top of **egg mixture**, sprinkle evenly:
¼ cup Parmesan cheese, freshly grated
Place pan in a preheated oven and bake until **eggs** are a *soft* set. Remove from oven and let set for 3 minutes. Cut into 6 wedges and serve immediately.

Option

■ For the *healthy* option, substitute **2 teaspoons olive oil** for **bacon**, **skim milk** for **milk**, and **4 egg whites** for **4 of the eggs**.

Bacon and Vegetable Frittata.

Biscuits and Gravy

Biscuits and gravy are one of America's favorite comfort foods. For the holidays or our family vacations, each family has a day when they are in charge of the menu. Jude is famous for his biscuits and gravy for breakfast, and it is a favorite with the entire family. It is easy and can feed the multitudes quickly.

Have prepared:
In a 1-cup Pyrex cup, combine:
¾ cup milk
1 teaspoon apple-cider vinegar
Set aside for 30 minutes.

Biscuits

Makes: 10 to 12
Bake: Preheated 350 degree oven
Time: 10 to 12 minutes

In mixer bowl with wire whip, combine:
2 cups unbleached flour
2 Tablespoons sugar
1 Tablespoon baking powder
½ teaspoon cream tartar

¼ **teaspoon soda**
½ **teaspoon salt**
Mix well.

Add to **dry ingredients**:
½ **cup cold lard or shortening**
With mixer on *stir* or *low* setting, cut in **cold lard or shortening** until **mixture** looks like coarse crumbs.

Remove bowl from mixer. Form a well in the center of the **dry mixture**, then add all at once:
prepared sour milk
Using a fork, stir until *just* moistened. Too much mixing may result in **biscuits** that are too tough and not as light as desired. **Dough** will be soft and sticky.

On **lightly floured** surface, gently roll **dough** in **flour** to coat. Knead the **dough** by gently folding and pressing **dough** about 10 to 12 times or until **dough** is nearly smooth. Roll or pat until **dough** is ½-inch thick. Cut with 2 ½-inch biscuit cutter and place on **greased** baking sheet 1 inch apart for crusty sides and touching for soft sides. Bake as instructed above until *golden brown.*

Gravy

Serves: 8

In a large skillet, brown:
1 pound ground pork sausage

In a small bowl, using a wire whisk, combine:
2 Tablespoons corn starch
½ **cup milk**
Mix and pour evenly over **sausage.**

Cook until **gravy** begins to thicken, then add:

1 ½ cups milk

salt and pepper to taste

To serve: Cut **biscuit** in half and pour **gravy** over it. Serve immediately and *enjoy*.

Jude and family: Roslin, Jude, and Gavin.

Chip Beef on Toast 🍎GF

In *Family Favorites*, there is a recipe for Dried Beef Dip, page 92. One of the most frequent comments was, "This recipe reminds me of chip beef on toast that my mother used to make when I was at home." When I found this recipe, I had the same thoughts, as Mom made this recipe and sometimes substituted asparagus for the dried beef as a Lenten dish.

Have prepared:
8 slices of bread for toasting

Serves: 4

Cut into strips or pieces:
¼ pound dried beef, thinly sliced or shaved*
Set aside.

In a skillet on medium heat, melt:
¼ cup (½ stick) butter

Add to **melted butter** and mix with a wire whisk to form a roux:
¼ cup white whole-wheat flour
⅛ teaspoon black pepper

*I have found dried beef, packaged or in a jar, is too salty.
I always get my dried beef at the deli and ask the clerk
to cut it as thin as possible or have it shaved.

Slowly add and stir constantly:

2 cups milk

Bring to a simmer.

Add:

prepared dried beef

Simmer for 5 minutes and serve on **2 slices of toast** per serving.

Options

- Use **unbleached flour** in place of **white whole-wheat flour**.
- Substitute **frozen or canned asparagus** in place of **dried beef**.
- GF   Substitute **1 ½ Tablespoons corn starch** for **white whole-wheat flour** and **gluten-free bread** for **toast**.

The latest addition to our family, Rocco Pierce, son of Leslie and Brian.

Hash Browns 🍎GF

Hash browns are a common side dish for breakfast and supper. They can be served many ways, plain, with cheese, bacon, onions, or all of the above. The most common potato is russet or Idaho, but I prefer the red or Yukon gold potatoes.

Serves: 4

Scrub, rinse:
4 medium red or Yukon gold potatoes
Leave **peelings** on or peel the **potatoes**.

In a large bowl, mix:*
4 cups water
1 Tablespoon lemon juice
Using a KitchenAid grater, grate **potatoes** into **prepared water** and allow to soak for 5 minutes. Drain the **potatoes** through a colander and pat off with paper towels to remove extra moisture.

Place a 10- to 12-inch cast-iron skillet over *medium* heat for 5 minutes. Add:
4 Tablespoons bacon fat, lard, or vegetable oil

Scatter evenly in the prepared pan:
grated potatoes

*Soaking the potatoes in lemon water prevents the potatoes from becoming dark or discolored.

Sprinkle over top of **potatoes**:

1 teaspoon salt

Cook for 4 minutes *without disturbing.*

Lower heat and flip **potatoes** and cook 5 more minutes. Serve immediately.

Back row: Fran with her brother Joe. Front row, left to right: Fran's sister Katy, niece Sarah, and sister Mary.

Hollandaise Sauce 🍎 GF

One of America's favorite breakfast entrées is Eggs Benedict, and one reason is the wonderful, creamy Hollandaise sauce. This sauce is also good on many foods including fish, beef, chicken, and vegetables; plus, it is easy and quick to make in the microwave. Make the sauce just before ready to use.

Makes: ¾ cup

In a 4-cup Pyrex bowl, add:
½ cup (1 stick) butter
Microwave on high for 20 seconds until **butter** is *soft*, not melted.

In a medium-sized glass bowl, combine:
3 egg yolks
1 Tablespoon lemon juice, freshly squeezed
Mix well.

Add to **egg mixture** and mix well:
softened butter
Microwave on high, stopping to whisk every 15 seconds. The **mixture** will be *lumpy* for the first two whiskings, but continue to microwave at 15-second intervals until **sauce** becomes *smooth* and *thick*. *Do not overcook.*

Add to the **thickened sauce:**
¼ teaspoon salt
⅛ teaspoon paprika
dash of pepper
Mix well and serve.

Eggs Benedict

Captain and Mrs. La Grand Benedict were frequent diners at Delmonico's, a famous New York restaurant. When Mrs. Benedict became uninterested in the usual menu offerings, she inquired for Chef Ranhofer to create something new. He asked if she had any ideas, to which she suggested what is known as Eggs Benedict.

Serves: 2

For each serving, split and toast:
2 English muffins

Top each half (4) with:
1 slice Canadian bacon, thinly sliced

Place on each piece (4) of **bacon**:
1 poached egg

Pour over each (4) **egg**:
Hollandaise sauce, page 251

Serve immediately.

Fish, Meat & Poultry

Sammy

Glossary

au jus. Served in its own juices.

baste. To moisten food during cooking with pan drippings or special sauce to add flavor and prevent drying.

braise. To cook by browning meat in a little hot fat, then covering and cooking in a small amount of liquid, water, milk, or stock. May be done in oven or browned on range top, then cooked in oven after liquid is added.

bread. To dredge with fine, dry bread crumbs.

broil. To cook meat quickly by placing under broiler in top of oven and cooking each side to desired brownness, turning only once or as needed.

coat. To cover with a thin film, such as flour on meat.

Crock-Pot. A trademark used for an electric countertop cooker that maintains a low temperature for many hours, allowing unattended cooking of pot roasts, stews, and other long-cooking dishes. This trademark often occurs in print without a hyphen. The generic term for a Crock-Pot is "slow cooker."

dredge. To coat lightly with flour or cornmeal, etc.

drippings. Fats and juices dripped from roasting or browning meats.

entrée. The main course.

glaze. To coat with a thin sugar, syrup, or jelly to give food a flavorful and glossy coating.

marinate. To allow food to stand in liquid in order to tenderize and add flavor.

panfrying. To cook in hot skillet by browning both sides in fat, then cooking at low temperature until done.

panbroiling. to cook slowly and uncovered in heavy skillet without added fat or water.

paste. A smooth mixture of two textures, usually flour and water, used as a thickener.

roasting. To bake uncovered in slow oven, without added liquids.

roux. Fat and flour gently blended over very low heat to form a thickener for gravies, soups, and sauces.

sauté. To quickly cook or brown food in small quantities of hot fat or oil.

score. To cut narrow grooves or gashes on meats such as ham.

simmering. To heat so bubbles come gently to surface and barely break; used in braising and stewing.

stewing. To cook meat, usually cut into pieces, completely covered with water.

Fish Tale

I had never been fond of fish. I always thought it was because as Catholics, we had to eat fish on Friday and during Lent. But in later years I realized it was because of the fishy taste and odor. If it smells or tastes fishy, I don't want to eat it, no matter how healthy it is. But now, most health experts highly recommend eating fish more than once a week and even designating a specific day for it, just as the Catholics did years ago. Isn't there an old saying, "What goes around comes around?"

Because of the nutritional emphasis on fish, I've taken a new attitude toward it and found there are ways to get rid of the fishy taste and odor, as well as some great recipes and ways of preparation so that even I enjoy fish. In this section of the book I pass along what I've learned about fish to make it tasty without fishy odor or taste.

First, I checked my older cookbooks, then searched the Internet for suggestions. But where I got most of my information was right here in Grand Island, Nebraska, thousands of miles from any oceans.

At a PEO dinner party, our guest speaker was the husband of one of our members. Sheri Medjo's husband, Terry, is a commercial Alaskan salmon fisherman. Every year from the end of May to September, he fishes for sockeye salmon. His program was very informative, so after the program I asked about recipes and if he would visit with me about salmon fishing, processing, and nutritional information. He came over one afternoon with a wealth of information.

Since salmon is a favorite of mine and widely popular with many people, and has such a high nutritional value, I thought I would feature wild Alaskan salmon in this section and share what I learned from Terry.

Story of Salmon

Alaskan salmon belongs to the genus *Oncorhynchus*, a name from two Greek words, "onco," meaning hook or barb, and "rhyno," meaning nose. There are five species of Alaskan salmon, king (Chinook), sockeye (red), coho (silver), chum (keta), and pink (humpy). The life cycle of Alaska salmon begins when the adult salmon return to their natal streams to spawn. The female salmon rolls to her side, beats her tail on the streambed to make a redd (nest); she deposits 2,000 to 3,000 eggs in the depression. A male salmon then releases mitt (sperm) on the upstream side of the redd to fertilize the eggs. After the process, the female goes upstream of the redd and beats her tail on the gravel to cover the eggs. The salmon eggs incubate and hatch in the gravel of the streambed. In spring the newly hatched salmon emerge from the gravel and begin their journey. Some species of salmon—pink and chum—migrate directly down the rivers to the sea, while others—king, sockeye, and coho—spend one to three years in freshwater rivers and lakes. In the ocean the young salmon eat plankton and smaller fish while evading predators such as birds, seals, whales, and other fish. Alaska salmon travel thousands of miles. Depending on the species, salmon take two to four years to grow to adulthood in the cold waters of the North Pacific Ocean. In the summer the instincts of the salmon lead them back to the Alaska streams where they were hatched, and the cycle begins again. All Alaska salmon die after spawning once in their lives

The industry is tightly regulated as to the number of fish taken so that there will be new generations of salmon. Sizes and types of nets are regulated, and Alaskan salmon fisherman must have a limited entry permit* to obtain a commercial fishing license.

*Limited entry permit: Number of licenses are limited for each fishing district in the State of Alaska. The number of permits and value vary according to the fish districts. They are a property right of the holder and may be sold, bought, and are inheritable.

On return of the salmon to their natal streams, commercial fishermen are allowed to catch salmon in the open ocean. After the salmon are caught, the fish are placed in RSW (refrigerated sea water) or in slush ice, then delivered to a tender (crab boat), which also has RSW. When the tender is full, it will deliver the refrigerated fish to the cannery where processing occurs.

Fresh salmon is only available at certain times of the year, usually from the end of May until the first of October. Fresh fish can be flown to market as far away as Europe or Japan in less than 48 hours after it has been pulled from the water. But if sockeye salmon is featured on the menu as "fresh" anytime after September until May, you may want to question the chef; most likely it is frozen salmon, not fresh.

Eating most any fish seems to be the healthy thing to do, but wild Alaskan salmon is the heavy hitter when it comes to nutrition. Besides high amounts of omega-3, salmon contains high-quality protein and amino acids. It provides a number of vitamins, especially vitamins D and B12. Another plus for wild Alaskan salmon is that studies have shown it to be the least contaminated fish, thriving in the cold waters of the northern Pacific and the freshwater streams and rivers of Alaska.

Even though I featured salmon after reading Terry's information, I realized that most fish are prepared the same way—grilling, planking, poaching, baking, and frying—so first read the Helpful Hints and then the methods of preparation.

Helpful Hints

- Even though fresh fish can keep up to 10 days, it is best to cook as soon as possible after purchase to avoid any fishy odor or taste.
- If fish does have any odor, place in a lemon bath for 20 minutes. Place **2 Tablespoons lemon juice** and **1 cup water** in a shallow pan. Place **fish fillets** into **water** and let set for 10 minutes on each side. Pat dry with paper towels and proceed with preparation.
- Usually when the **fish** is breaded, the **seasonings** are in the **breading**, so most of the time the **seasonings** do not penetrate the **fish fillet**. After the **fillets** have had their citrus bath,

I pat the **fillets** with a paper towel and lightly sprinkle the **seasoning** directly on the skinless side of the **fish**. I love the herb **tarragon**, especially on **chicken**, so I thought I would try it on **fish**, and I liked the flavor. **Dill** is another good seasoning as are other **dry herbs (rosemary, marjoram, parsley)**. **Salt** and **pepper** should be mixed in the **flour**.

■ There are many **sauces** that you can serve with **fish**, such as **Asian glaze** and **tartar sauce** (page 267), that enhance the flavor of **fish**. Now I enjoy eating **fish** more than I ever did.

Terry Medjo holding a king (Chinook) salmon.

Bristol Bay, Alaska, is the world's largest sockeye salmon fishery, and most fillets coming out of Bristol Bay are frozen within hours of being removed from the sea. Next time you order or purchase salmon, ask where the salmon is from. If it's sockeye salmon and has been previously frozen, chances are good that it's from Bristol Bay.

Methods of Cooking Fish

Cuts of Fish

Yes, there are cuts of fish. If you are like me, you may not have known or paid any attention to this fact, but it can make a difference in how long you cook fish, whether there are bones in the fish, and whether you like a more dense fish or less so. Of course, there is whole fish and a number of cuts, but we are dealing here with the way we usually buy and prepare fish. The two basic cuts of fish are steaks and fillets.

Fish steaks. The fish is a crosscut of the whole fish, producing a thicker, more even cut. It is easier to handle and does not break up easily as fillets in the cooking process. Steaks are usually cut from larger fish such as salmon, swordfish, halibut, and tuna.

Fish fillets. Fillets are removed from the side of fish. If it is a larger fish, it may be cooked whole or even cut into steaks. More often it is smaller, flatter, and thicker in the middle with tapering ends. It is usually boneless. It is typical of tilapia.

It is interesting to note, filet mignon is spelled with one L and fish fillets are spelled with two Ls, but they are completely different animals.

Grilling Fish

Grilling is one of the oldest cooking methods known. It is also a fast, healthy way to preserve the natural flavors and nutrients of fish and other seafood. There are a few tips to make grilling easier.

1. The grill needs to be *thoroughly* clean before you begin grilling.
2. Make sure the grill is *hot* before you start cooking.
3. Brush oil on the grill to prevent sticking.
4. Fish cooks best over a *medium-hot* fire.

Grilling

1. If fish is frozen, rinse off any ice glaze with cold water and pat dry with paper towel.
2. Cut large fish steaks into meal-sized portions before grilling. This makes it easier to turn the portions on the grill.
3. Brush fish with oil lightly just before cooking to prevent sticking.
4. Always start to grill fish with *skin side up*; this allows the natural fat carried beneath the skin to be drawn into the fillet, keeping it moist. *Turn the fish only once.*
5. Cook fish approximately 10 minutes per inch of thickness. Fish continues to cook after its removed from the heat, so take it off the grill just as soon as it is opaque.
6. Check doneness by sliding a sharp knife tip into the center of the thickest part of a cooking fish portion; check color. Remove from heat just as soon as it turns from translucent to opaque throughout.

Planking

Planking is roasting food on a wood plank over fire. It is a time-honored tradition arising from a northwest-style of cooking using aromatic pieces of wood, such as cedar. Salmon was the original food of choice for planking. Purchase precut planks at barbecue or grill shops or larger grocery stores. You could also go to your local lumberyard and purchase untreated hardwoods such as cedar, oak, hickory, and maple. Do not use pine or other soft woods, as they are too resinous.

1. Cut planks into any size you desire, but be certain that the plank will fit your grill.
2. Presoak the plank in water 30 minutes to 2 hours. Pat planks dry with paper towels and spray coat cooking oil on one side of the plank: place seafood on oiled side.
3. If fish is frozen, rinse off any ice glaze with cold water and pat dry with paper towel.
4. Season *lightly*. You don't want to overpower the flavor you get from the plank.
5. Preheat one side of the grill to medium heat, with no heat on the other, indirect side. Place the planked seafood on the grill on the indirect side (not over direct heat) and close the lid.
6. Turn the heat down to medium.
7. Check the seafood frequently for doneness after 10 minutes.
8. To glaze seafood, brush on **Asian Glaze** (page 267) or **barbecue sauce** during the last 5 minutes of grilling and planking; cover and let it cook to a sheen.
9. Seafood changes from translucent to opaque as it cooks and continues to cook after it is removed from the heat. Cook just until opaque throughout.

Poaching

Poaching is a good way to prepare lean fish such as tilapia, red snapper, bass, and other white fish. (You can also poach fatty fish such as salmon or trout.) Poaching preserves the moisture, adding flavor without using fat. Many recipes call for preparing a fish broth to poach your fish. This might be easy to do on the coast but not so in the middle of the country. I don't know where I could find fish bones to make a broth or sauce. When I made Linguine and Clam Sauce, I used canned clam juice, and it is available in this area, so this is what I would recommend. Chicken broth or white wine is also recommended.

1. If fish is frozen, rinse off any ice glaze with cold water and pat dry with paper towel.
2. Prepare the poaching liquid in a sauté pan with enough liquid to measure 1 inch.
3. Add to the **clam juice**, **chicken broth**, or **white wine** your favorite spices, such as **fresh or dried parsley**, **oregano**, **savory**, **thyme**, **marjoram**, **tarragon**, and my favorite, **freshly squeezed garlic**.
4. Cover the pan and allow the mixture to come to a boil, then turn to low heat and simmer for 20 minutes to allow the spices to infuse into the liquid. Set aside.
5. Bring poaching liquid back to a full, rolling boil, then turn heat back to lowest setting. When boiling settles down, place fillets into liquid, and cover for 5 minutes or until the fish meat looks translucent. Increase time 2 or more minutes if fillets are thick.
6. Remove fillets from liquid, *drizzle* with **extra virgin olive oil**, sprinkle with **salt and pepper**, and garnish with **lemon slices**.

Oven Roasting

Oven roasting fish is simple, fast, and delicious. It takes approximately 20 minutes before it is ready to serve. Cod or any white fish seem to be the fish of choice; it can be plain or breaded. I also found a recipe for oven-fried fish, and I call it the best of both worlds. I prepared it on live television in a 15-minute segment. Easy! Easy!

1. If fish is frozen, rinse off any ice glaze with cold water and pat dry with a paper towel.
2. In small bowl, combine your favorite spices for fish, such as **parsley**, **marjoram**, **oregano**, **savory**, **thyme**, **lemon zest**, **tarragon**, and **bay leaf** (remove stem).
3. Place in spray-coated 9 × 13 glass baking dish the frozen, fresh, or thawed fish. *Sprinkle* with **lemon juice** or **white wine**. Season with **salt and pepper** and rub in your favorite spices.
4. Cover with lid or foil wrap and bake in preheated oven at 375 degrees for 10 minutes. Remove wrap, pour **2 to 3 Tablespoons melted butter** over fish; return to oven and bake 7 to 10 minutes for frozen fillets and 4 to 7 minutes for fresh or thawed fillets. Cook until fish is opaque throughout.

Frying

1. If fish is frozen, rinse off any ice glaze with cold water and pat dry with a paper towel.
2. Heat skillet (I use a cast-iron skillet) over medium to high heat.
3. Season fish on meat side with your favorite fish **spices** and **salt and pepper**.
4. Lightly dredge your fish in **flour**, shaking off the excess.
5. When pan is good and hot, add **canola oil** and follow with **butter**. When the foaming subsides, place **fish** in pan *skin side down*. Shake pan for a few seconds to prevent the fish from sticking.
6. Cook until a golden crust appears on the fish. Carefully turn the fish, gently shaking to prevent the fish from sticking, and brown the other side.
7. Remove and place on a warm plate. Garnish with **lemon slices**.

Oven Fried

This is the best of both worlds. Brown fish on both sides in an oven-proof skillet, then place the skillet in the oven to finish the cooking. While the fish is in the oven, you can set the table, make a salad, or do any last preparation for dinner. Quick and easy!

1. Preheat oven to 400 degrees.
2. Follow instructions above under Frying for preparation of the **fish**.
3. In an oven-proof skillet on medium to high heat, place **fillets** and brown both sides, approximately 1 minute on each side.
4. Place skillet in oven and bake for approximately 10 minutes or until fish appears opaque.
5. Serve on a *warm* plate, garnish with **lemon slices**, and serve immediately.

Salmon Soufflé 🍎 GF

During our Feingold days, this was one of our favorite main dishes, especially during Lent and on Fridays. Any recipe that has the word "soufflé" in it frightens me, but this recipe is so easy. When you get such a wonderful result, your family and friends will think you are a "chef" rather than a cook.

Have prepared:
lightly greased soufflé bowl (2 quart); set aside

Serves: 4 to 6
Bake: Preheated 350 degree oven
Time: 20 to 25 minutes

Separate:
3 large eggs
Place **egg whites** in mixer bowl and **egg yolks** in small bowl. Slightly beat **egg yolks** using a wire whisk; set aside.

In 8-cup Pyrex bowl, melt:
3 Tablespoons butter

Add to **melted butter** and mix well with a wire whisk:
3 Tablespoons unbleached flour
1 cup milk
1 teaspoon salt
white pepper to taste
Microwave on high for 2 to 3 minutes until **mixture** thickens.

Add to **above mixture**:
1 (6-ounce) can salmon, flaked and bones crushed
prepared egg yolks
Set aside.

In mixer bowl with wire whip attachment, beat until *stiff* peaks form:
3 egg whites
Fold in **salmon mixture** and gently pour into prepared soufflé dish or deep baking dish.

Bake as instructed above or until *golden brown*. Serve immediately.

Option

■ GF   Substitute **gluten-free flour** for **unbleached flour**.

Grandchildren Zoey, Sammy, and Gracie were guests with Grandma on Channel 13.

Salmon Patties 🍎 ♥ GF

In our family salmon patties were one of our favorite fish dinners. Another name for this recipe is salmon cakes. We always used canned red-sockeye salmon, never pink salmon. There is quite a difference in the taste of the two salmons. The red-sockeye salmon is the filet mignon of canned salmon. It is preferred because of its rich orange-red flesh and is considered more flavorful. This is a recipe you could also use if you had leftover salmon or any other fish.

Serves: 4

Drain and reserve the **liquid**:
1 (14.75-ounce) can red-sockeye salmon

In a mixing bowl, add:
reserved salmon liquid
½ cup bread crumbs, page 3
1 Tablespoon white or yellow onion, finely chopped
1 large egg
Mix well.

Add to above mixture:
red-sockeye salmon
Mix well.

In a skillet, on medium to high heat, add:
1 Tablespoon coconut or canola oil
To form the patties, spoon the **salmon** into four portions in the skillet and fry crisp on the first

side; then turn and cook well on the other side. Garnish with **lemon slices** and serve immediately with **tartar sauce** (recipe below).

Option

- ■ GF Substitute **gluten-free bread or cracker crumbs** for **bread crumbs**.

Tartar Sauce 🍎♥GF

In a small bowl, combine all ingredients using a wire whisk:
1 cup mayonnaise
1 Tablespoon horseradish
1 teaspoon Worcestershire sauce
1 clove garlic, freshly squeezed
3 Tablespoons sweet pickle relish
Place in a small serving bowl. Chill.

Asian Glaze 🍎♥GF

In a medium bowl with a wire whisk, combine:
3 Tablespoons pure maple syrup
2 teaspoons ginger
2 teaspoons lime juice
2 teaspoons soy sauce
1 ½ teaspoons garlic, freshly squeezed

Brush or spoon ½ **to 1 teaspoon on each seafood portion** or **all onto large fillet or salmon side.**

Pecan-Crusted Tilapia   🍎 ♥ GF

When Dave and I ate pecan-crusted tilapia at a restaurant in Omaha, it became one of our favorite entrées. The restaurant removed it from the menu, so I tried to find a recipe for bread crumbs with pecans. I decided to revamp the bread crumb recipe that I use for the Chicken Florentine/Lemon Parsley Chicken, page 64.

Have prepared:
a baking sheet lined with waxed paper. Set aside.

Serves: 6
Bake: Preheated 400 degree oven
Time: 10 to 12 minutes

In a food processor, add:
½ cup (20 pecan halves) pecans
¾ cup bread crumbs, page 3
Process the **mixture** until it has a coarse texture. Place the crumbs in a 9 × 13 baking pan and set aside.

Get ready:
6 to 8 tilapia fillets
If frozen, rinse off ice glaze with **cold water** and pat dry with a paper towel.

Sprinkle lightly on meat side with:
parsley
dill
tarragon

In a bread pan, add:

1 cup milk

In a second bread pan, combine:

1 cup white whole-wheat or unbleached flour

½ teaspoon salt

¼ teaspoon pepper

Dip, one at a time, each **fish fillet** in this order: Dredge the **fish fillet** in the **seasoned flour**, then dip the **dredged fish** into the **milk**; coat both sides with the **seasoned pecan bread crumbs**. Place on the prepared baking sheet. Continue until all **fillets** are coated. Place in freezer or refrigerator until ready to use.

In a large oven proof skillet on *medium* to *high* heat add:

enough canola oil to cover bottom of skillet

1 tablespoon butter

When the foaming of the **butter** subsides, place **fish** in pan *skin side down*. Shake pan for a few seconds to prevent the **fish** from sticking. Cook until a *golden crust* appears on the **fish**, approximately 1 minute on each side. Carefully turn the **fish** and gently shake to prevent the **fish** from sticking and brown the other side.

Place skillet in oven and bake for approximately 10 minutes or until **fish** appears opaque.

Serve on a *warm* plate, garnish with **lemon slices**, and serve immediately.

Options

- **GF** Substitute **gluten-free bread or gluten-free cracker crumbs** for **bread crumbs**.
- **GF** Substitute **gluten-free bread flour** for **whole-wheat or unbleached flour**.

Oven-Fried Fish 🍎 ♥ GF

My sister, Mary, was a guest with me on our local Channel 13's (NTV) *The Good Life*. We had to make at least two recipes in a "live" 15-minute segment. Because it was during Lent, we decided to do meat-less recipes. I did Oven-Fried Fish, and Mary did the Walnut Penne Pasta. There was enough time for me to make a simple **tartar sauce**, page 267. A wonderful meal was prepared a few minutes.

....

Serves: 4
Bake: Preheated 400 degree oven
Time: 10 minutes

In 9 × 13 pan, combine:
1 cup water
1 Tablespoon lemon juice

In **lemon juice water**, place:
4 white fish fillets
Soak **fish** 10 minutes on each side

Remove fillets from water, pat dry with paper towel, and lightly sprinkle over each **fillet**:
salt
white pepper
tarragon

In gallon-size Ziploc bag, combine:
¼ cup corn meal
1 Tablespoon unbleached or white whole-wheat
2 Tablespoons pecans, finely chopped
1 Tablespoon melted butter

Seal bag and shake well. Add **fillets** one at a time to bag, shake well, and place on platter. Let stand for 5 minutes to dry.

In a oven-proof skillet on *medium* to *high* heat, add:

2 Tablespoons coconut or canola oil

Place **fillets** in skillet and brown each side, approximately 1 minute on each side. Then place skillet in oven and bake as instructed on page 270.

Garnish with **lemon slices** and serve immediately with **tartar sauce**, page 267.

Option

■   GF   Substitute **gluten-free bread flour** for **whole-wheat or unbleached flour**.

Family photo.

Scallops and Sugar Snap Peas 🍎 GF

It had been many years since I had seen or heard from our Italian cousins who live in Cheyenne. The last time I remember was at Nonna's funeral in 1987. One evening the phone rang; on the caller ID was Cheyenne, Wyoming. When I answered it, a voice said, "This is your cousin Ernie Brazzale. Our daughter, Becca, has enrolled in Hastings College, and we are going to help her move. We were wondering if we could stop by for a visit." I said, "Yes, and you are welcome to stay with us." This call renewed our relationship and friendship, and now we spend every other Thanksgiving at my sister Mary's home in Kansas. Mary extends an invitation to all the cousins and their families, and we have a Thanksgiving potluck dinner. We feast, hunt, and play Polish poker. Nonno and Nonna would be so happy to see us all together. While visiting Ernie and Melinda in Cheyenne, Ernie made this delicious dish, and I want to pass this recipe on to you.

Have prepared:
Basic White Rice, page 277

Serves: 4

In a deep frying pan, melt until foaming:
½ cup (1 stick) butter

Add:
2 garlic cloves, freshly squeezed
Sauté for 1 minute.

Katy Lingo and Ernie Brazzale.

Add:
1 (12-ounce) package frozen sweet snap peas
6 sliced mushrooms
¼ teaspoon salt

¼ teaspoon cracked black pepper

Cover and simmer on low heat until **peas** are *crisp tender*.

Add:

1 pound bay scallops

¼ cup white wine

Cover and steam for approximately 2 minutes until **scallops** are done. *Do not overcook.*

In a 1-cup Pyrex cup, using a wire whisk, add:

¼ cup milk

2 Tablespoons corn starch

Blend until smooth.

Slowly add **above blend** to the:

prepared scallop mixture

Simmer until **sauce** thickens. Immediately remove from heat and keep covered until ready to serve.

Serve over a bed of **rice**, page 277.

Option

■   Substitute **shrimp** for **scallops**.

Beef Burgundy   GF

When we got our first Crock-Pot, this is one of the first recipes I tried. It was one of Chris's favorites, and he recently asked me about this recipe. I had totally forgotten about it and had no idea where to find it. Later, I was at an auction and bought a Crock-Pot; in it came a small recipe book. As I was looking through the book, I found the lost recipe. I noticed the recipe had some ingredients I no longer use, such as beef bouillon cubes and margarine; so I have revised this recipe.

Serves: 4 to 6

In a large Crock-Pot, set on high, melt:
2 to 4 Tablespoons butter

Add to **melted butter**:
2 pounds beef stew meat, cut in 1 ½-inch cubes
Cook until **meat** is browned.

Add to Crock-Pot:
⅓ cup white or yellow onions, finely chopped
1 clove garlic, freshly squeezed
¼ cup carrots, finely chopped
1 cup beef broth, page 16
1 cup Burgundy or any dry red wine
1 Tablespoon tomato paste
½ teaspoon salt
½ teaspoon black pepper

Though fresh thyme is more flavorful than dried, it rarely lasts more than a week. Depending on how it is used in a dish, the whole sprig (single stem snipped from the plant) may be used or the leaves removed and the stems discarded. Remove leaves from stems by either scraping with the back of a knife or by pulling through the fingers or tines of a fork.

1 bay leaf

½ teaspoon thyme

Cover and cook on low for 6 to 8 hours.

To thicken the **gravy**, remove from Crock-Pot **1 cup beef juices** and set aside.

In a medium bowl using a wire whisk, add:

¼ cup white whole-wheat or unbleached flour

Slowly add:

reserved beef juices

Mix well, then add to beef in Crock-Pot, stir well.

Half an hour before serving, place in a 4-cup Pyrex bowl:

4 slices nitrate/nitrite-free bacon, cut in small strips

Microwave on high until **bacon** is crisp, stirring once during cooking. After cooking, drain off grease and place **bacon** on a paper towel to continue to drain until crispy and dry. Set aside.

In a medium skillet, melt:

2 to 3 Tablespoons butter

Add to **melted butter** and sauté for 2 minutes:

¼ to ½ cup fresh mushrooms, sliced

Add **mushrooms** and **bacon** to the Crock-Pot and mix well.

Serve with **rice** (page 277) or **noodles** (page 35, **GF** 40–41). Garnish with **parsley**.

Options

- ■ GF Substitute **1 ½ Tablespoons corn starch** for **white whole-wheat or unbleached flour.**
- ■ GF Substitute **¼ cup gluten-free flour** for **white whole-wheat or unbleached flour.**

Pepper Steak Stir-Fry 🍎 ♥ GF

While traveling to Manzanillo, Mexico, with our friends Luke and Shirley Coniglio, I saw this recipe in a magazine. Pepper steak is my favorite Asian dish. No matter the choices on the menu, I always seem to order it. This recipe appeared to be the same or similar to the ones I have ordered at different restaurants. When we arrived at our hotel, Dolphin Cove Inn, we had to walk and climb steps to get to the restaurant, so we thought we could dine in some nights since our rooms had a complete kitchen. This was our first "dine-in" dinner in Mexico.

....

Have prepared:
Basic White Rice, page 277

Serves: 4

In a 12-inch skillet, heat on *high* or *medium* heat:
2 teaspoons canola oil
1 ½ pounds beef steak, thinly sliced*
1 clove garlic, freshly squeezed
¼ teaspoon salt
Cook for 3 minutes or until just browned, stir occasionally, then transfer to medium bowl.

*It will be easier to cut your steak in thin strips if the
meat is partially frozen.

To skillet add:

1 medium red bell pepper, thinly sliced

1 medium green bell pepper, thinly sliced

1 small white or yellow onion, thinly sliced

2 Tablespoons water

pinch salt

Cover and cook until **peppers** are *crisp tender*, approximately 5 minutes. Stir occasionally.

While **peppers** are sautéing, in a small bowl, using a wire whisk, mix until smooth:

1 Tablespoon corn starch

1 Tablespoon soy sauce

2 Tablespoons brown or raw sugar

3 Tablespoons water

¼ teaspoon black pepper

Then add to the skillet and simmer 1 minute or until thickened. Add the **prepared beef** and **juices** to skillet. Cook 1 minute or until **beef** is heated through. Serve on a bed of **rice**.

Options

- For a slightly sweeter flavor, use **teriyaki sauce** for **soy sauce**.
- Substitute **pork** for **steak**.
- Substitute **broccoli** for **peppers**.
- Use **maple syrup** for **brown or raw sugar**.

Perfect Basic White Rice   GF

Serves: 4

In a medium sauce pan with heat on *high*, add:

2 cups water

1 teaspoon salt
1 teaspoon butter
Bring to a boil.

Add to **water**:
1 cup white rice
Stir and cover with good-fitting lid and reduce heat to *medium low*. You will know the temperature is correct if a little steam is visible leaking from the lid. A lot of steam means the heat is too high.
Cook for 20 minutes. DO NOT LIFT LID. The steam trapped inside the pan allows the **rice** to cook properly. Remove from heat and fluff with a fork. Serve immediately

Left to right: Luke and Shirley Coniglio with Mary and Frank Stovall.

Umami. Japanese for "delicious taste," umami is produced by certain amino acids and is best described as "savory"—rich in flavor released by cooking, curing, or aging. Examples of umami foods include seared and cured meats, aged cheeses, fish sauce, green tea, soy sauce, and cooked tomatoes.

Meat Loaf 🍎GF

Meat loaf was a staple meal when growing up in the '50s. I found a recipe with sweet bell peppers, and I liked the extra flavor the peppers gave the meat loaf. I prefer red, yellow, or orange peppers rather than green peppers because they are milder in taste.

Serves: 4 to 6
Bake: 350 degree oven
Time: 1 hour

In a medium bowl, combine:
2 pounds (80/20) ground beef
2 large eggs
½ to ¾ cup bread crumbs, page 3
¼ small white or yellow onion, finely chopped
½ bell pepper, finely chopped
1 clove garlic, freshly squeezed
1 teaspoon salt
½ teaspoon ground pepper
Place the **meat mixture** in a glass loaf pan and make an indentation the top of the **meat**.

Fill the indentation with:
¼ to ½ cup ketchup
Bake as instructed above.

Option

■   GF   Substitute **gluten-free bread or crackers** for **bread crumbs**.

Roasted Chicken Dinner 101 GF

On one of the programs on Channel 13's *The Good Life*, I demonstrated how to roast a chicken. The time it takes to prepare a chicken for roasting is minimal, plus you save money and get three times more food. Check the prices below and see the benefits of cooking from scratch.

Serves: 4 to 6
Bake: Preheated 350 degree oven
Time: 2 to 3 hours

Remove **giblets** and wash the 4 to 5 pound *fully thawed* **chicken**. Place the **chicken**, *breast side down*, on a solid cutting board. Bend the whole **leg** firmly to the outside until the **ball** of the thighbone pops from the hip socket; repeat on the other side. Using a sharp knife and/or kitchen scissors, cut the **back** on both side to the **ribs**, cutting across the backbone. Remove the **back**. Then cut off the **tips** of the wings. Place the **back**, **neck**, and **wing tips** in an 8-cup Pyrex bowl. Set aside to make microwave **chicken broth**, page 13.

Place in the cavity of the **chicken**:
2 stalks celery, leaves and all
½ small onion
Pull the skin across the **vegetables** and place *breast side up* in a baking pan.

Sprinkle the outside with:
salt and pepper
tarragon and parsley flakes
Bake in a covered pan or use a foil tent and bake as instructed above. Remove the cover for the last 20 minutes to allow the **chicken** to brown.

Save the **drippings** from the **roasted chicken** and refrigerate. Separate the **chicken fat** from the **chicken gelatin**, place into small plastic bags, and store in the refrigerator. **Chicken fat** is a good substitute for **butter** when making **gravy**. The **chicken gelatin** is excellent for making **soup**.

To serve: Place **roasted chicken** in the center of a *warm* platter and arrange the **vegetables** around the **chicken**.

Option

■ About 1 hour before **chicken** is completely cooked, add ½ **to 1 cup water and cut vegetables** (**potatoes**, **carrots**, **onions**, and **celery**). Check **vegetables** for tenderness.

Chop sage leaves very finely and use in small amounts. The raw, fresh leaves are a little hairy and have a strong flavor. Added toward the end of cooking, sage can bring a distinctive taste to pork, veal, venison, and risotto dishes, and the dried leaves are good for stuffings and with poultry, fish, carrots, and potatoes. The flowers can be used to make summer teas.

What Do You Save by Cooking from Scratch?
(prices from 2013)

Cooking from Scratch

Chicken, 5 lb., on sale	$3.20
Celery @ 1.29	$0.40
Potatoes @ .98 per lb.	$0.60
Onions, 1, @ .98 per pound	$0.50
Carrots, 1, @ .98	$0.30
Total	**$5.00**

This home-cooked chicken will provide:	Price if purchased at the store:	
Chicken dinner for two	Rotisserie chicken, 1 lb., 13 oz.	$6.95
46 oz. chicken broth by using chicken back, wing tips, and neck	46 oz. can chicken broth	$2.98
Chicken drippings, fat, and gelatin	Chicken base, 1 small jar	$4.15
	Chicken consommé	$2.98
1 lb. chicken breast for sandwiches	1 lb. deli chicken breast	$6.95
Chicken for chicken salad	1 lb. deli chicken salad	$5.98
With chicken broth and remaining vegetables: chicken soup	4 cans chicken soup @ .98/can	$3.92
	Total	**$33.91**
		$33.91
		-$5.00
	You save $28.91	

Lard 🍎 ♥ GF

In the 19th century, lard was used in a similar fashion as butter and was widely used during World War II because it was cheaper. By the late 20th century, lard was considered less healthy because of high saturated fatty acids and cholesterol content; but unlike the highly touted margarines and vegetable shortenings, unhydrogenated lard contains no trans fats. In the 1990s, a partial rehabilitation of this fat became recognized by chefs and bakers. This trend was driven by the negative publicity of trans fat content in shortenings and vegetable oils. Now the "bad boys", lard and coconut oil, have become again "knights in shining armor" with American cooks. But remember, industrially produced lard, including most lard sold on the shelves in supermarkets, is often treated with bleaching and deodorizing agents, emulsifiers, and antioxidants, such as BHT, which prevent spoilage. Most packaged foods on grocery store's shelves have many of these additives and preservatives to give their products a long shelf life. *Untreated lard needs to be refrigerated or frozen.*

Lard is rendered pig fat, commonly used as a cooking fat or shortening. Lard can be obtained from any part of the pig, but leaf lard is obtained from the fat surrounding the kidneys and inside the loin. Lard may be rendered two ways, wet or dry. In wet rendering, pig fat is boiled in water, and the lard that is insoluble is skimmed off. In dry rendering, which is most common, the fat is cooked in a large pan in the oven or on the stove. Smaller amounts can be rendered in the Crock-Pot. But if you have a large amount of fat, the oven is the quickest method to use.

Dry Rendered Lard

Bake: Preheated 225 degree oven
Time: 1 hour or until all fat is melted

In a large roasting pan place:
chopped pig fat

Roast slowly for 30 minutes to one hour until fat has melted; **protein particles** and **connective tissue** will be floating on the top. Skim off the **solid particles** and set aside.

Pour through a mesh colander lined with a double layer of cheesecloth:
liquid fat
To prevent breakage, cool slightly before pouring into quart-size glass canning jars. Store in refrigerator or freezer. Frozen, it will keep indefinitely.

Crock-Pot Rendering

If you have a smaller amount of pig fat to render, the Crock-Pot or slow cooker is an easy way to do it. The wonderful thing about the slow cooker is the heat is even in the pot and there is less chance of burning. You can start it on high setting, then when the fat starts to melt, turn it to low. In order to keep an eye on the cooking process, set your timer at 30-minute intervals. You can remove the melted fat at this time and the remainder of the unmelted fat will cook faster.

Before cooking, chop ½-inch squares or grind and place in Crock-pot on *high* setting
5 to 7 pounds leaf pork fat (fat around kidneys and loin)
¼ cup water
Water helps transfer heat from Crock-Pot into **cold fat** without scorching it. Cover with a lid for one hour. After 1 to 2 hours, remove lid to allow any remaining **water** to evaporate and reduce your setting to *low* to keep the **partially rendered mixture** simmering lightly. The volume of the contents will decrease as **fat** renders into **lard**.

When **mixture** is about half liquid and half solid, start removing some of the **rendered lard** to help the remaining chunks to cook down further. Strain **lard** to remove the solid pieces called "cracklings." Continue to cook until all **fat** is melted. Strain and pour into quart-sized glass canning jars. Place in refrigerator or freeze.

Pies

Gracie

Glossary

condensed milk. Milk made with sugar added, reduced to thick consistency by evaporation. Usually found in cans. Not to be confused with evaporated milk, which is thinner and has no added sugar.

cream pie. Filling of pudding made from eggs, butter, flour, milk, or other liquids. May have additional flavors such as chocolate or ingredients such as bananas.

crimp. To seal edges of a two-crust pie by pinching the top and bottom crust together with the finger or by pressing them with a fork or crimper.

cut in. Combining fat with dry ingredients using two knives, a fork, or a pastry blender.

dot. To scatter small bits of butter over top of food.

flake. To break lightly into small pieces with a fork.

lard. Solid cooking fat rendered from pork, softer and more oily than butter, margarine, or shortening.

lattice-top pie. A top crust made by interweaving strips of pie dough.

meringue. Stiffly beaten mixture of egg whites and sugar used to cover a pie and browned in the oven.

pie. A baked dish of fruit, or meat and vegetables, typically with a top and base of pastry.

pie shell. Single pie crust baked *before* filling; used most often with cream pies.

render. To make lard by separating fat from muscle and tissue of pork by means of heat.

shortening. Fat used in frying, baking, or other cooking; includes butter, lard, margarine, vegetable oil. Gives baked goods, particularly pies, their tender, flaky quality. (See ingredient section, page 4, for further details.)

single-crust pie. A pie with no top crust, baked *after* filling, usually a custard or pumpkin pie.

steep. To extract flavor, color, or other qualities from substances, e.g., fruit, by allowing them to stand in hot water for a period of time.

temper. To add a small amount of cooked mixture to beaten eggs before returning it to rest of egg mixture.

two-crust pie. A pie made with a bottom crust, filled (often with fruit), then topped with a second crust, sealed together, and baked.

Helpful Hints

■ The pie plate that I prefer is a 9 × 1 ¾-inch glass plate. Disposable foil pie plates are usually smaller. If it is necessary to use one, use a deep-dish style measuring 8 ¾ × 1 ¾ inches.

■ Shiny metal does not bake the **undercrust** well because it deflects the heat.

■ If the **pastry dough** is crumbly and hard to roll, add **water, 1 teaspoon at a time**, just until the **pastry** is evenly moistened.

■ Roll out **pie crust** at room temperature.

■ To prevent **crust** from being tough, **use less water**. Toss the **flour mixture** and **water** together only until all of the **flour** is moistened. Don't overmix.

■ Use a pastry cloth and cover for your rolling pin; this helps keep the **dough** from sticking.

■ To prevent a soggy **crust**, fix any cracks in the **dough** with a **scrap of dough** before adding **filling**.

■ Make several slits in the top to allow the steam to escape, preventing excessive bubbling.

■ Bake in a hot oven. If the temperature is too low, the **bottom crust** will not bake properly.

■ For a glazed top crust, brush lightly with an egg white.

■ For a **sugar crust**, brush the top with **milk or water** and sprinkle with **sugar**.

■ When baking a **pastry shell**, place a smaller pie tin, such as an 8-inch disposable tin, lightly in the **pie shell** for 10 minutes. Remove and allow the **pastry** to brown. This prevents the **pastry** from puffing.

■ An 8-inch pie cuts into 5 to 6 pieces; a 9-inch pie cuts into 7 to 8 pieces.

During World War II, Grandpa and Grandma lived with us. Grandma was a slow-moving, genteel lady from Missouri; she took her time with everything she did. So you can imagine living in the same house with my spirited Italian mother who wanted things done in a "flash." But Grandma was a godsend because my dad and grandpa drove to work everyday twenty-five miles south to the Hastings Naval Ammunition Depot, the largest naval ammunition plant in the country. My mother, a legal secretary, worked 40 miles west in Kearney. All their jobs were war-related. Grandma stayed home and took care of my brother Jon and I. Consequently, she did the majority of the housework and cooking. She was a fabulous cook, and pies were her specialty. She was famous for her sour cream raisin pie (a caramelized two-crusted pie, page 276 in *Family Favorites*), apple (page 274 in *Family Favorites*), and minced meat, Jon's favorite. When she cooked, we would often hear her hum, and I find myself doing the same thing. I guess it is because we enjoyed what we were doing. After World War II, they moved a few blocks away, but they would often invite us to stay overnight, and we would play canasta, a popular card game. She always fixed us our favorite foods; mine were apple pie, stewed tomatoes, and Irish spaghetti.

After my cousin Max, their grandson, passed away, I found this picture. I think it might be Grandpa and Grandma's wedding picture.

Pie Pastry for Two Crusts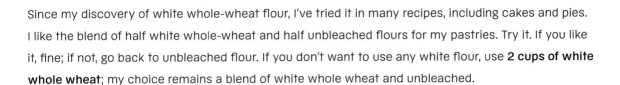

Since my discovery of white whole-wheat flour, I've tried it in many recipes, including cakes and pies. I like the blend of half white whole-wheat and half unbleached flours for my pastries. Try it. If you like it, fine; if not, go back to unbleached flour. If you don't want to use any white flour, use **2 cups of white whole wheat**; my choice remains a blend of white whole wheat and unbleached.

In mixer bowl with wire whip attachment, add:
1 cup white whole wheat flour
1 cup unbleached flour
½ to 1 teaspoon salt

Then add:
¾ cup cold lard or shortening
With a spatula or knife, cut **lard** or **shortening** into small pieces. With your mixer on *stir* or *low* speed, using wire whip attachment, cut the **lard** or **shortening** into the **flour** until pieces are the size of small peas. *Do not overmix.*

Remove the mixer bowl from the mixer. Sprinkle over the **mixture**:
1 Tablespoon cold water
Gently toss with a fork.

Repeat above, sprinkling **1 Tablespoon water** at a time over dry parts until all **flour** is moistened:
total 5 to 7 Tablespoons cold water

On a **lightly floured** surface, flatten half of the **dough** and roll out to about ⅛-inch thickness, forming a 12-inch circle. Place into a 9-inch glass pie plate ... avoid stretching. Prepare the **filling**.

For **top crust**, repeat the above instructions, except the **top crust** should be slightly thinner than the **bottom crust**. Cut slits or a design on the **crust** to allow steam to escape. Fold in half and *carefully* place over top of the **filling**.

Trim both **crusts** to ½-inch beyond the edge of the pie plate. Fold the **top crust** under the **bottom crust**. Seal and crimp the edge.

Prepared single-crust pie shell before baking.

Smaller pie tin placed over crust before baking.

Options

■ **One-Crust Pie**

The above recipe makes 2 one-crust pie shells.

For 1 one-crust pie shell:

Roll out the **dough** as instructed for a **bottom crust**. Fold **extra pastry dough** back and under, forming a high, fluted edge to hold the **filling**. Pour most of the filling into **pastry-lined** pan. To prevent spilling, pour in **remaining filling** after the **pie** is placed on the oven rack.

Weaving pastry strips over pie filling.

Prepared lattice crust.

■ **Baked Pastry Shell**

Makes: 2
Baked: Preheated 450 oven
Time: As instructed below

Roll out your **dough** as you would for the **bottom crust**. Place it in pie plate and avoid stretching to prevent shrinking. Fold **extra pastry dough** back and under, forming a high, fluted edge to hold the **filling**. Prick **pastry** generously on the bottom, sides, and edges *with the tines of a fork* to prevent puffing during baking. *Lightly* place a smaller pie tin, e.g., 8-inch disposable pie pan, over the **crust**. Bake for 10 minutes, remove the 8-inch pie pan, and allow the **crust** to brown, approximately 5 minutes. Watch closely. (See illustrations on page 368.)

Lattice Crust

Have prepared:
Pie Pastry for Two Crusts, above; use **1 crust** to line the bottom of a 9-inch glass pie plate

After rolling top crust, cut into ½- to 1-inch strips.

In a pastry-lined glass pie plate, transfer:

desired filling

Trim **bottom pastry** to ½ inch beyond edge of plate.

Weave the **strips** on top of the **filling** to make a lattice design. Press ends of **strips** into rim of the **bottom crust**. Fold **bottom pastry** over **strips**; seal and crimp edge. See illustrations on page 291.

Helpful Hints

- A baker's pin is a rolling pin (no handles) made out of a single dowel of hardwood about two inches in diameter. The pin covers the entire dough all at once to make the process of flattening and evening the crust easier and faster. (Suggestion from our daughter Leslie.)
- Be sure your **lard** is *cold* and not melted or in liquid form. You will have difficulty making a crust if it is melted or liquid. Place it into the refrigerator or freezer until it is in a solid form, either cold or frozen.

Fran and Arlene Hansen (left and middle) presenting a gift to their exercise instructor, Sheeré Gleason (right).

Crumbs for Pie and Dessert Crusts

When I prepare crumbs for various pie and dessert crusts, I usually do the whole box or package and make all three kinds, starting with the lightest and ending with the darkest.

Process in your food processor until you have a fine crumb. Start with **vanilla wafers**, then the **Graham crackers**, and finally the **chocolate cookies**. Wipe out the food processor bowl before doing the **chocolate cookies** (no need to wash). Store in airtight containers. **Crumbs** do not need to be refrigerated. You can get about *4 crusts out of a 1-pound box*. Recipes using these ingredients generally call for ¼ **cup sugar**. **Chocolate cookies** *do not* require any additional **sugar**.

Graham Cracker or Vanilla Wafer Crust

Serves: 8
Bake: Preheated 350 degree oven
Time: 10 minutes

In a medium bowl, using a fork, combine;
1 ½ cups (Graham cracker or vanilla wafers) crumbs
¼ cup sugar
¼ cup (½ stick) melted butter
Mix well until **crumbs** are *evenly* coated with **butter**. Press into a 9- to 10-inch glass pie plate. Bake as directed above or until slightly browned. Set aside and cool.

Chocolate Cookie Crust

In a medium bowl,using a fork, combine:

1 ½ cups cookie crumbs

¼ cup (½ stick) melted butter

Mix well until **crumbs** are *evenly* coated with **butter**. Press into a 9- to 10-inch glass pie plate. Bake as directed above or until slightly browned. Set aside and cool.

Options

- Substitute **ginger snaps** for **Graham crackers**.
- Substitute **vanilla cookies** for **chocolate cookies**.

Left to right: Justin, Jared, and Skhyler Schaffer.

Blueberry Pie

Whenever I go through a buffet dessert line, I usually pick blueberry or pecan pie. These are two pies I seldom make. With all that is written about the benefits of eating blueberries, this pie could be a healthy dessert as well as a delicious one. If you use white whole-wheat flour for a crust, you have added benefits. This Blueberry Pie won second place at the 2010 Nebraska State Fair.

Have prepared:
Pie Pastry for Two Crusts, page 289; use **1 crust** to line the bottom of a 9-inch glass pie plate

Serves: 8
Bake: Preheated 400 degree oven
Time: 50 minutes

In an 8-cup Pyrex glass bowl, combine:
2 cups water
½ cup blueberries
Microwave on high for 5 minutes. Stir, set aside and allow to steep for approximately 15 minutes or more.

In an 8-cup Pyrex glass bowl, combine and mix well with a wire whisk:
¾ cup sugar
pinch of salt
⅓ cup corn starch

Add slowly to **above mixture**:
steeped blueberry water
Mix until all **ingredients** are *dissolved*. In microwave, cook on high for 3 ½minutes. Stir and

return to microwave for an additional 3 ½ minutes. When the **solution** appears thick and clear, it is ready; if not, return to the microwave for 1 ½-minute intervals until it becomes thick and clear.

Add:
3 ½ cups frozen blueberries
½ teaspoon lemon zest
2 teaspoons lemon juice
1 Tablespoon butter
Mix well and allow the **filling** to cool before pouring into the **prepared pie crust**. Top the **filling** with a **lattice crust**, pages 291–292. Sprinkle **granulated sugar** over the top. Place aluminum foil over the **pie**. Bake in hot oven for 40 minutes; remove the foil and continue to bake for 10 minutes or until crust is *lightly* browned. Cool on a wire rack.

Healthful Hints

- **Blueberries** have been found to slow down visual loss and may lower the risk of age-related macular degeneration.
- **Blueberries** are low in calories, less than 100 calories for 1 cup.
- **Blueberries** are high in magnesium, which plays an important role in bone development.

Fresh Peach Pie

In 2012 I entered this recipe into the Nebraska State Fair. When the judge was examining the pie, she said, "I don't understand how the filling has such a good color." Well, the secret is in this recipe! I received a second-place ribbon.

Have prepared:
Pie Pastry for Two Crusts, page 289; use **1 crust** to line the bottom of a 9-inch glass pie plate

In a large bowl, combine:
1 cup water
1 Tablespoon lemon juice
5 medium peaches (5 cups), peeled and thinly sliced; *reserve peelings and pits*
Allow to steep for 15 minutes to prevent **peaches** from browning. Drain **peaches** and reserve **peach water**. Set aside.

In an 8-cup Pyrex bowl, combine:
reserved peelings and pits
1 cup reserved water
Cover bowl with paper towel, microwave for 5 minutes, and allow to steep for 30 minutes. This naturally colors and flavors the **water**. This is the secret to the pie **filling**'s hue.

Pie Filling

Serves: 8
Bake; Preheated 400 degree oven
Time: 50 minute

In an 8-cup Pyrex bowl, combine:

¾ cup sugar

¼ cup corn starch

dash of salt

¼ teaspoon nutmeg

dash of cinnamon

Mix well with wire whisk.

Then *slowly* add:

1 cup prepared peach peeling water

Stir until smooth. Place in the microwave on high and cook for 5 minutes or until the **mixture** slightly thickens.

Add:

2 Tablespoons butter

Set aside and allow to cool.

Add:

prepared peaches

Mix well and pour into **prepared crust**. Top the **pie** with the **lattice crust**, pages 291–292. Place aluminum foil loosely over the **pie**. Bake in a hot oven for 40 minutes. Remove the foil and bake 10 minutes more or until the crust is *slightly* browned. Cool on a wire rack.

Helpful Hints

- **Juices**, such as **lemon** and **lime**, can help keep **peaches** from discoloring.
- **Peaches** ripen faster when placed in paper bags.
- Add sliced **peaches** to cereals or use as a topper on waffles and pancakes or as a light snack.
- When combining **peaches** and other **fruits** into a fruit salad, add a bit of **orange juice concentrate** to keep it brightly colored and tasty.

Healthful Hints

■ **Peaches** contain chemical compounds called phytochemicals, which act as antioxidants.

■ A medium **peach** has *no fat* and only 37 calories.

■ **Peaches** are a good source of vitamins C, A, and B.

Grandpa, Grandma, Frances, and Jon.

Key Lime Pie

Graham Cracker Crust

Bake: Preheated 350 degree oven
Time: 10 to 12 minutes

In a medium bowl, using a fork, combine:
1 ½ cups graham cracker crumbs
¼ cup sugar
1 teaspoon cinnamon
1/2 teaspoon nutmeg
pinch of salt
¼ cup (½ stick) butter, melted
Mix well until **crumbs** are evenly coated with the **butter**. Press into a 9- to 10-inch glass baking plate. Bake until slightly browned as directed above. Cool. Set aside.

Filling

Serves: 8
Bake: Preheated 325 degree oven
Time: 15 minutes

Place in mixer bowl with wire whip attachment, beat on high speed for eight minutes:
4 large egg yolks
zest of one lime, finely grated

Gradually add and beat seven minutes:

1 (14-ounce) can sweetened condensed milk

Add and beat on high for two minutes:

½ cup squeezed Key lime juice

Pour **filling** into **prepared pie shell**. Bake as instructed above or until **filling** is set. Refrigerate 3 hours. Serve with a **dollop of whipping cream**, page 230, and top with a thin **slice of lime**.

Helpful Hints

- It is essential to beat **ingredients** the required times. Set your timer!
- To get maximum amount of any citrus **zest**, brush both sides of the grater with a pastry brush.
- Substitute **regular lime juice** for **Key lime juice**.

Sour. This mouth-puckering sensation is caused by acids in lemons, limes, yogurt, sourdough bread, and other foods. Scientists aren't sure how it works or even its precise biological purpose.

Eva Marie Saint's Heavenly Apple Pie 'The Rest of the Story'

Eva Marie Saint ate at Nonna's more than once while filming *My Antonia* at Stuhr Museum. She and her husband came back to the kitchen and asked for the recipe for my grandma Calhoun's Sour Cream Raisin Pie. I told her it was a family secret, and I was writing a cookbook, so I couldn't give it to her. She told me she was from California and assured me that she would not give the recipe to anyone, but I had memorized the recipe and at that time had never written it down. After *Family Favorites* was published with the recipe in it, I wrote her and offered her a complimentary copy. She wrote me back after receiving the book and sent me this recipe she had submitted in 1973 to the *Kennedy Center Performing Artists Cookbook*. She wrote, "My children and grandchildren love making it; we all love it." This is her recipe and the delightful note I received.

Eva Marie Saint

Miss Saint, an academy award winning actress, has appeared at the Kennedy Center in "Lincoln Mask" and "Summer and Smoke" with much critical acclaim. She says her recipe below is "sooooo easy to make!"

HEAVENLY APPLE PIE

1 cup sugar
1 cup flour
1 stick unsalted butter
3 Pippin apples

3 tablespoons lemon juice
1 cup cold water
2 tablespoons cinnamon

1
Grease glass pie plate and preheat oven to 350°.
2
Cut thin slices of Pippin apples and soak them in cold water and lemon juice at least ten minutes.
3
Knead butter and flour together, then add sugar to dough.
4
Spread one half dough in pie dish, add sliced apples and sprinkle with cinnamon.
5
Pat bits of remaining dough on top of apple slices, then bake in oven for one hour.
Yield: one pie.

Dear Grace,
In 1973 the Kennedy Center in Washington DC published a Performing Artists Cookbook. I contributed the Heavenly Apple Pie recipe. A friend of mine kept it as a secret but her son gave it to me. My children, grandchildren are making it, we all love it —
E.M.S.

Cream Pies

My sister Mary called and said, Cordell, her grandson, wanted to have a grandmothers and aunt pie contest. Grandmothers were Mary, Carol Anderson, and myself (Aunt Fran) as contestants. All three contestants felt there was an ulterior motive in this contest and that it was a way to get three homemade pies. Mary made a rhubarb pie, and I made a coconut cream pie. Carol was to make a cherry pie but was unable to come. The judges were Cordell and his brother, Lucas. Surprise! Surprise! There was a three-way tie. Even Carol won! I think Mary's grandsons are on their way to being great politicians because this was a good example of a politically correct pie contest.

I entered this pie into the 2014 Nebraska State Fair and won a first-place blue ribbon.

Coconut Cream Pie

Have prepared:
1 single-crust pie shell, page 290

Serves: 8

In an 8-cup Pyrex glass bowl, combine and mix well:
½ cup sugar*
¼ to ⅓ cup corn starch
dash of salt

Gradually add, mixing well:

1 ½ cups milk

Microwave on high for 3 ½ minutes. Stir. Return the **mixture** to microwave and continue cooking on high in 1-minute intervals until **mixture** thickens.

Separate into 2 small bowls:

4 large eggs

Reserve **egg whites** for the **meringue** and set aside.

In the other small bowl, combine:

4 egg yolks

½ cup milk**

Mix well with wire whisk. Add **egg yolk mixture** to the **pudding**, mixing well. Microwave for 2 to 3 minutes on *high*; stir well.

Stir in:

2 Tablespoons butter

1 to 1 ½ cups flaked coconut***

Mix well and pour into **prepared pie shell**.

Top the **pie** with **meringue**, page 309. Sprinkle ⅓ **cup flaked coconut** over **meringue** before baking. Cool on a wire rack. Store in refrigerator until ready to serve.

*I reduce sugar to ½ cup because of the sugar in
the coconut.
**I have found that you can temper your eggs with cold
milk.
**I omit vanilla extract from this pie because I feel it
overpowers the coconut flavor.

Option

- **Banana Cream Pie:** Omit **coconut**. Before adding **filling**, cover the *bottom* of the **pie shell** with **3 medium sliced bananas**. Top with **meringue**, page 309.

Coconut Cream Pie.

Lucas and Cordell judging the pies.

I was the winner because Lucas asked me to dance.

Lemon Meringue Pie 🍎

When I demonstrate making cream pies using the microwave, many people are amazed at how easy it is compared to using a double boiler. (I consider the double boiler a dinosaur.) This technique goes back to the late '70s when my mother got her first microwave, an Amana Radarange, along with the *Amana Radarange Cookbook*, so I'm amazed that this is such a "revelation." These pies are quick, easy, and delicious.

Have prepared:
1 single-crust pie shell, page 290

Serves: 8

In an 8-cup Pyrex glass bowl, combine and mix well:
1 cup sugar
¼ to ⅓ cup corn starch
dash of salt

Gradually add, mixing well:
2 cups water
Microwave on high for 3 ½ minutes. Stir. Return the **mixture** to microwave and continue cooking on high in 1-minute intervals until **mixture** thickens.

Separate into 2 small bowls:
4 large eggs
Beat **egg yolks** in a small bowl with a wire whisk. Temper **egg yolks** with a small amount of **hot liquid**. Return **egg yolk mixture** to the **pudding**, mixing well. Microwave for 2 to 3 minutes on high; stir well. Reserve **egg whites** for the **meringue**, page 309.

Stir in:

1 to 2 Tablespoons lemon zest

⅓ cup lemon juice, freshly squeezed

2 Tablespoons butter

Mix well and pour into **prepared pie shell**.

Top the **pie** with **meringue**, page 309. Cool on wire rack. Store in refrigerator until ready to serve.

Helpful Hint

■   Use a pastry brush to remove any extra **lemon zest** from outside and inside of the grater.

Left to right: Katy, Mom, Mary, Dad, Jim, Joe, Grandpa, Aunt Marie, Grandma, Jon.

Meringue Fat Is the Enemy GF

Greg called one Sunday morning, pleading, "Mom, I'm making a coconut cream pie, and I have beaten these egg whites to death, but they are not getting fluffy. What should I do?" I quietly said, "Was there any egg yolk in the egg whites?" He said, "YES, just a little! That shouldn't make any difference, should it?" "Yes, it does." I told him to throw them out and start over. The enemy of whipped egg whites is fat. Just a little egg yolk, fat, butter, or oil in the bowl will keep your meringue from forming at all. Rule number one: You need to take special care when separating eggs to avoid mixing in any yolk with the whites. Check the Helpful Hints.

Bake: Preheated 400 degree oven
Time: 8 to 10 minutes

In a mixing bowl with a wire whip attachment, beat until *soft* peaks form:
3 to 4 egg whites
¼ to ½ teaspoon cream of tartar
dash of salt
½ teaspoon vanilla extract

Gradually add, a little at a time:
½ cup sugar
Beat until all **sugar** is dissolved and *stiff* peaks form. Using a spatula, spread meringue over hot pie filling. Push the meringue into the tips of the pastry's edge so the pie is completely sealed. Then make swirls and peaks in the meringue for an attractive top.

Bake as directed above or until meringue is golden brown. Cool gradually on a wire rack in a slightly warm place. A chill can cause the meringue to fall.

Helpful Hints

- Separate your **eggs** when they are cold. Be sure the **egg whites** are free of any **yolk**.
- Beat your **egg whites** at room temperature.
- Dip the knife in water (don't wipe it off) before cutting each slice of a **meringue pie**.

Still have problems with your meringue weeping? Here are some remedies:

- Add ¼ **teaspoon corn starch** to the **egg whites**, **salt**, and **cream of tartar**. Follow above instructions.
- If **meringue** shrinks, beat **meringue** until *stiff* peaks form and **sugar** is completely dissolved.
- If your **meringue** beads or weeps, check oven temperature to see if it is *too low*.
- If your **meringue** leaks, spread **meringue** on the **filling** while it is still hot, sealing it *well* to the edges of the pastry.

Greg Schaffer.

Salads & Sandwiches

Glossary

chop. To cut into coarse or fine pieces with a knife or chopper.

crisp. To make firm and brittle by placing vegetables in very cold water or in a cold, moist place.

cube. To cut into equal, six-sided pieces, ¼ to ½ inch in size.

dice. To cut into equal, six-sided pieces, smaller than cubes, probably no more than ¼ inch maximum in size.

grate. To rub food against a grater to tear it into bits and shreds of various sizes.

greens. Any of the lettuces or other leafy green vegetables that often form the basis of a salad.

mayonnaise. A creamy homemade or commercial dressing composed of egg yolks and vinegar or lemon juice. Differentiated from commercial salad dressing such as Miracle Whip by its more piquant taste.

pare. To cut off the skin or outer covering of a fruit or vegetable, such as an apple or potato, with a knife.

peel. To remove the skin or outer covering of a fruit or vegetable, such as a tomato, peach, or banana, with a knife.

piquant. Pleasantly sharp, stimulating to taste, and appetizing.

shred. To tear or cut into long, narrow pieces.

toss. To combine ingredients with a repeated lifting motion.

vinaigrette. A salad dressing basically composed of vegetable or olive oil, vinegar, and seasonings.

The Proper Way to Make and Dress an Italian Salad

To make a true homemade Italian dressing, remember the vital ingredients, oil and vinegar, separate. Shaking the ingredients in a bottle or blending them will emulsify them somewhat. But the *first part* of your dressing will invariably have *more oil and less vinegar*, and the *second part* will have *more vinegar and less oil*. As stated in most Italian cookbooks, the true and proper Italian dressing is a process, not an item; a verb, not a noun. It is not taking a salad dressing and pouring it over a salad; it is central to and an active part of putting a salad together. I learned this early in my married life.

When Dave and I were newlyweds, my cooking bible was *Cooking for Two*. It had very simple recipes using canned soups, packaged ingredients, and helpful hints for a tasty meal. Of course, I was trying to impress my husband with my culinary skills, and he seldom complained except for my Italian dressing. Dave said, "I don't know what it is, but your dressing just doesn't taste like your mom's."

So I went home to Mother, and she instructed me on "how to dress an Italian salad." My first mistake was using vegetable oil. My second mistake... I used garlic salt. Can you believe it? Me? The lover of garlic in all things who now never uses garlic salt or powder?

The only ingredients needed are **extra virgin olive oil**, **freshly squeezed garlic**, **apple-cider vinegar**, and **salt** (**pepper** can be added if needed)—but they are absolutely essential. You must use these exact ingredients. Proportions are something you will learn. I have broken the process down into steps to help you get started. Getting the desired taste is up to you.

Italian Salad 🍎 ♥ GF

Serves: 6 to 8

Wash **greens** ahead of time. Place them in a colander and allow them to drain well because *water will dilute the flavor* of the **dressing**. Place the **lettuce** in the refrigerator to crisp, about 1 hour.

Chop:
1 bunch or head of lettuce

Add, mostly for color:
1 small carrot, grated
1 small wedge red cabbage, coarsely chopped

Add:
1 garlic clove, freshly squeezed
Mix **ingredients** well and place in a resealable bag or container; refrigerate until ready to use. This allows the **garlic** to permeate the **chopped greens** and eventually flavor the **dressing**. It also helps to preserve the **greens**, keeping them fresh, crisp, and green.

Just before serving, place the **prepared salad ingredients** in a large bowl. Sprinkle *lightly* with:
salt

Add in a *thin* stream (just enough to coat the **salad greens** and **vegetables**):
extra virgin olive oil
Toss gently; do not overuse because this will make the **lettuce** soggy.

Add:

apple-cider vinegar

This **ingredient** should be added sparingly, as you want just a hint of tartness, not a **salad** with bite. Again, toss the **salad** gently.

Taste! Taste! And taste again! It is important to taste after each addition and correction.

- If **salad** is too dry, add, very sparingly, **more olive oil**.
- If you want more **garlic** flavor, add **another clove of garlic**. Do not overdo; you can add more later, if necessary.
- If the **salad** is too tart, sprinkle with a little **salt**.
- To increase the tartness, add, by drops, **more vinegar**.

When you are satisfied with the flavor, your **salad** is ready to serve.

The mistake many people make with **dressings** is adding an array of **seasonings**. More is not always better. Don't drown the wonderful **oil** flavor. Remember, **seasonings** are to *enhance* the **oil**.

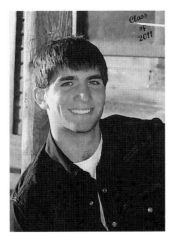

Riccardo Parigi, Mary's foreign-exchange student.

Salad Mix 🍎 ♥ GF

It is so convenient to run to the supermarket to buy a salad mix for dinner.... It's expensive, too. The most reasonably priced salad mix is with iceberg lettuce with a sprinkling of carrots and red cabbage. My suggestion is to buy a head of romaine lettuce, a bag of carrots, and a small head of red cabbage, and make your own mix at a fraction of the cost. Follow these simple instructions, and you will never buy a mix again.

Serves: 6–8

Wash the **leaves** (discarding any wilted or discolored **leaves**) and place in a colander:
1 head romaine lettuce
Place in refrigerator for ½ hour. This crisps the **leaves**.

Prepare:
1 medium carrot, peeled and grated
1 small slice of red cabbage, diced (you don't need a lot)

Tear or cut into bite-size pieces:
freshened romaine lettuce leaves
Place into a large plastic bag.

Add:
prepared carrots
prepared red cabbage
1 garlic clove, freshly squeezed
Place into a tie or Ziploc plastic bag. Shake *well* and refrigerate until ready to use.

Options

- For variety, choose **lacy-leafed escarole**, **endive**, and **young spinach**.
- **Scallions**, **leeks**, and **onions**, thinly sliced ... or **zucchini**, **cucumbers**, or **celery**, finely sliced or chopped.
- Small flowerets of **cauliflower** and/or **broccoli**, **chopped bell peppers**, **olives**, etc.
- **Tomatoes** ... add just before serving because this juicy **vegetable** will make the **salad** soggy.
- Substitute **natural wine** or **balsamic vinegars** for all or part of the **apple-cider vinegar**. Use **salt and pepper** to individual taste.

Helpful Hints

- Select **salad greens** with care; discard any *wilted* or *discolored* **leaves**.
- **Leaf lettuce**: Wash each **leaf** separately, place in colander, and refrigerate for ½ hour. This freshens and crisps the **leaves**.
- Wash **iceberg (head) lettuce** *core end down* in colander and refrigerate for 1 hour before cutting; remove the core and tear or cut into bite-size pieces.
- **Cabbage** and **lettuce** should be heavy in proportion to size and solid to touch.

Grape Berry Gelatin ● ♥ GF

This is one of our favorite gelatin salads and a great choice for almost any diet because you don't need to add any extra honey or sugar. I received many positive comments from dieters and diabetics who said this recipe fit their diets because of the use of unsweetened fruit juice; plus, they liked the tart taste better than the sweet taste of regular Jell-O. And with the additional benefits of no artificial colors, flavors, or sweeteners, they were excited!

Serves: 6

In a 9 × 9 serving bowl, add:
¼ cup cold water

Sprinkle over **water**:
1 package Knox unflavored gelatin
Allow it to stand for 2 minutes until the **liquid** absorbs the **gelatin**.

Add to the softened gelatin:
¾ cup hot, unsweetened Concord grape juice
Stir the **gelatin** until it dissolves completely.

Add and stir well:
additional cup cold unsweetened grape juice

1 cup IQF raspberries*
1 cup fresh cut strawberries**
1 cup IQF or fresh blueberries
Stir well and place in refrigerator until the **gelatin** sets, approximately 2 to 3 hours.

Options

- Add **1 to 2 Tablespoons honey or stevia** for a sweeter taste.
- Use **other flavors of all-natural juices**, such as **raspberry**, **cherry**, **strawberry**, and **assorted berries**. I find a good assortment of **regular and frozen juices** from Old Orchard.
- Add **beet or cherry juice** for color.

Healthful Hints

- Does **grape juice** offer the same heart benefits as red wine? Some research studies suggest that **red and purple grape juice** may provide some of the same heart benefits, minus the alcohol. This includes lowering LDL (bad) cholesterol, reducing the chance of blood clots, and maintaining a healthy blood pressure.
- **Raspberries** contain about 10 times more antioxidants than tomatoes. The high levels of antioxidants in **raspberries** make it a great cancer-fighting **fruit**.
- The heart shape of the **strawberry** is the first clue that this **fruit** is good for you; it protects your heart, increasing your HDL (good) cholesterol, lowering your blood pressure, and possibly guarding against cancer.

*Use frozen raspberries in this salad; fresh raspberries
may lose their shape when added to the grape juice.
**Use fresh strawberries in this salad: frozen get mushy
and do not retain their shape.

Orange, Banana, and Walnut Gelatin  GF

This was my father's favorite gelatin salad. What could be healthier for you than a salad with walnuts, bananas, and orange juice without any artificial colors or flavors? By using unsweetened orange juice, it is another salad that is a good option for a diabetic or someone who is on a weight-loss diet.

Have prepared:
1 (12-ounce) can orange juice, diluted according to directions

In a 9 × 9 serving dish add:
¼ cup cold water

Sprinkle over water:
1 package Knox unflavored gelatin
Let stand for 2 minutes to allow the **liquid** to absorb the **gelatin**.

Add to the **softened gelatin**:
¾ cup hot orange juice
Stir well until **gelatin** is dissolved.

Then add:
1 cup cold orange juice
Stir well and place in the refrigerator for approximately 20 to 30 minutes until it begins to slightly set.

Add to the **cooled gelatin**:
3 bananas, sliced

½ **cup walnuts, coarsely chopped**

¼ **cup celery, thinly sliced**

Place in refrigerator until the **gelatin** sets, approximately 2 to 3 hours.

Option

- 🐝 For a sweeter taste, add **1 to 2 Tablespoons of honey or stevia** to the **softened gelatin** before adding the **hot orange juice**.

Healthful Hints

- **Oranges** are juicy and sweet and are known for their high concentration of vitamin C.
- **Bananas** are one of our best sources of potassium, an essential mineral for maintaining blood pressure and heart function.
- **Walnuts** contain the most antioxidants of all nuts and are the richest in omega-3 fatty acids.

Banana-Walnut Gelatin Salad in Orange Juice.

Grape Berry Gelatin.

Cranberry Sauce and Jelly 🍎❤GF

When Thanksgiving and Christmas are near, you see sacks of cranberries in the produce department. Dishes using cranberries are usually a must for holiday dinners, whether homemade or canned. The jelly or sauce can be made several days before the dinner, and the recipes are rather easy and foolproof. Cranberries can be frozen, so buy extra packages and eat them throughout the year. They are good, easy to make, and healthy.

Whole Cranberry Sauce

In an 8-cup Pyrex glass bowl, bring to a boil in microwave on *high* setting:

1 cup water
1 cup sugar
Stir well until all **sugar** is dissolved, approximately 3 minutes.

Add:
1 (12-ounce) package fresh cranberries
Microwave on high for 4 to 5 minutes until **cranberries** burst. Remove, let cool for 10 minutes; place in a serving (Grandmother's crystal) bowl. The **cranberry sauce** will thicken as it cools. Cover and refrigerate until serving time.

Cranberry Jelly

In a serving (Grandma's crystal) bowl, combine:
¼ cup cold water
1 package Knox unflavored gelatin
Sprinkle **gelatin** over **water**; allow **gelatin** to softened, approximately 2 minutes.

Follow recipe for Cranberry Sauce, page 322.

After **cranberries** have cooked, press the **cranberries** through a wire strainer with the back of a big spoon, frequently scraping the outside of the strainer until no pulp is remaining. Allow **cranberries** to cool about 10 minutes, pour in prepared bowl, and stir to combine **cranberries** with **softened gelatin**. Cover and refrigerate until serving time.

Options

- Substitute **orange juice** for **water**.
- Add **pecans**, **orange zest**, and/or **celery** for a different taste.

Healthful Hints

- **Cranberries** are good for the heart. They help to lower bad cholesterol levels and help to prevent plaque from forming on the arterial wall.
- Studies show that **cranberries** are good for the brain and can help to improve memory.
- For optimum health benefits, consume **fresh cranberries**, make your own **juice**, or buy **unsweetened 100% pure cranberry juice**.

Blueberry Orange Salad 🍎 ♥ GF

Not only is this salad delicious and healthy, it has a beautiful presentation. Many times the foods that have the best eye appeal are the easiest to make.

Blueberry Vinaigrette

Makes: 2 cups

In a food processor, combine;
1 cup extra virgin olive
1 cup frozen blueberries
1 Tablespoon Dijon mustard
2 Tablespoons brown sugar
¾ teaspoon salt
½ teaspoon white pepper
½ teaspoon paprika
Process until **mixture** is smooth. Chill for 1 hour.

Salad

Serves: 8

Toss with **1 ½ cups dressing**:
2 pounds salad greens
Divide between 8 salad plates

On each plate of **greens**, add:

½ **cup (4 cups needed) canned mandarin oranges**

½ **cup (4 cups needed) fresh blueberries**

Spread *evenly* over the top of **greens**.

Sprinkle over top of **fruits**:

¼ **cup granola (2 cups needed)**, page 240

Drizzle remaining **salad dressing** over tops of **salads**. Serve immediately.

Healthful Hints

- **Blueberries** are high in fiber: 1 cup contains 4 grams of fiber.
- **Blueberries** may help reverse age-related memory loss, thanks to the antioxidants called flavonoids.
- **Blueberries** have a favorable impact on blood sugar regulation.

Beet Walnut Salad 🍎 ♥ 🐝 GF

When our son, Greg, graduated from law school in California, we celebrated by dining at a wonderful restaurant in Santa Monica; on the menu was a beet salad. I have always liked any kind of beets—canned or fresh, hot or cold, pickled, buttered, or Harvard style—so this was a salad I wanted, and it was indeed wonderful. By tasting and examining it and asking a few questions of our waitress, I was able to develop my own version. If you like beets, you won't be disappointed.

Have prepared:
beets

Bake: Preheated 400 degree oven
Time: 30 to 45 minutes

On a baking sheet, place:
3 medium beets, scrubbed and trimmed
Bake as instructed above. Cool, peel, dice, and set aside.

Vinaigrette

In a food processor, add:
½ cup apple-cider vinegar
2 Tablespoons honey
2 Tablespoons roasted and diced beets
1 teaspoon mustard
¾ teaspoon salt
Process on *high*.

While processing, gradually add:

1 cup extra virgin olive oil

Transfer into a bottle and refrigerate until 30 minutes before serving.

Salad

Serves: 8

In medium bowl, combine:

remaining diced beets

1 crisp, tart apple, unpeeled and diced

Mix well; set aside.

In large bowl, combine:

1 pound mixed greens

1 head romaine lettuce, coarsely chopped

3 green onions (some green tops), finely chopped

Toss **greens** well with:

1 cup of dressing

Divide between 8 salad plates.

On each plate of **greens**, place:

prepared diced beets and apple mixture, divided equally

1 Tablespoon crumbled bleu cheese

1 Tablespoon walnut pieces, roasted

Shake **vinaigrette** well. Drizzle lightly over **salad**.

Serve immediately. Remaining **dressing** can be stored in refrigerator for several weeks.

Abuela's Chicken Potato Salad 🍎 ♥ GF

Potato salad is always a must when having a picnic. In *Family Favorites*, it was my traditional potato salad that my family loves (page 296), and Dave's Uncle Benny's Hot German Potato Salad was another favorite (page 298). While celebrating my sister Mary and brother-in-law Laurel Goddard's anniversary, my niece, Alison (Calhoun) Barrios, made her mother-in-law's Venezuelan potato salad. The day it was made, the salad was good, but the following day, it was delicious. Some foods, such as meatballs, chili, and potato salad, need extra time for ingredients to blend. So this is a good example of a recipe you can make a day before the big event... it is worth all the time and effort. Enjoy!

In a medium sauce pan, over *medium* heat, combine:

3 cups water

½ teaspoon salt

¼ teaspoon tarragon

3 chicken breasts

Cook until **chicken** is tender enough to shred, approximately 45 to 60 minutes. Remove **chicken** from **water**, set aside, and allow **chicken breasts** to cool. Reserve water.

Peel:

6 to 8 medium red potatoes, evenly diced

3 to 4 medium carrots, coarsely chopped

To reserved chicken broth, add:

prepared potatoes

prepared carrots

Cook until **vegetables** are *al dente* (they should have a bite)*

In a large bowl, add:

shredded chicken breast

Layer over top of **chicken**:

¼ to ½ head shredded green cabbage

Drain above vegetables* and place on top of:

cabbage and chicken

The **cabbage** will cook just enough from the steam of the **vegetables**.

Add:

1 medium vidalia onion, finely chopped

Cover bowl with a lid. Set aside.

In a small bowl, blender, or food processor, add:

1 cup mayonnaise

¼ to ½ cup vinegar (your choice)**

⅛ to ¼ cup canola or extra virgin olive oil

1 clove garlic, freshly squeezed ***

1 ½ teaspoons salt

¾ teaspoon oregano

¼ teaspoon cumin

¼ teaspoon allspice

¼ teaspoon curry

Mix or blend well and pour over **salad** ingredients. Mix thoroughly.

*Save and freeze vegetable broth for another recipe.

**Do not use balsamic vinegar.

***Alison uses 1 Tablespoon Adobo spice for

individual spices.

In an 8-cup Pyrex bowl , microwave on high until crispy:

1 pound nitrate/nitrite-free bacon, thinly sliced

Transfer **bacon** onto a paper towel to drain and cool.

Before ready to serve, rinse with **warm water**:

1 (12-ounce) bag frozen sweet peas

Drain and add to **salad** and mix thoroughly

Add:

prepared bacon

Mix thoroughly and refrigerate for at least 1 hour or overnight for the **ingredients** to blend. It tastes the best a day or two later.

Luis and Alison Barrios with Luis
Christopher and Kiara Vita

Carbonara Pasta Salad

Wednesday's papers have the supermarkets' specials and also a section of the paper with recipes. One Wednesday when reading the paper, this recipe caught my eye, "Pasta Carbonara Salad." Spaghetti carbonara was a favorite with my customers, so I read further to see how this salad was made. Lately, I've noticed most recipes in the newspapers (we get two dailies) use "trendy" ingredients, the kind we usually don't have in our cupboards. So, I ventured down to our supermarket and checked to see how much this would cost me if I were to make this salad with the ingredients they suggested. It was a whopping $30 salad. Too much for me! So I revised this recipe to use the ingredients I had on hand and must say it was a delicious salad and at a fraction of the cost. I had all the ingredients listed in this recipe except the nitrate/nitrite-free bacon that cost $6.96 for 12 ounces. That was my only cost. **In this recipe, the original ingredients and their prices are listed in parentheses.**

Bring a large pan of **water** to a boil and add:

1 teaspoon salt

1 (16-ounce) box rotini pasta

Cook according to package directions. Drain well, then spread on baking sheet with sides to cool.

In a 8-cup Pyrex glass bowl, microwave on high until crispy:

9 ounces (9 slices) nitrate/nitrite-free bacon, thinly cut* (9 oz. pancetta, $14.95 or $4.99/3 oz.)
Transfer **bacon** onto paper towel to drain and cool.

*Fresh bacon can be thinly cut using kitchen scissors.

Frozen bacon can be thinly cut with a knife.

Add to **bacon grease** and microwave until tender about 4 to 6 minutes:
1 cup frozen sweet peas (fresh peas) (fresh peas were not available)
Transfer **peas** to plate with **bacon**.

In a blender or food processor, combine to make **dressing**:
3 egg yolks
3 cloves garlic, freshly squeezed
1 Tablespoon mustard (dijon mustard, $2.79)
2 Tablespoons apple-cider vinegar (white balsamic vinegar, $5.49)
1 Tablespoon lemon juice
Process **mixture** until combined.

Then add in a *slow* stream:
½ cup canola oil (mild olive oil, $8.99)

Season to taste with:
salt and pepper

In a large bowl, combine :
cooled pasta
crisp bacon
prepared peas
above dressing
1 cup Parmesan cheese, freshly grated
½ cup white or yellow onion, finely chopped (scallions, $2.98 per pound)
Mix well, cover, and refrigerate for at least 1 hour.

(Total original ingredients: $33.24)

Before serving, microwave until warm and add to **salad**:
1 cup half-and-half
Sprinkle with **extra Parmesan cheese** if needed. Serve immediately.

Reuben and Runza Sandwiches

I can't remember which one was eaten first by our family, but they remain favorites and are a must whenever we get together. Both are closely tied to Nebraska culture... The Reuben originated in Omaha, and the Runza was brought to Nebraska by German immigrants and adopted by Nebraskans of all nationalities.

Reuben Sandwich

There are several claims as to who invented the Reuben Sandwich. One in particular revolves around a delicatessen in New York City. However, the story that seems most authentic, particularly to Nebraskans, and has some documentation, comes from Omaha, Nebraska.

It seems an Omaha grocer, Reuben Kulakofisky, is generally credited with inventing the Reuben. From 1920 to 1935, he was part of a group who met weekly to play poker at Omaha's premier hotel, the Blackstone. They nicknamed themselves the "committee" and included the hotel's owner, Charles Schimmel. They enjoyed eating at these gatherings, and the sandwich may have been a group effort.

It first gained local fame when Schimmel put it on the Blackstone's lunch menu. It was also served in another Schimmel hotel, Lincoln's famous Cornhusker. The only known fact about the Reuben is its appearance on the 1937 Cornhusker Hotel menu. It also won a national food contest, entered by a former hotel employee.

Today you will find the Reuben on many restaurant menus. One complaint I have about restaurant Reubens is they use too much corned beef and sauerkraut in their sandwiches. I like a sandwich that is easy to eat and doesn't make a mess because they are too thick. I prefer a sandwich where you can taste the melted cheese as well as the corned beef and kraut. If you're not in agreement, you can change the ingredients according to your taste. Enjoy this wonderful sandwich.

Serves: 6

On a large skillet or griddle, place:
6 slices rye bread lightly buttered on one side (buttered side down)

Spread on nonbuttered side:
Thousand Island Dressing, page 344

Layer on each slice of **bread**:
1 slice Swiss cheese
2 Tablespoons sauerkraut, drained
2 slices corned beef, thinly sliced
Cover each **sandwich** with a second slice of **lightly buttered rye bread** with **Thousand Island dressing** spread on the inside.

Turn griddle on *medium* heat and grill the sandwich until lightly browned; then turn the sandwich over and grill the other side until lightly browned. Serve with a **kosher dill pickle**.

Bierocks (Runzas)

In Nebraska and neighboring states, there is a popular and traditional German yeast dough pocket, baked with a ground beef and cabbage filling, known as a "runza." It has its origins in Russia, where the Germans emigrated at the invitation of the Russian czar, who wanted to use their farming skills to cultivate the fertile Volga River and Black Sea regions. The Russians promised the Germans, or Russia Deutchlanders (as they were known), they could keep their ethnicity, live autonomously, and not be required to serve in the Russian army. When the Russians reneged on these promises, many Germans left Russia, and many came to the United States, particularly the Midwest. They brought their runza-type sandwich to Nebraska, especially those who had lived around the Volga River. In 1949 Sarah "Sally" Everett and her brother Alex Brening started the Runza Hut on a dirt road on the edge of Lincoln, Nebraska. In 1966 her son Don Everett began franchising the Runza trademark and now has more than 70 stores. They are also a popular vendor at football games in Memorial Stadium at the

University of Nebraska in Lincoln. The name Runza has been copyrighted, but many a Nebraska cook, German or not, has a favorite runza-type recipe. There are many claims on the Internet as to what is the authentic recipe. My first recipe came from Barb Meyer, a wonderful cook and friend; this is her recipe I am using.

A runza, also called a bierock, is a yeast dough bread pocket with a filling consisting of hamburger, onions, cabbage, and seasonings. They are baked in various shapes; in Nebraska, the runza is usually baked in a rectangular shape. The bierocks of Kansas, on the other hand, are generally baked in the shape of a bun. While on the Feingold diet, the runza was a mainstay for our school lunches. With the advent of the microwave oven in the late '70s, runzas could be easily reheated at school. To have plenty of runzas for the week, I usually doubled my recipe in order to have enough to freeze to eat at a later date. You can use any yeast bread recipe or you can buy frozen bread dough. I suggest my recipe for White Whole-Wheat Bread; using this recipe, you are getting all the nutrients of whole wheat.

Makes: 24
Bake: Preheated 350 degree oven
Time: 20 to 25 minutes

Have prepared:
1 recipe White Whole-Wheat Bread (dough), page 128, or **Basic White Bread (dough)**, page 126 in *Family Favorites*

In a large skillet, add:
2 pounds (80/20) hamburger
1 medium white or yellow onion, finely chopped
salt and pepper to taste
Sauté until brown and no longer pink. Drain off the grease, then return **beef mixture** to the pan.

Cover **beef mixture** with:
1 medium head green cabbage, finely chopped
Cook until cabbage is done, approximately 30 to 45 minutes. Set aside to cool.

On a **floured** surface, roll out **bread dough** to approximately ½-inch thickness and cut into 5 × 5-inch squares. Place ½ **cup hamburger mixture** in the center of the square and fold by bringing each corner of the square to the center; seal edges. Place the sealed side down on a lightly **greased** baking sheet. Allow the **dough** to rise for the second time. Bake as instructed above.

Option

- **Cheese Runza:** In the center of the **dough**, add **1 folded slice of white American cheese**, then add ½ **cup cabbage/hamburger mixture**. Fold, seal, and bake as instructed above.

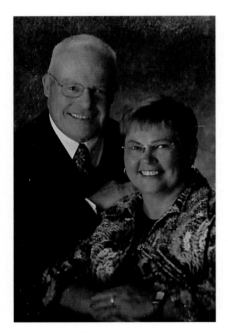

Jerry and Barb Meyer.

Grand Island's Fifties Favorites

Kathy Grasmick Patton posted these two recipes on Facebook in a special section called, "If you grew up in Grand Island, NE, you remember…"

In the '50s there were two drive-ins the teen-agers frequented the most, Nifty's, on South Locust, and Hight's at Five Points near Grand Island Senior High. After school and on weekends these places were hopping with '50s music, carhops, and their staple burger, fries, and malts. One of the most prized jobs as a teenager was to be a carhop at the Nifty because you were where the action was. The Nifty burger was crumbled ground beef and was served on a hamburger bun with mustard and dill pickles. Hight's burger was a Bar-B-Beef recipe that was served on a coney bun. Both were wonderful if you could afford the quarter to buy one. When you were a senior in high school and had a weekly allowance of one dollar, you had to choose carefully. But for all of us who were born and raised here, what a delight it was to get these recipes. Several class reunion organizers have said they will be using these recipes for their class reunions. Thank you, Kathy!

Nifty Burgers

Serves: 24

In a 6-quart or larger Crock-Pot, combine and cook on *high* setting:
5 pounds (80/15) ground beef
1 large white or yellow onion, finely chopped
Brown and crumble **ground beef** and drain off **fat**.*

*Place drained juices in a small bowl, cool, and remove
fat. Return juices to meat.

Turn the Crock-Pot on *low* setting and add:

¼ **cup mustard**

¼ **cup horseradish**

¼ **cup Worcestershire sauce**

½ **cup ketchup**

1 **teaspoon salt**

1 **cup water**

Stir well, then cover and let simmer for 30 minutes, stirring occasionally. The Nifties seem to taste better if they steam all day on the *low* or *warm* setting.

To serve: Use a large, serrated spoon and press the hot, crumbly **ground beef** to remove most of the **juices** and place on a **hamburger bun**. Top with **mustard** and **dill pickle slices**.

Hight's Drive Inn Bar-B-Beef

Because many people need to restrict their salt intake, I have revised this recipe using fresh and natural seasonings. For those of you who are interested in the original seasonings, I have included the recipe on the next page under "Original Seasonings."

Serves: 8 to 10

In a Crock-Pot, combine

2 **pounds (85/15) ground beef**

1 **clove garlic, freshly squeezed**

¼ **cup (½) medium yellow or white onion, finely chopped**

Brown and crumble **beef mixture**.

Sprinkle on **browned ground beef** and mix well:

⅓ **cup Cream of Wheat**

1 **teaspoon salt**

1 ½ teaspoons chili powder

¼ teaspoon cayenne (red) pepper

Adjust **seasonings** according to taste.

In a medium bowl, combine and mix well:

2 cups water

½ cup tomato paste

¼ cup barbecue sauce

Combine with **ground beef**. Let simmer for 30 minutes and serve hot on **coney buns**.

Original Seasonings

In small bowl, combine and mix well:

⅓ cup salt

1 cup chili powder

3 teaspoons garlic salt

4 teaspoons onion salt

½ teaspoon cayenne salt

Add **2 to 4 teaspoons of above mixture** to the **ground beef**. Store **remaining seasonings** in container with lid and use as needed.

Barbecued beef presentation.

Nifty Burger presentation.

Grilled Cheese Sandwich

The grilled cheese sandwich is one of many classic comfort foods, usually served with a bowl of Cream of Tomato Soup. It is one of the first and easiest grilled sandwiches made.

Preheat a skillet or grill on *medium* heat.

Generously **butter** one side of a **slice of bread**. Place bread *butter side down* and add:
1 slice cheese (your choice)

Butter a *second slice of bread* on one side and place on the top of the **sandwich** *butter side up*. Grill until lightly browned.

Flip over and continue to grill until the **cheese** is melted.

See photo on page 359.

Mustard 🍎♥🐝GF

One afternoon there was a package on our front porch. The package was from Bob Thomazin, a classmate from high school. In the package was a jar of homemade mustard, gourmet popcorn, and a very nice note. The mustard had some zing and was very tasty. When I sent him a thank-you note, I asked for the recipe. Here it is!

Dressing 🍎 GF

Ranch Dressing

At dinner time whenever we are at Tony and Cari's home, I notice the first item on the table is ranch dressing. They use it on everything: salads, dipping their fresh vegetables, french fries, and chips. I remember in the early '70s Hidden Valley Ranch Dressing was the rage. It came in seasoning packets that were mixed with buttermilk and mayonnaise; it later became a bottled dressing. It is mainly used for salads and commonly used as a dip for carrots, broccoli, chips, chicken wings, etc. I made this dressing, one with buttermilk and the other with soured milk, and had a taste test for Dave and Sandie, my editor. They picked the dressing made with soured milk. That recipe is less expensive and will be our recipe, but you have the option to use buttermilk.

Makes: 2 cups

In 1-cup Pyrex cup, combine:
½ cup (whole or 2%) milk
½ teaspoon vinegar or lemon juice
Set aside for at least 5 minutes.

In medium bowl, using a wire whisk, combine:
½ cup sour cream
½ cup mayonnaise
1 Tablespoon white or yellow onions, finely chopped
1 Tablespoon parsley
1 garlic clove, freshly squeezed
¼ teaspoon black pepper, coarsely ground
prepared milk

Mix well and pour into a covered container. Refrigerate.

Options

- Substitute **buttermilk** for **soured milk**.
- Add or substitute **chives** for **onions**.
- Add **dill**, **paprika**, or **ground mustard** for added flavor.

Honey Mustard Dressing 🍎🐛GF

Honey Mustard Dressing is used for salads and as a dip for vegetables, just as Ranch Dressing is. It is especially good on ham and chicken as a glaze. It has that wonderful sweet-sour taste that most people enjoy.

Makes: 2 cups

In medium bowl, using wire whisk, combine:

1 cup mayonnaise
⅓ cup honey
⅓ cup prepared mustard, page 341
1 ½ Tablespoons lemon juice
Mix well and pour into a covered container. Refrigerate.

Thousand Island Dressing 🍎GF

Makes: 2 cups

In a small bowl, combine:
1 cup salad dressing
2 Tablespoons chili sauce
¼ cup sweet pickle relish
1 teaspoon paprika
Keep any unused portion refrigerated

Options

- Substitute **ketchup** for **chili sauce.**
- Add **1 Tablespoon bell pepper** and/or **1 ½ Tablespoons chopped onions**.
- Prior to serving, add a **chopped, hard-cooked egg** to the **dressing**. Chill any unused portion.

French Dressing 🍎GF

Makes: 1 ½ cups

In a blender, combine:
1 cup extra virgin olive oil
¼ cup apple-cider vinegar
¼ cup lemon juice
½ teaspoon salt
½ teaspoon dry mustard
½ teaspoon paprika
Beat all **ingredients** together and keep in a covered bottle. Shake well again to mix before using as it separates.

Soups

Glossary

"Stock is to soup what flour is to cake."

broth *or* **stock.** A flavorful liquid made from cooking water with meat, chicken, fish, or vegetables and seasonings. It can be strained and served without further additions or it can be the basis of other soups, containing additional ingredients, e.g., noodles, rice, etc. It can also be used in gravies and stews and to enhance the flavor of many dishes. Broth or stock can be either bouillon or consommé:

> **bouillon.** Brown broth or stock, usually made from beef, 2/3 meat to 1/3 bone. Browning the meat before adding the liquid gives it additional flavor and color.

> **consommé.** White broth or stock, usually made from chicken, turkey, veal, or fish.

> **jellied bouillon or consommé.** Homemade bouillon or consommé will usually jell if chilled overnight. One to two teaspoons of jellied bouillon or consommé combined with one cup of water equals one cup of broth.

bisque. A rich cream soup usually containing vegetables or shellfish.

borscht. A soup of Russian origin made mainly from beets.

chowder. A thick soup usually containing onions, potatoes, corn, tomatoes, and often milk and shellfish.

Crock-Pot. A trademark used for an electric cooker that maintains a low temperature. This trademark often appears, incorrectly, without a hyphen in print. (See *slow cooker*.)

degrease. To remove fats from the surface of stock, soups, or stews, usually by cooling in the refrigerator so that the fats rise to the top and harden for easy removal.

roux. A cooked mixture of melted butter or other fat and flour used for thickening sauces and soups.

simmer. To remain at or just below the boiling point, usually forming tiny bubbles.

slow cooker. A countertop electrical appliance that maintains a relatively low temperature for many hours, allowing unattended cooking of pot roast, stew, and other long-cooking dishes.

Soup

A group of hunters from Florida come every October to hunt pheasants at my brother-in-law Laurel and sister Mary Goddard's ranch in northwest Kansas; Mary has a hunting business called Seven 2 Bar Adventures. Every year she has asked me to come and help her cook. Mary and I went to Italy in 1990, and Mary has gone back numerous times; she also has had several foreign-exchange students from Italy. When the hunters come, she wants to fix real Italian meals that include many courses. The day starts out with a hearty hunter's breakfast ... eggs, bacon, pancakes, etc., then a hearty lunch prepared by Carol Anderson using all of her culinary skills of a rancher's wife, and finally in the evening a true Italian dinner with many different courses. It begins with an appetizer (antipasto), first plate (soup, pasta, or risotto), second plate or main course (meat and vegetables), then dessert, and finally to cap the dinner off, a liquor, such as grappa or lemoncello. In 2013 Mary and I had to also do the lunches, and I suggested that we have a lighter meal such as soup and sandwiches. Our soups were chili and chicken and barley; the sandwiches were made with ham and beef salad on potato rolls. For dessert we made an assortment of homemade cookies. When the hunters came in, Jorge exclaimed, "Soup! I've been thinking of soup all morning long. You must have read my mind." The guys were all happy to sit down to a lighter meal.

Soup is as old as the art of cooking. In fact, the word *restaurant* originally meant *soup*. It came from the French word *restorier*, meaning to restore. In 16th-century France people believed soup had restorative powers. An enterprising chef painted a sign over his door, "Restaurer," to tell people he served soup. In time, of course, restaurant came to mean a place where all kinds of food were served.

We still think of soup as having restorative or curative powers. Soup serves two purposes: It stimulates the appetite and provides wholesome nourishment. Italian and Jewish mothers, in particular, have long believed that chicken soup has medicinal powers. Following that tradition, I always made chicken soup for my family when they were ill.

When our family was young, I made the broth the traditional way in a large kettle, simmering it for hours. Then came the Crock-Pot. I would fill it with water, add meat or chicken with seasonings, and let it cook all day. Then I would cool it overnight before refrigerating.

Now I make broths in the microwave. Simple. It is ready sooner and is so basic to cooking that it is in my Staples section, pages 13–16. Also in Staples are other sources of chicken flavoring, such as chicken fat and gelatin that are drippings from a roasted chicken, or beef drippings or other meat stock from drippings of ground beef or beef roasts. Whenever you have a recipe calling for broth or stock, just use these recipes or the supply you may have made to keep on hand.

Back, left to right: Fran and Byran Frates. Front, left to right: Jorge Hernandez, Robert Day, Tom Braxton, and Nacho.

Chicken and Barley Soup 🍎 ♥ GF

My favorite soup was beef and barley. When I was young, Mom would always have Campbell's Beef and Barley Soup on hand for a fast lunch when there wasn't any cafeteria at our school. On the back of a barley package,I found a recipe for chicken and barley soup, and I must say I like this almost as much as the beef and barley. This gives a person who doesn't eat red meat a choice.

Serves: 10 to 12

In a Crock-Pot on *high,* sauté until golden brown:
2 Tablespoons butter
¼ cup celery, finely chopped
¼ cup white or yellow onions, finely chopped

Add and cook thoroughly on *high*:
1 or 2 slightly thawed, skinless, boneless chicken breasts, diced*
¼ teaspoon parsley
½ teaspoon tarragon
sprinkle lightly with **salt and white pepper**
Sautéing the **chicken breasts** before adding the **liquid** gives additional flavor and color.

Add and continue to sauté:
2 to 3 medium carrots, peeled and diced
2 to 3 medium red potatoes, peeled and diced

*It is easier to cube boneless chicken breast if it is
slightly frozen rather than thawed or fresh.

Add and bring to a boil:

8 cups strained and defatted chicken stock, pages 13–14

When the **broth** comes to a boil, add:

½ cup pearled barley

Allow it to simmer on *low* until **barley** is cooked, approximately 30 to 60 minutes.

Add ½ hour before serving:

1 cup frozen sweet peas or 1 (15-ounce) can sweet peas with juice

Place the Crock-Pot on *warm* until ready to serve. If the **soup** becomes too thick, add **more broth** or **water**.

Options

■ This recipe can be prepared in a large pan on the stove.
■ **Broth** can be from **drippings** from other **chicken** dishes. See page 14.
■ **GF** Substitute **brown rice** for **barley**.

Laurel and Mary Goddard.

Ham and Barley Soup

After eating the large, calorie-laden dinners of the holiday season, I look forward to lighter foods, such as a wonderful soup. If your traditional choice for Christmas dinner is ham, the soup we most associate with it is "Ham and Beans." If you don't care for this, Ham and Barley might be a nice option. I use my recipe for Beef and Barley and substitute ham and ham broth for beef. This can be made on the stove or in your Crock-Pot; I prefer the Crock-Pot.

Serves: 10 to 12

The day before:
Remove any **extra ham** from the **ham bone** and dice the **meat**. Set aside in the refrigerator.

In a Crock-Pot, place:
ham bone
8 to 10 cups water
Cook on *high* until the **broth** begins to simmer, then reduce the Crock-Pot setting to *low* and continue to cook for 6 to 8 hours. Turn off the Crock-Pot and allow the **broth** to cool in the Crock-Pot overnight.

The following day:
Remove the **ham bone** from the **broth**; remove any **remaining ham** from the **bone** and return **ham** to the **broth**. Discard the **bones**. Place **ham broth** in a large bowl and set aside in refrigerator.

In Crock-Pot, sauté on *high* until transparent and tender:
2 Tablespoons butter
1 Tablespoon olive oil
½ cup white or yellow onion, finely chopped

½ cup celery, chopped

2 medium red or Yukon gold potatoes, diced

2 medium carrots, chopped

Cover and cook until *crisp tender*; stir occasionally. Approximate cooking time is 45 minutes.

Add and bring to a boil:

prepared broth

salt to taste

5 to 10 drops Tabasco sauce

Then add:

½ cup regular pearl barley

Once the **broth** returns to a boil, cover and turn the Crock-Pot setting to *low*. Let the **soup** simmer until time to serve, approximately 1 hour.

About ½ hour before serving, add:

1 (15-ounce) can sweet peas with juice

2 to 3 cups diced reserved ham*

God's Pharmacy

Celery, bok choy, rhubarb, and many more look just like bones. These foods specifically target bone strength. Bones are 23% sodium, and these foods are 23% sodium. If you don't have enough sodium in your diet, the body pulls it from the bones, thus making them weak. These foods replenish the skeletal needs of the body.

*The ham retains its flavor when added to the broth just before serving.

Minestrone Soup

Minestrone Soup (zuppa) is a thick soup of Italian origin made with vegetables, often with the addition of pasta, rice, and meat. The most common ingredients are carrots, onions, celery, and tomatoes. The earliest origin of this soup predates the second century BC. During this time, it was a simple but filling soup (porridge of spelt flour) cooked in salt water with whatever vegetables were available. It is a very versatile soup; it can be a vegetarian soup or made with any type of meat, chicken, or fish broth. When Mom and Nonna fixed minestrone soup, it was to use up the leftover vegetables in the refrigerator or the vegetables from the garden. When I was in college, the vegetables in the soup were the vegetables that were served the day before in the cafeteria. They must have had some Italian cooks in the kitchen!

Serves: 10 to 12

In a large stock pot or Crock-Pot over *medium* heat, add and saute:

3 Tablespoons olive oil

1 Tablespoon butter

1 medium white or yellow onion, finely chopped

3 cloves garlic, freshly squeezed

2 stalks celery, finely chopped

2 carrots, diced

2 medium red or Yukon gold potatoes, diced

½ teaspoon crushed rosemary

Cover and reduce to *simmer* or *low*. Cook until **vegetables** are *crisp tender*.

Add to the **vegetables**:

4 ½ cups stock (chicken, meat, or vegetable), pages 13–15

1 teaspoon oregano

2 teaspoons basil
salt and pepper to taste
1 (15-ounce) can cannellini beans
2 cups tomatoes, coarsely chopped
Simmer for 30 to 40 minutes or longer.

When the **broth** is simmering, add:
½ cup bow-tie pasta
Cook until tender.

To serve:
Ladle **soup** into a bowl and **sprinkle grated Parmesan cheese** over the top.

Corn Chowder 🍎GF

Living in Huskerland, it is a must that I should feature a recipe with corn. Growing up in Nebraska, corn season was one of my favorite times of the year; I loved sweet corn. Many times what we had as our main meal was corn on the cob, along with fresh garden tomatoes and cucumbers. Corn harvesting also provided a summer job for many teenagers. I detasseled corn for five summers, and this money was my money to spend on school clothes. Sweet corn has become sweeter since hybrid varieties, such as Kandy Korn, have been developed, so this makes corn chowder even more delicious.

Serves: 8

On a cutting board, cut **corn kernels** from **cob**, then scrape the **cob** with the back of a knife to release the **milk**:
4 ears (2 ½ cups) sweet corn*
Place in a medium bowl and set aside.

In a 4-cup Pyrex cup, microwave on *high*:
4 slices nitrite/nitrate-free bacon, cut in small pieces
Continue to microwave on *high* until **bacon** is crisp. Remove and drain on a paper towel. Set aside.

To the **bacon drippings**, add:
1 medium white or yellow onion, finely chopped
2 medium red or Yukon gold potatoes, peeled and finely diced

*You can use frozen or canned corn.

prepared corn

1 teaspoon salt

1 teaspoon paprika

Sauté for 10 to 20 minutes until **potatoes** are *crisp tender*.

Add to **above vegetables**:

2 Tablespoons unbleached or white whole-wheat flour

Stir well and cook for 2 to 3 minutes.

Add:

5 cups milk

5 drops Tabasco sauce

Continue to stir and cook 10 minutes or until thick and creamy.

Before serving, stir in:

1 cup fresh spinach, coarsely chopped

Garnish with:

crumbled bacon bits

Option

- **GF** Substitute **2 Tablespoons gluten-free flour** or **1 Tablespoon corn starch** for **unbleached or white whole-wheat flour**.

Cream Soup   GF

Cream soups, such as broccoli, asparagus, and tomato, are usually used as a luncheon entrée and served with a sandwich or salad; but they can also be used as an ingredient in many recipes such as casseroles, hot vegetable dishes, or meats. Whenever I eat cream of tomato or asparagus soup, memories go back to Fridays and Lent when Mom would have it ready for me as I hurried home for a quick lunch during the school year. It was always served with a grilled cheese sandwich. This, to me, is true comfort food!

Basic Cream Soup

Makes: about 1 cup, approximately the same amount contained in a 10-ounce can of soup

In an 8-cup Pyrex pitcher, melt:
2 Tablespoons butter

Add to **butter** and microwave on *high* until transparent:
½ teaspoon garlic, freshly squeezed
1 teaspoon onion, minced

Add and stir constantly with a wire whip until blended:
3 Tablespoons white whole-wheat or unbleached flour
Cooked in microwave on *high* until **mixture** becomes bubbly; stir well.

Add:
any vegetables or liquids that are called for (except broccoli and asparagus that are added later)

Add and cook in microwave on *high* until smooth and thick:
1 cup milk, stock, or other liquids as indicated
salt and pepper to taste

To serve, add an **additional cup milk**, **water**, or **other liquid** to the recipe and heat.

For more detailed recipes, see below.

Option

■ GF Substitute **1 ½ Tablespoons corn starch or ¼ cup gluten-free flour** for **unbleached or white whole-wheat flour.**

Cream of Tomato Soup ● ♥ GF

Serves: 2

In 8-cup Pyrex bowl, melt:
2 Tablespoons butter
Microwave on *high* for 30 seconds.

Add and mix well:
¼ cup white whole-wheat or unbleached flour
Microwave for 1 minute on *high*.

Add to **above mixture**:
1 cup tomato juice, V8 Vegetable Juice, or Bloody Mary Mix, page 118 (my choice)
Microwave on *high* until **mixture** thickens, 2 to 3 minutes.

Add:

1 cup milk (whole, 2%, 1%, or skim)

¼ to ½ teaspoon sugar

salt and white pepper to taste

Cook in microwave on *high* until **soup** thickens and is hot.

Option

- ■   GF   Substitute **1 ½ Tablespoons corn starch or ¼ cup gluten-free flour** for **unbleached or white whole-wheat flour**.

Tomato soup with grilled cheese sandwich.

Cream of Broccoli or Asparagus Soup 🍎 ♥ GF

Have prepared:
½ to 1 cup steamed broccoli or asparagus

In 8-cup Pyrex bowl, melt and mix well:
2 Tablespoons butter
1 Tablespoon white or yellow onions, finely chopped
1 Tablespoon celery, finely chopped
Microwave on *high* for 2 minutes.

Add and mix well:
¼ cup white whole-wheat or unbleached flour
Microwave on high and cook for 1 minute.

Add:
1 cup warm milk
1 to 1 ½ cups shredded cheddar cheese
¼ teaspoon dry mustard
Mix until **cheese** melts into roux, then microwave on high for 2 minutes.

Add to **above mixture** and mix well:
prepared broccoli or asparagus
1 cup milk
salt and white pepper to taste
Microwave on high until **soup** thickens and is hot.

Option

- ■   GF   Substitute **1 ½ Tablespoons corn starch or ¼ cup gluten-free flour** for **unbleached or white whole-wheat flour**.

Vegetables

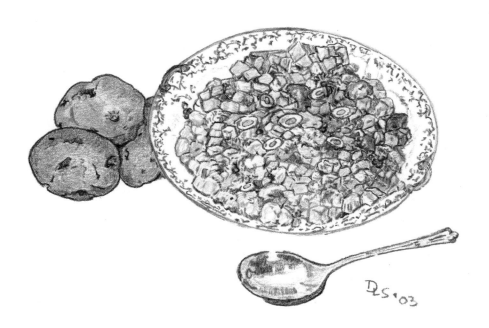

Glossary

au gratin. Vegetables topped with a lightly browned crust of bread crumbs and cheese.

blanch. To place briefly in boiling water for easier removal of skin or to set color and preserve nutrients.

chop. To cut into small pieces.

crisp. To make firm and brittle by placing vegetables in very cold water or a moist, cold place.

dice. To cut into small cubes smaller than ¼ inch.

julienne. To cut vegetables, fruits, or cheese into matchstick-like strips.

mince. To cut or chop into very small pieces.

parboil. To boil vegetables until partially cooked. Similar to blanching.

pare. To peel or trim away the rind or skin of a fruit or vegetable.

refresh. To run cold water over foods that have been parboiled in order to stop the cooking process quickly.

steam. To cook in the steam that rises from a pan of boiling water or other liquid. Food is placed in a basket or insert that fits over the steaming water and does not allow the food to touch the water.

toss. To combine ingredients with a repeated lifting motion.

Helpful Hints

- Choose bright green **asparagus** with compact, firm tips and smooth, tender skin. Handle **asparagus** like flowers. Trim the butt end off the **asparagus** and refrigerate upright, standing in **an inch of water**.
- To keep **cauliflower** white while cooking, add a little **milk** to the **water**. **Lemon juice** works, too.
- When boiling **corn**, add **sugar** to the **water** instead of **salt**. **Salt** toughens **corn**.
- **Lettuce** keeps better if you store it unwashed in the refrigerator.
- Wash **iceberg lettuce** with the core intact. This prevents dirt from washing into the **lettuce**; then remove the **core** by hitting it sharply on your kitchen counter. The **core** will loosen and pull out easily.
- When storing **romaine** or **leafy lettuce** once it is cut, place in a sealed container with **1 clove of freshly squeezed garlic** per head, allowing the **garlic** to permeate the **greens**. The **garlic** is helpful in keeping the **cut lettuce** fresh and crisp for approximately a week.
- Buy **mushrooms** before they are open, when **stems** and **caps** are attached firmly.
- There will be fewer tears with **onions** if you cut the **root end** off the **onion** last or place the **onion** in the deep freeze for four to five minutes before cutting.
- To freshen **parsley** for garnish, cut off the bottom of the **stems** and place in a glass of **cold water**.
- Cutting a thin slice from the end of a **potato** speeds up the baking time.
- When cutting **julienne potatoes**, soak in **lemon water** for approximately one hour to prevent discoloring after they are cooked.
- Let **raw potatoes** stand in **cold water** at least 1 hour before frying to increase crispness. Be sure to dry **potatoes** before adding to frying pan.
- To keep **mashed potatoes** hot, leave in mixer bowl, cover, and place bowl in a pan of **hot water**.
- To keep **mashed potatoes** fluffy, add a **pinch of baking powder**.
- To hasten the ripening of **tomatoes** or **avocados**, put them in a brown paper bag and leave at room temperature for a few days.
- Do not use **soda** to keep **vegetables** green. It destroys vitamins and minerals and makes the **vegetables** soggy.

Real Mashed Potatoes ♥ GF

Serves: 8

In a large saucepan, cook until tender:
8 medium red potatoes
1 teaspoon salt
Drain the **potatoes**, saving the **potato water** for soups, sauces, breads, or gravies.

In a mixer bowl, using wire whip attachment, beat until fluffy:
prepared potatoes
2 Tablespoons butter
½ to 1 cup hot milk or half-and-half
Cover until ready to serve.

Helpful Hints

■ If you drain the **potato water** into a mixer bowl, it will warm the bowl before you put in the **potatoes**. Let it set a minute or two, then pour the **water** into a quart jar and refrigerate for future use.

■ When warming **milk**, add the **butter** so it will be melted and warm. This helps **potatoes** retain their heat.

■ To keep **mashed potatoes** fluffy, add a **pinch of baking powder**.

Good Gravy 🍎GF

To save washing another pan, make **gravy** in the roasting pan or skillet in which you cooked your **meat**. Place pan on stove over *medium* to *high* heat.

Add to **meat**, **chicken**, or **turkey drippings**:
1 to 2 Tablespoons unbleached flour or white whole-wheat flour
Mix well to form a smooth paste.

Using a wire whisk, gradually add and stir constantly:
1 to 2 cups water, milk, potato water, or chicken stock
salt and pepper to taste
Cook until thickened. *Wonderful!*

Option

■   GF   Substitute **1 ½ Tablespoons corn starch or ¼ cup gluten-free flour** for **unbleached or white whole-wheat flour**.

Asparagus 🍎 ♥ GF

Asparagus is a versatile vegetable. It can be eaten cold, warm, or hot. To prepare asparagus, break off the tough ends as far down as snaps easily. You can leave the stalks whole or cut into pieces.

....

Have prepared:
1 baking sheet sprayed with **canola or olive oil**

Serves: 4
Bake: Preheated 400 degree oven
Time: 12 minutes

On prepared baking sheet, arrange in a single layer:
1 bunch (1 pound) fresh asparagus, trimmed
Bake as instructed above or until *fork tender*.

In 1-cup Pyrex cup microwave or on the stove in a small pan, melt:
2 Tablespoons butter

Remove from heat, add to **melted butter**:
1 Tablespoon soy sauce
1 Tablespoon balsamic vinegar
Arrange **asparagus** on a serving platter and pour **above mixture** on **asparagus**.

Serve immediately.

Roasted Root Vegetables 🍎 ♥ GF

While visiting Chris's family in Alabama, Maria fixed these vegetables. What a blend of flavors. I couldn't remember the last time I had eaten parsnips, rutabaga, or turnips. It was a very attractive and tasty dish.

Serves: 6 to 8
Bake: Preheated 375 degree oven
Time: 45 minutes

Have prepared:
1 baking sheet sprayed generously with **olive or canola oil**

Peel, cut into chunks, and place in a large bowl:
4 to 5 carrots
1 parsnip
1 beet
1 yam or sweet potato
1 rutabaga
1 turnip
2 medium white or yellow onions
3 medium to large potatoes
5 garlic cloves

Toss, coating **vegetables** with:
3 Tablespoons extra virgin olive oil
2 Tablespoons melted butter
Place on prepared baking sheet.

Sprinkle lightly:

salt and pepper

1 teaspoon rosemary

1 teaspoon thyme

Bake as instructed above. Stir **vegetables** occasionally until *fork tender*.

To serve: Transfer **vegetables** to a *warm* platter. Serve immediately.

God's Pharmacy

A sliced carrot looks like the human eye. The pupil, iris, and radiating lines look just like the human eye ... and, yes, science now shows carrots greatly enhance blood flow to and function of the eyes.

When we purchased our home in 1983, the previous owner told us that this window was an unsigned Tiffany window. We have never contacted an appraiser to verify this. We named the window the "Olympic Torch."

Harvard Beets   ♥ GF

Serves: 4 to 6

Boil in large sauce pan on *medium* heat:
3 medium to large beets
enough water to cover beets
Cover pan with a lid; cook until tender, about 45 to 60 minutes.

Peel, slice, or cube **beets**. Set aside. Reserve **beet peeling** (see Beet Juice Food Coloring, page 370).

In a 4-cup Pyrex cup, melt:
2 Tablespoons butter

Add to **melted butter**:
1 Tablespoon corn starch
1 Tablespoon sugar
¼ teaspoon salt
Mix well.

Add to above mixture:
½ cup apple-cider vinegar
Microwave until thick. Set aside.

In a medium sauce pan, combine:
prepared sauce
prepared beets
Mix well and heat thoroughly.

To serve: Place in a *warm* serving bowl and serve immediately.

Option

■ You can use **canned beets**.

Beet Juice Food Coloring

In 4-cup Pyrex cup combine:
beet peelings
½ cup water
Cover top of cup with a paper towel, Microwave for 3 minutes and allow to steep for 1 hour. Press out **juice** from the **beet peelings**. You can repeat this several times. Store the **juice** in a small, resealable plastic bag and freeze. Add to **gelatins**, **frostings**, or any other **food** you wish to color.

Healthful Hints

■ The powerful phylonutrients that give **beets** their deep crimson color may help ward off cancer. Betanin pigment from **beets** has been shown to lessen tumor growth.

■ **Beets** are high in immune-boosting vitamin C, fiber, and essential minerals such as potassium and manganese.

■ **Beets** may help fight inflammation because of their unique source of glycine betaine, a nutrient that helps protect cells, proteins, and enzymes.

Baked Beans

Whenever someone asks me to bring something to a dinner or picnic, I often offer to bring baked beans. This was my mother's recipe, and it is so easy. I always use regular canned beans that are not flavored, and now I have been able to buy nitrite/nitrate-free bacon at our local supermarket.

Serves: 4 to 6
Bake: Preheated 350 degree oven
Time: 30 to 45 minutes

In a 9 × 9 glass baking dish, combine:
2 (16-ounce) cans pork and beans
2 Tablespoons brown sugar
1 ½ Tablespoons ketchup
Mix well.

Layer over the top of **beans**:
4 to 6 strips nitrite/nitrate-free bacon, cut in half
Bake as instructed above until the **bacon** begins to crisp.

God's Pharmacy

Kidney beans actually heal and help maintain kidney function, and, yes, they look exactly like the human kidneys.

Creamed Potatoes and Peas ♥ GF

Something we all looked forward to was the first produce from our garden. Radishes were always first, followed by green onions, sweet peas, and potatoes. From this produce, Mom would make creamed potatoes and sweet peas; we could hardly wait for dinner.

Serves: 4 to 6

Bring to boil a large pan of water over *high* heat and add:
1 pound unpeeled new red potatoes, quartered
Boil for 15 to 20 minutes until *fork tender*. Drain and cover with a lid. Set aside.

In a medium sauce pan, combine:
1 cup water
2 cups fresh or frozen sweet (new) peas
Boil until tender, approximately 6 to 7 minutes. *Do not overcook.* Drain and place in a small dish. Set aside.

In same pan, sauté:
2 Tablespoons butter
1 green onion, finely chopped
Cook until **onions** are transparent.

To the **onion mixture**, using a wire whisk, add:
2 Tablespoons unbleached flour
Mix well to form a paste.

Gradually add:

1 cup milk

salt and pepper to taste

Stir constantly until the **sauce** is slightly thickened.

Add:

prepared potatoes

prepared peas

Cook until reheated. Serve immediately.

Option

■ **GF** Substitute **gluten-free flour** or **1 ½ Tablespoons corn starch** for **unbleached flour**.

Italian Red Peas

This is a recipe that was my Aunt Eleanor Brazzale's. It was one of their family's favorite vegetables. It is a quick and easy recipe for a vegetable side dish.

In a medium saucepan, melt until *foaming*:
4 Tablespoons (½ stick) butter
Do not burn.

Add:
1 clove garlic, freshly squeezed
Sauté until **garlic** is slightly browned.

Add:
1 (14-ounce) can sweet peas
2 Tablespoons tomato paste
Mix and simmer on *low* heat until **mixture** starts to bubble and is heated through.

Serve immediately.

Left to right: Ernie and Tony Brazzale.

Appendix

Feingold Diet

The Feingold diet was developed by Ben F. Feingold, MD, to treat hyperactivity. It eliminates synthetic food additives, synthetic flavors, and synthetic preservatives, and one class of synthetic sweeteners:

- Synthetic colors (FD&C and D&C colors)
- Synthetic flavors (several thousand different chemicals)
- Synthetic preservatives: (BHA, BHT, and TBHQ)
- Artificial sweeteners (Aspartame, Neotame, and Alitame)

There are thousands of synthetic flavorings used in prepackaged foods, from a variety of sources, most of which are not noted on the label. Safety and neurotoxicity studies are not required for these chemicals because the level of risk is considered too small to be of legal importance. The Feingold diet seeks to minimize the ingestion of these synthetic ingredients.

Contrary to popular misconception, soft drinks, chocolate, and sugar have never been eliminated on the Feingold diet, although moderation is encouraged. Families can often continue to eat the types of foods they normally eat, including desserts.

There has been much debate about the benefits of the program since it was introduced over thirty years ago, but there is no doubt that changing to the Feingold diet helped Fran Schaffer's son manage his ADHD more effectively.

The safe-food list for your area may be obtained with a membership to the Feingold Association. This list is invaluable for anyone who wants to eat foods without additives. If more consumers were to choose additive-free foods, more manufacturers would offer them.

This entry was developed in large part from information found on Wikipedia. For more information on the Feingold diet, visit www.wikipedia.org/wiki/Feingold_diet or www.feingold.org. There are also a number of Feingold-related sites that you can find by doing a keyword search through any search engine.

The Hamilton-Donald Home

Part of the pleasure of dining at Nonna's was the unique setting in the historical Hamilton-Donald Home. It is architecturally significant as a particularly fine example of the Neoclassic Revival Style that was popular at the turn of the 20th century. The most striking feature is the sweeping entry with its colossal, full-height portico supported by eight large wooden columns with Corinthian capitals. Other features include lavish amounts of leaded, beveled, and stained glass and ornate woodworking. There is a ballroom on the third floor that now serves as the living room.

The house, constructed in 1906, is historically significant because of its association with the growing and changing community of Grand Island. Successful bankers and merchants built palatial homes as symbols of their growing success.

In 1983 Fran and Dave Schaffer purchased the house and opened Nonna's Palazzo Restaurant. The second and third stories were the Schaffer's private residence. Dave and Fran have spent a great deal of their time and resources in restoring the mansion to its original grandeur. It was placed on the National Register of Historic places on March 13, 1986. In February 2000 the mansion was nationally televised as a feature of Bob Villa's *Restore America* on HGTV. Though Nonna's Palazzo is no longer open, the Schaffers continue to live in their beloved home.

Nonna's Palazzo Restaurant

Fran Schaffer was the proprietor of Nonna's Palazzo Restaurant, located on the edge of downtown Grand Island, Nebraska, right on Second Street, the Highway 30 route through the city. The forty-five-seat restaurant was noted for its simple but elegant "homemade gourmet" style and gracious settings on the first floor of the historically significant Hamilton-Donald Home. Nonna's was open to the public on Thursday, Friday, and Saturday nights, and by special arrangement for private lunches, dinners, and other special occasions. The menu featured pastas, sauces, breads, and desserts, with a special of the week from Fran's recipe collection of Italian specialties. True to her philosophy of cooking, Fran made almost everything from scratch and used all-natural ingredients whenever possible.

Bibliography

Better Homes and Gardens Cookbook. Des Moines: Meredith Publishing Company, 1941, 1942, 1943.

Better Homes and Gardens Old-Fashioned Home Cooking. Des Moines: Better Homes and Garden Books, 1990.

Cox, Jeff and Marie-Pierre Moines. *The Cook's Herb Garden.* New York City: D K Publishing, 2010.

Crocker, Betty. *Betty Crocker's Picture Cookbook.* New York: McGraw-Hill Book Co. and General Mills, Inc., 1950.

Longacre, Doris Janzen. *More-with-Less Cookbook.* Scottdale, Pennsylvania: Herald Press, 1978.

Root, Waverly, editors of Time-Life Books, and Fred Lyon, photographer. *The Cooking of Italy (Foods of the World).* New York City: Time-Life Books, 1968.

Schaffer, Frances. *Shortcuts to Gourmet Cooking & Family Favorites.* Lincoln, Nebraska: Infusionmedia, 2008, 2009.

Tonn, Maryjane Hooper, ed. *The Ideals Family Cookbook.* Milwaukee: Ideals Publishing, 1972.

Online resources included Google searches and Wikipedia.

Index